BEITRÄGE ZUM AUSLÄNDISCHEN UND INTERNATIONALEN PRIVATRECHT

HERAUSGEGEBEN VOM

MAX-PLANCK-INSTITUT FÜR AUSLÄNDISCHES UND INTERNATIONALES PRIVATRECHT

Direktor: Professor Dr. Hans Dölle

24

II

1 9 5 3

WALTER DE GRUYTER & CO.
BERLIN

J. C. B. MOHR (PAUL SIEBECK)
TÜBINGEN

DIE ZWEISEITIGEN STAATSVERTRÄGE ÜBER ANERKENNUNG AUSLÄNDISCHER ZIVILURTEILE

Eine kritische Untersuchung

von

Dr. WALTER JELLINEK
Professor an der Universität Heidelberg

Zweites Heft: Vertragstexte und Register

1953

WALTER DE GRUYTER & CO.
BERLIN

J.C.B. MOHR (PAUL SIEBECK)
TÜBINGEN

Gedruckt mit Unterstützung der Deutschen Forschungsgemeinschaft

Satz: Walter de Gruyter & Co., Berlin W 35
Druck: Buchkunst, Berlin W 35

Inhaltsverzeichnis

Vorbemerkung

Die Verträge sind rein alphabetisch geordnet, auch steht der im Alphabet frühere Staat immer an erster Stelle. Da jede Seite als Überschrift die Staaten nennt, zu denen der Vertragstext gehört, kann man den gesuchten Text unmittelbar, ohne Hilfe des Inhaltsverzeichnisses aufschlagen. Den Abschluß bilden der Haager Entwurf und das Haager Questionnaire von 1925 sowie die Haager Zusätze von 1928.

Man findet:

England unter Großbritannien,
San Domingo unter Dominikanische Republik,
Sardinien unter Italien,
Königreich der Serben, Kroaten und Slowenen unter Jugoslawien,
Tunis unter Frankreich/Tunis,
Ungarn unter Österreich-Ungarn.

Anhang

Texte

Aargau—Baden

Übereinkommen
zwischen dem Großherzogthum Baden und dem Kanton Aargau, betreffend die gegenseitige Vollstreckbarkeit der Urtheile und den Vollzug von Ersuchschreiben in bürgerlichen Rechtssachen. Vom 23. August/28. September 1867. Badisches Regierungsblatt 1867, S. 426.

Art. 1. Erkenntnisse in bürgerlichen Rechtssachen, mit Einschluß der Handelssachen, welche von den zuständigen Gerichten des einen der kontrahirenden Staaten auf gegenseitige Verhandlungen oder auf Ausbleiben oder Versäumniß des Beklagten erlassen sind, werden, nachdem sie die Rechtskraft beschritten haben, auch in dem andern Staate vollziehbar, vorausgesetzt, daß die Betheiligten den in Artikel 3 und 4 enthaltenen Bestimmungen genügen.

Den Erkenntnissen der Gerichte stehen rechtskräftige Schiedssprüche gleich.

Art. 2. Die Frage der Zuständigkeit wird nach den Gesetzen desjenigen Staates geprüft und entschieden, in welchem das Erkenntniß zum Vollzuge kommen soll.

Art. 3. Diejenige Partei, welche auf Grund eines in dem einen Staate ergangenen Urtheiles oder Schiedsspruches Zwangsvollstreckung auf das in dem andern Staate befindliche Vermögen erwirken will, hat eine beglaubigte Fertigung des Urtheiles oder Schiedsspruches nebst Urkunde über die geschehene Eröffnung und ein Zeugniß der Gerichtskanzlei über die Rechtskraft vorzulegen.

Art. 4. Diejenige Partei, welche den Vollzug des Urtheiles oder Schiedsspruches verlangt, hat die in Artikel 3 bezeichneten Ausweise der zuständigen Behörde vorzulegen, welche zu prüfen hat, ob das Urtheil oder der Schiedsspruch nach denselben als zuständig erlassen und rechtskräftig zu betrachten, somit der Vollzug zuzulassen sei. Diese zuständige Behörde ist im Kanton Aargau das Obergericht, im Großherzogthum Baden das Gericht erster Instanz desjenigen Bezirks, in welchem die belangte Partei ihren Wohnsitz oder Aufenthalt hat oder die Sache gelegen ist.

Art. 5. Beide kontrahirende Staaten verpflichten sich ferner, Zustellungen, Ladungen und Ersuchschreiben um Vornahme gerichtlicher Handlungen in bürgerlichen Rechtssachen durch ihre Behörden vollziehen zu lassen, soweit die Gesetze des Landes, an dessen Behörde das Ansuchen gestellt wird, nicht entgegenstehen, auch auf Verlangen Bescheinigung über die geschehene Zustellung zu erheben und mitzutheilen.

Art. 6. Für die Besorgung der Zustellungen und Ersuchschreiben sollen gegenseitig keine Kosten und kein Porto berechnet werden.

Art. 7. Gegenwärtige Übereinkunft ist auf fünf Jahre abgeschlossen und bleibt fünf weitere Jahre in Kraft, wenn sechs Monate vor Ablauf dieses Zeitraums keine der beiden Regierungen ihren Rücktritt erklärt, und so fort von fünf zu fünf Jahren.

So geschehen Karlsruhe den 23. August 1867.

Gegeben in Aarau den 28. Herbstmonat 1867.

Ägypten-Palästina

Convention between Egypt and Palestine concerning reciprocal enforcement of judgments. Signed at Cairo, January 12, 1929. Texte officiel anglais. SdN. 94 (1929) S. 10.

Art. 1. In this Convention, unless the context otherwise requires, "judgment" means any judgment or order given or made by a Court in any civil or commercial proceedings, or by any religious Court established by law, whether before or after the passing of this convention, whereby any sum of money is made payable, and includes an award in proceedings on an arbitration if the award has, in pursuance of the law in force in the place where it was made, become enforceable in the same manner as a judgment given by a Court in that place.

"Original Court" in relation to any judgment means the Court by which the judgment was given.

"Registering Court" in relation to any judgment means the Court by which the judgment was registered.

"Judgment creditor" means the person by whom the judgment was obtained, and includes the successors and assigns of that person.

"Judgment debtor" means the person against whom the judgment was given, and includes any person against whom the judgment is enforceable in the place where it was given.

Art. 2. The judgment given by any civil or commercial court or religious court established by law in Palestine and Egypt shall be enforceable in the territories of each of the two countries in accordance with the procedure, and subject to the conditions, hereinafter provided:

Art. 3. 1. The party seeking to enforce in Egypt a judgment of a Palestinian Court shall apply within one year of the date of the judgment for an order of exequatur. Such order shall be granted in the form of an "ordonnance sur requête" by the President of the Court of First Instance of the Mixed or Native Court (as the case may be) of the place or one of the places in which execution is to be effected.

2. The rules as to application to set aside such an order, the periods of limitation, and in general all the rules of procedure applicable under the relevant law in Egypt to an "ordonnance sur requête" shall apply to an order of exequatur issued in Egypt in pursuance of this convention.

3. The party seeking to enforce in Palestine a judgment of an Egyptian Court may apply within one year of the date of the judgment, to the President of the District Court of the District within which the judgment is to be enforced for the registration of the judgment in the Court.

4. An order for registration in Palestine shall be liable to be set aside upon application by the judgment debtor in accordance with the proce-

dure from time to time prescribed for setting aside the registration of a judgment under the Reciprocal Enforcement of Judgments Ordinance 1922, or any other Ordinance substituted therefor.

Art. 4. 1. The judgment creditor shall, in support of his application, produce a certified copy of the judgment of which he seeks execution, in the form prescribed by the law of the country from which the judgment emanates and being enforceable therein. The seal and signature of the authority granting the certified copy shall be legalised in the case of an Egyptian judgment by the Minister of Justice or his representative and in the case of a Palestinian judgment by the Chief Secretary of the Government of Palestine or his representative.

2. Unless a judgment which it is sought to enforce under this convention is one which under the law of the country in which it was obtained was capable of being enforced, notwithstanding any appeal or opposition, the judgment creditor shall satisfy the President of the Court to which the application is made that no appeal or opposition is pending.

Art. 5. The President of the Court to which an application for the enforcement of a judgment is made shall not examine the merits of the case. He shall not refuse an order of exequatur or of registration (as the case may be), except in the following cases:

(a) If the Original Court acted without jurisdiction;

or (b) If the judgment debtor, being a person who was neither ordinarily resident, nor possessing a commercial establishment, nor at the date of the entry of the action carrying on business within the jurisdiction of the Original Court, nor a party to a commercial contract, the subject matter of the action, which was intended to be executed, wholly or in part, within the jurisdiction of that Court, did not voluntarily appear or otherwise submit or agree to submit to the jurisdiction of that Court, particularly by choosing a place of service within that jurisdiction;

or (c) If the judgment debtor, being a defendant in the proceedings, was not duly served with the process of the Original Court and did not appear, notwithstanding that he was ordinarily resident or was carrying on business within the jurisdiction of that Court or agreed to submit to the jurisdiction of that Court;

or (d) If the judgment has given effect to a cause of action which for reasons of public policy could not have been entertained by the Court of the country in which execution is demanded;

or (e) If execution of the judgment is incompatible with the international Treaties and Agreements in force within the country in which execution is demanded;

or (f) If a contradictory judgment between the same parties and upon the same facts has been given by the Courts of the country in which execution is demanded;

or (g) if there has been fraud by the other party to the action calculated to influence the decision of the judges or if the documents on which the decision is based have since been recognised or declared judicially to be false.

Art. 6. The order of exequatur or of registration shall invest the foreign judgment with the same force and effect, and proceedings may be taken thereon, as if it had been a judgment originally obtained by the

Court of the country in which execution is sought. The Court of which the President has granted the order of exequator or of registration shall have the same control and jurisdiction over the judgment as it has over similar judgments given by itself so far as relates to execution.

Art. 7. Nothing contained in this convention shall apply to any judgment of a Court in Egypt or Palestine being:

(a) A judgment purporting to adjudicate on the title to or the right to possession of immovable property elsewhere than in Egypt or in Palestine (as the case may be), or to adjudicate as to any mortgage or charge or easement on such property;

(b) A judgment against the Government of Palestine or the Government of Egypt or any Officer thereof in respect of any act done by such Officer in the course of his duty;

(c) A judgment given by a Consular Court or other Foreign Court in Egypt established in virtue of the Capitulations or other international conventions.

Art. 8. (1) The present convention is made for a period of five years and shall come into force fifteen days after the date of signature.

(2) If neither of the contracting parties shall have notified to the other one year before the expiration of the said term of five years its intention to discontinue the present convention, the convention shall continue in force for a further period of one year, and so on from year to year until the expiration of one year from the date on which notification of the intention to denounce it was given.

Done in duplicate, in English and Arabic, both texts being authentic.

Cairo, the 12th day of January, 1929.

Argentinien—Italien

Convenzione tra l'Italia e la Repubblica Argentina per la reciproca esecuzione delle lettere rogatorie e dei giudicati. 1 agosto 1887. Raccolta ufficiale delle leggi 1902 I, S. 45.

Art. 8. Le sentenze definitive in materia civile e commerciale proferite dalle autorità giudiziarie di ciascuna delle parti contraenti avranno completa e reciproca esecuzione negli Stati dall' altra parte come quelle dei proprî tribunali.

Per tale effetto sarà però necessario che i tribunali competenti della circoscrizione ove deve eseguirsi la sentenza, secondo le rispettive leggi di procedura, la dichiarino esecutiva, dopo aver citato gl'interessati in un giudizio sommario, nel quale si esaminerà solamente:

1° se la sentenza la cui esecuzione viene richiesta sia stata proferita dall' autorità giudiziaria competente;

2° se le parti debitamente citate abbiano assistito al giudizio personalmente o per mezzo di un mandatario legale, o se sieno state dichiarate contumaci in conformità dei vigenti codici di procedura;

3° se il giudicato derivi dall' esercizio di un' azione personale e la obbligazione od obbligazioni da eseguirsi non sieno proibite dalle leggi dello Stato richiesto;

4° se la sentenza non contenga disposizioni contrarie all' ordine pubblico o al diritto pubblico dello Stato medesimo.

La esecuzione della sentenza potrà essere richiesta per la via diplomatica o direttamente dalla parte interessata; avvertendosi che, allorquando essa venga richiesta per la via diplomatica, se la parte interessata non avrà costituito un procuratore, questo le verrà nominato d'ufficio dal magistrato che deve decidere sul giudicato, e dovrà essa soddisfare al procuratore il pagamento di ogni legittima sua competenza.

L'autenticazione della sentenza sarà fatta in conformità delle leggi di ciascun paese, aggiungendovisi la legalizzazione finale del Ministero degli affari esteri.

Art. 9. La presente convenzione entrerà in vigore il giorno in cui ne saranno scambiate le ratifiche, e durerà indefinitamente; però potrà cessare, se una delle parti contraenti notificasse ufficialmente all' altra, sei mesi prima, la sua risoluzione di modificarla o di farla cessare.

In fede di che, i rispettivi plenipotenziarî hanno firmato la presente convenzione e vi hanno apposto il loro sigillo.

Fatto a Roma, in doppio originale, addì primo di agosto dell' anno mille ottocento ottanta sette.

Belgien—Frankreich

Convention

entre la France et la Belgique sur la compétence judiciaire, sur l'autorité et l'exécution des décisions judiciaires, des sentences arbitrales et des actes authentiques. Du 8 juillet 1899. Bulletin des lois de la République Française 1900 II, S. 658.

Titre Ier

De la compétence.

Art. 1er § 1er En matière civile et en matière commerciale les Français, en Belgique et les Belges en France sont régis par les mêmes règles de compétence que les nationaux.

§ 2. Toutefois les Belges ne peuvent invoquer en France l'article 14 du Code civil pour traduire d'autres étrangers devant les tribunaux français que s'ils ont été autorisés par le gouvernement français à établir leur domicile en France, et tant qu'ils continuent d'y résider.

§ 3. L'article 15 du Code civil cesse d'être applicable dans les rapports entre Français et Belges.

Art. 2. Si le défendeur n'a ni domicile ni résidence en France ou en Belgique, le demandeur belge ou français peut saisir de la contestation le juge du lieu où l'obligation est née, a été ou doit être exécutée.

Les Belges conserveront en France les droits que leur confère, en matière commerciale, l'article 420 du Code de procédure civile, aussi longtemps que cette disposition restera en vigueur.

Art. 3. § 1er Lorsqu'un domicile attributif de juridiction a été élu dans l'un des pays pour l'exécution d'un acte, les juges du lieu du domicile élu sont seuls compétents pour connaître des contestations relatives à cet acte.

Si cependant le domicile n'a été élu qu'en faveur de l'une des parties contractantes, celle-ci conserve le droit de saisir tout autre juge compétent.

§ 2. Tout industriel ou commerçant, toute société civile ou commerciale de l'un des deux pays, qui établit une succursale dans l'autre est réputé faire élection de domicile, pour le jugement de toutes les contestations concernant les opérations de la succursale, au lieu ou celle-ci a son siège.

Art. 4 § 1er Les tribunaux de l'un des États contractants renvoient, si l'une des parties le demande, devant les tribunaux de l'autre pays les contestations dont ils sont saisis quand ces contestations y sont déjà pendantes ou quand elles sont connexes à d'autres contestations soumises à ces tribunaux. Ne peuvent être considérées comme connexes que les contestations qui procèdent de la même cause ou portant sur le même objet.

§ 2. Le juge devant lequel la demande originaire est pendante connaît des demandes en garantie et des demandes reconventionnelles, à moins qu'il ne soit incompétent à raison de la matière.

Art. 5. Le juge français ou belge, compétent pour statuer sur la demande en validité ou en mainlevée d'une saisie-arrêt, l'est également pour connaître de l'existence de la créance, à moins qu'il ne soit incompétent à raison de la matière, et sauf le cas de litispendance.

Art. 6. Toutes les contestations relatives à la tutelle des mineurs ou des interdits sont portées devant le juge du lieu où la tutelle s'est ouverte.

Art. 7. § 1er Seront, dans chaque pays, portées devant le juge du lieu de l'ouverture de la succession, les actions en pétition d'hérédité, les actions en partage et toutes autres entre cohéritiers jusqu'au partage, les actions contre l'exécuteur testamentaire, les actions en nullité ou en rescision de partage et en garantie des lots, les actions des légataires et des créanciers contre les héritiers ou l'un d'eux.

§ 2. La compétence relative à ces actions est limitée en Belgique suivant l'article 47 de la loi du 25 mars 1876.

Art. 8. § 1er Le tribunal du lieu du domicile d'un commerçant français ou belge, dans l'un ou l'autre des deux pays, est seul compétent pour déclarer la faillite de ce commerçant. Pour les sociétés commerciales françaises ou belges ayant leur siège social dans l'un des deux pays, le tribunal compétent est celui de ce siège social.

Les commerçants des deux nations, dont le domicile n'est ni en France ni en Belgique, peuvent être, néanmoins, déclarés en faillite dans l'un des deux pays s'ils y possèdent un établissement commercial. Dans ce cas, le tribunal compétent est celui du lieu de l'établissement.

§ 2. Les effets de la faillite déclarée dans l'un des deux pays par le tribunal compétent, d'après les règles qui précèdent, s'étendent au territoire de l'autre. Le syndic ou curateur peut, en conséquence, prendre toutes mesures conservatoires ou d'administration et exercer toutes actions comme représentant du failli ou de la masse. Il ne peut, toutefois, procéder à des actes d'exécution qu'autant que le jugement en vertu duquel il agit a été revêtu de l'exequatur, conformément aux règles édictées par le titre II ci-après. Le jugement d'homologation du concordat rendu dans l'un des deux pays aura autorité de chose jugée dans l'autre et y sera exécutoire d'après les dispositions du même titre II.

§ 3. Lorsque la faillite déclarée dans l'un des deux pays comprend une succursale ou un établissement dans l'autre, les formalités de publicité exigées par la législation de ce dernier pays sont remplies, à la diligence du syndic ou du curateur, au lieu de cette succursale ou de cet établissement.

§ 4. Les effets des sursis, concordats préventifs ou liquidations judiciaires, organisés par le tribunal du domicile du débiteur dans l'un des deux États, s'étendent, dans la mesure et sous les conditions ci-dessus spécifiées, au territoire de l'autre État.

Art. 9. Les mesures provisoires ou conservatoires organisées par les législations française et belge peuvent, en cas d'urgence, être requises des autorités de chacun des deux pays, quel que soit le juge compétent pour connaître du fond.

Art. 10. Pour tous les cas où la présente convention n'établit pas de règles de compétence commune, la compétence est réglée dans chaque pays par la législation qui lui est propre.

Titre II.

De l'autorité et de l'exécution des décisions judiciaires, des sentences arbitrales et des actes authentiques.

Art. 11. Les décisions des cours et tribunaux rendues en matière civile ou en matière commerciale dans l'un des deux États ont dans l'autre l'autorité de la chose jugée, si elles réunissent les conditions suivantes:

1° Que la décision ne contienne rien de contraire à l'ordre public ou aux principes du droit public du pays où elle est invoquée;

2° Que, d'après la loi du pays où la décision a été rendue, elle soit passée en force de chose jugée;

3° Que, d'après la même loi, l'expédition qui en est produite réunisse les conditions nécessaires à son authenticité;

4° Que les parties aient été légalement citées, représentées ou déclarées défaillantes;

5° Que les règles de compétence rendues communes aux deux pays par la convention n'aient pas été méconnues.

Art. 12. Les décisions des cours et tribunaux, rendues dans l'un des deux États, peuvent être mises à exécution dans l'autre État, tant sur les meubles que sur les immeubles, après y avoir été déclarées exécutoires. Les décisions belges rendues exécutoires en France n'y entraîneront pas hypothèque judiciaire.

L'exequatur est accordé par le tribunal civil du lieu où l'exécution doit être poursuivie. Il a effet dans toute l'étendue du territoire.

Le tribunal saisi de la demande d'exécution statue comme en matière sommaire et urgente. Son examen ne porte que sur les points énumérés dans l'article précédent.

Art. 13. En accordant l'exequatur, le juge ordonne, s'il y a lieu, les mesures nécessaires pour que la décision étrangère reçoive la même publicité que si elle avait été prononcée dans le ressort où elle est rendue exécutoire.

Art. 14. Le jugement qui statue sur la demande d'exequatur n'est pas susceptible d'opposition. Il peut toujours être attaqué par la voie de l'appel dans les quinze jours qui suivent la signification à partie. L'appel est jugé sommairement et sans procédure.

Art. 15. Les sentences arbitrales rendues dans l'un des deux États ont dans l'autre l'autorité de la chose jugée et peuvent y être rendues exécutoires si elles satisfont aux conditions exigées par les nos 1, 2, 3 et 4 de l'article 11.

L'exequatur est accordé par le président du tribunal civil de l'arrondissement dans lequel l'exécution est poursuivie.

Art. 16. Les actes authentiques, exécutoires dans l'un des deux pays, peuvent être déclarés exécutoires dans l'autre par le président du tribunal civil de l'arrondissement où l'exécution est demandée.

Ce magistrat vérifie si les actes réunissent les conditions nécessaires pour leur authenticité dans le pays où ils ont été reçus et si les dispositions dont l'exécution est poursuivie n'ont rien de contraire à l'ordre public ou aux principes de droit public du pays où l'exequatur est requis.

Art. 17. Les hypothèques consenties dans l'un des deux pays n'auront d'effet à l'égard des immeubles situés dans l'autre que lorsque les actes qui en contiennent la stipulation auront été rendus exécutoires par le président du tribunal civil de la situation des biens.

Ce magistrat vérifie si les actes et les procurations qui en sont le complément réunissent toutes les conditions nécessaires pour leur authenticité dans le pays où ils ont été reçus.

Art. 18. Dans les cas prévus par les articles 15, 16 et 17, la décision du président a effet dans toute l'étendue du territoire. Elle est susceptible d'appel.

La cour statue comme en matière d'appel de référé.

Art. 19. La présente convention ne sera applicable qu'aux décisions rendues par les cours et tribunaux postérieurement au jour où elle sera devenue obligatoire dans les deux pays.

Elle ne déroge pas à la convention internationale conclue à la Haye, le 14 novembre 1896, et relative à la procédure civile.

Elle n'enlève aux Français aucun des droits que leur confère la loi belge du 25 mars 1876, tant qu'elle sera en vigueur.

Art. 20. La présente convention est conclue pour cinq ans à partir du jour de l'échange des ratifications. Dans le cas où aucune des hautes parties contractantes n'aurait notifié, une année avant l'expiration de ce terme, son intention d'en faire cesser les effets, la convention continuera d'être obligatoire encore une année et ainsi de suite, d'année en année, tant que l'une des parties ne l'aura pas dénoncée.

Art. 21. La présente convention sera soumise à l'approbation des pouvoirs législatifs.

Les ratifications en seront échangées à Paris aussitôt que faire se pourra, et la convention entrera simultanément en vigueur dans les deux pays au jour fixé par les parties contractantes.

En foi de quoi les plénipotentiaires respectifs ont signé la présente convention qu'ils ont revêtue de leurs cachets.

Fait à Paris, en double exemplaire, le 8 juillet 1899.

Belgien—Großbritannien

Convention between Belgium and Great Britain and Northern Ireland for the reciprocal enforcement of judgments in civil and commercial matters. Signed at Brussels, May 2nd, 1934. SdN. 173 (1936), S. 293.

Art. 1. In this Convention:

(1) The words "His Majesty the King and Emperor" shall mean His Majesty the King of Great Britain, Ireland and the British Dominions beyond the Seas, Emperor of India;

(2) The words "territory of one (or of the other) High Contracting Party" shall be interpreted as meaning:

(a) On the part of His Majesty the King and Emperor, the United Kingdom (England and Wales, Scotland and Northern Ireland) and any territories to which the Convention applies by reason of extensions under Article 11, or accessions under Article 13; and

(b) On the part of His Majesty the King of the Belgians, Belgium and any territories to which the Convention applies by reason of extensions under Article 12.

(3) The words "superior court" shall be deemed to mean:

(a) In the case of the United Kingdom, the House of Lords, and for England and Wales, the Supreme Court of Judicature (Court of Appeal and High Court of Justice) and the Courts of Chancery of the Counties Palatine of Lancaster and Durham; for Scotland, the Court of Session; and of Northern Ireland, the Supreme Court of Judicature;

(b) And in the case of Belgium, the Court of Cassation, all Courts of Appeal, Tribunals of First Instance and Tribunal of Commerce.

All other courts in these territories shall be deemed to be "inferior courts" for the purpose of this Convention.

(4) The word "judgment" means any decision of a court however described (judgment, order and the like) by which the rights of the parties are finally determined.

(5) (a) The words "original court" shall be deemed to mean, in relation to any judgment, the court by which such judgment was given; and the words "court applied to" the court in which it is sought to obtain recognition of a judgment, or to which an application for registration or grant of exequatur is made;

(b) The words "judgment debtor" mean the person against whom the judgment was given in the original court, and include any person against whom judgment is enforceable in the country of the original court; and the words "judgment creditor" mean the person in whose favour the judgment was given, and include his successor and assigns.

Art. 2. (1) Judgments pronounced after the date of the entry into force of the present Convention by a superior court in the territory of one High Contracting Party, other than judgments rendered on appeal from inferior courts, shall, whatever the nationality of the judgment creditor or debtor, be recognised and enforced in the territory of the other in the cases and upon the conditions laid down in Articles 3 to 8 inclusive of the present Convention.

(2) Nothing in the present Convention shall be deemed to preclude the recognition and enforcement in the territory of one High Contracting Party, in accordance with the municipal law for the time being in force in the country concerned, of judgments pronounced by a court in the territory of the other High Contracting Party, being judgments to which the present Convention does not apply, or judgments given in circumstances where the provisions of the present Convention do not require such recognition or enforcement.

Art. 3. (1) Judgment in civil and commercial matters, given by any superior court in the territory of one High Contracting Party, and executory in the country of the original court, although still open to proceedings by way of opposition, appeal or setting aside shall, in the courts of the territory of the other, be recognised in all cases where no objection to the judgment can be established on any of the grounds hereinafter enumerated, that is to say, unless:

(a) In the case in question the jurisdiction of the original court is not recognised under the rules of Private International Law with regard to jurisdiction observed by the court applied to;

(b) The judgment was given in default, and the judgment debtor did not appear in the proceedings and satisfies the court applied to that he did not actually acquire knowledge of the proceedings in reasonable sufficient time to act upon it. It is understood that in all cases where it is proved that notice of the proceedings has been duly served on the defendant in conformity with the provisions of Articles 3 or 4 of the Convention signed between the High Contracting Parties on June 21st, 1922, it shall be deemed to be conclusive evidence that the defendant actually acquired knowledge of the proceedings;

(c) The judgment is one which is contrary to the public policy of the country of the court applied to;

(d) The judgment is in respect of a cause of action which had already at the date when it was given, as between the same parties, formed the subject of another judgment which is recognised under the law of the court applied to as final and conclusive;

(e) The judgment has, in the opinion of the court applied to, been obtained by fraud;

(f) In the opinion of the court applied to, the judgment was given against a person, defendant in the proceedings, who under the rules of public international law was entitled to immunity from the jurisdiction of the original court, and did not submit to the jurisdiction of the original court; or is sought to be enforced against a person who is entitled under the rules of public international law to immunity from the jurisdiction of the court applied to;

(g) The judgment debtor satisfies the court applied to that proceedings by way of appeal, opposition or setting aside have been instituted against the judgment in the country of the original court.

It is understood that if such proceedings have not been actually instituted, but the time for lodging an appeal, opposition or application to set aside has not expired under the law of the country of the original court, the court applied to may, if it thinks fit, adjourn its decision on the recognition of the judgment so as to allow the judgment debtor a reasonable opportunity of instituting such proceedings.

(2) Recognition of a judgment shall not be refused merely on the ground that the original court has applied, in the choice of the system of law applicable to the case, rules of Private International Law different from those observed by the court applied to.

(3) The recognition of a judgment under paragraph (1) of this Article means that such judgment shall be treated as conclusive as to the matter thereby adjudicated upon in any further action as between the parties (judgment creditor and judgment debtor) and as to such matter shall constitute a defence against further action between them in respect of the same cause of action.

Art. 4. (1) Notwithstanding the provisions of Article 3 (1) (a) and without prejudice to the provisions of paragraphs (2) and (3) of the present Article, the original court shall be recognised as possessing jurisdiction in all cases:

(a) Where the judgment debtor was in respect of the matter, which is the subject of the judgment, a plaintiff or counter-claimant in the proceedings in the original court;

(b) Where the judgment debtor, being a defendant in the proceedings in the original court submitted to the jurisdiction by voluntarily appearing in the proceedings. It is understood that the expression "voluntarily appearing in the proceedings" does not include an appearance merely for the purpose of protecting property situated within the jurisdiction of the original court from seizure, or of obtaining the release of property seized, or for the purpose of contesting the jurisdiction of the original court;

(c) Where the judgment debtor, being a defendant in the proceedings in the original court, had before the commencement of the proceedings agreed, in respect of the subject matter of the proceedings, to submit to the jurisdiction of the original court or of the court of the country of the original court;

(d) Where, at the time when the proceedings were instituted, the judgment debtor, being a defendant in the original court, was resident in the country of the original court, or, being a company or other body corporate, had its head office in the country of the original court;

(e) Where the judgment debtor, being a defendant in the original court, had, within the country of the original court, either a commercial establishment or a branch office, and the proceedings were in respect of a transaction effected through, or at, such establishment or branch office.

Nevertheless, the jurisdiction of the original court shall not be recognised in the cases referred to in sub-paragraphs (d) and (e) above if the judgment debtor satisfies the court applied to that the bringing of the proceedings in the original court was contrary to an agreement between the parties under which the dispute in question was to be settled otherwise than by proceedings in the courts of the country of the original court.

(2) The provisions of paragraph (1), of this Article do not apply to judgments where the subject matter of the proceedings is immovable property, nor to judgments in rem in respect of movable property. Nevertheless, in these cases the jurisdiction of the original court shall be recognised if such property was situated within the country of the original court.

(3) The provisions of paragraph (1) of this Article do not apply:

(a) To judgments in matters of family law or status (including divorces or other judgments in matrimonial causes);

(b) To judgments in matters of succession, or the administration of the estates of deceased persons;

(c) To judgments in bankruptcy proceedings, or proceedings for the winding up of companies or other bodies corporate.

In the case of judgments given in proceedings of the kind referred to in the present paragraph, the jurisdiction of the original court shall be recognised in all cases where such recognition is in accordance with the rules of Private International Law observed by the court applied to.

(4) Recognition of the jurisdiction of the original court shall not be refused on the ground that the original court had no jurisdiction under the law of its own country, if the judgment is executory in the country of the original court.

Art. 5. (1) Judgments, to which the present Article applies, given by a superior court in the territory of one High Contracting Party shall be enforced by the courts of the territory of the other High Contracting Party in the manner and upon the conditions set out in Articles 6 to 8 inclusive.

(2) The judgments to which the present Article applies are judgments in civil or commercial matters, including judgments for the payment of a sum of money as compensation upon the claim of an injured party appearing as "partie civile" in criminal proceedings:

(a) Which are capable of being executed in the country of the original court although still open to proceedings by way of opposition, appeal or setting aside;

(b) Whereby a definite sum of money is made payable, including judgments for the payment of costs in civil or commercial matters;

(c) To the recognition of which none of the objections set out in Article 3 can be established.

(3) The provisions of this Article do not apply to judgments for the payment of a sum of money for any form of taxation, State or Municipal, or for the payment of penalties.

Art. 6. (1) In order that any judgment of a superior court in the territory of His Majesty the King and Emperor should be enforced in Belgium, it is necessary that an application for the grant of an exequatur accompanied by a certified copy of the judgment issued by the original court, including full particulars as regards the proceedings and the causes of action in respect of which it was given, should be made in Belgium in accordance with the procedure of the court applied to, to the Tribunal of First Instance of the district where the execution is sought.

(2) Any judgment in respect of which a certified copy has been issued by the original court shall be deemed to have been a judgment which was capable of execution in the country of the original court at the time the certified copy was issued.

(3) If such application is made, exequatur shall be granted unless the judgment debtor satisfies the court applied to:

(a) That the judgment debt has been wholly satisfied, or

(b) That the right to enforce the judgment debt is not vested in the person by whom the application is made.

Art. 7. (1) In order that any judgment of a superior court in the territory of His Majesty the King of the Belgians should be enforced in the United Kingdom, it is necessary that an application for its registration accompanied by a certified copy of the judgment issued by the original court, including the reasons therefor, should be duly made:

(a) In England and Wales to the High Court of Justice;

(b) In Scotland to the Court of Session;

(c) In Northern Ireland to the Supreme Court of Judicature, in accordance with the procedure of the court applied to.

(2) All Belgian judgments which bear the executory formula prescribed by Belgian law shall be deemed to be capable of execution in Belgium within the meaning of Article 5 (2) (a). The formula at present in force is that set out in the Annex to the present Convention.

(3) If such application is made, registration shall be granted unless the judgment debtor satisfies the court applied to:

(a) That the judgment debt has been wholly satisfied, or

(b) That the right to enforce the judgment debt is not vested in the person by whom the application is made.

Art. 8. (1) Where an exequatur has been granted in respect of any judgment under Article 6 or where any judgment has been registered under Article 7, such judgment shall, as from the date of registration or grant of exequatur, be as regards all questions relating to its execution in the country of the court applied to in the same position as a judgment originally given by the court applied to at the date of registration or grant of exequatur, and the court applied to shall have the same control and jurisdiction over the judgment, in so far as related to its execution, as it has over similar judgments given by itself.

(2) A copy of any judgment, certified by the original court and attested with its seal, shall be accepted without the necessity of further legislation.

(3) The procedure for the registration of a judgment under Article 7, and the procedure for the grant of an exequatur to a judgment under Article 6, shall be simple and summary, and no deposit by way of security for costs or cautio iudicatum solvi shall be required of any person making application for such registration, or for the grant of an exequatur.

(4) A period of not less than six years, running from the date of the judgment of the original court, if no proceedings have been taken against the judgment in the country of the original court, or from the date of the judgment given in the last instance if such proceedings have been taken, shall be allowed for the purpose of making an application for registration under Article 7 or for the grant of an exequatur under Article 6.

(5) It is understood:

1. That, if it is found by the court applied to that the judgment debt, whose enforcement is sought by registration under Article 7 or by exequatur under Article 6 has been partly but not wholly satisfied, registration or exequatur shall be granted so as to permit of its execution in respect of the unpaid balance provided that the judgment is otherwise one which satisfies the conditions laid down in the present Convention;

2. That if it is found by the court applied to that a judgment, whose enforcement is sought by registration under Article 7 or by exequatur under Article 6, is one under which sums of money are payable in respect of different heads of claim, and that reasons for the refusal of the registration or executory declaration exist in respect of some, but not of all, the grounds of claim, registration or exequatur shall be granted in respect of the sums of money due under those portions of the judgment to the enforcement of which no objection under the provisions of this Convention is established;

3. That if under a judgment a sum of money is payable, which is expressed in a currency other than that of the country of the court applied to, the law of the country of the court applied to shall determine if, and if so in what manner, the amount payable under the judgment may or shall be converted into the currency of the court applied to for the purposes of the satisfaction or enforcement of the judgment debt.

(6) When granting registration or exequatur, the court applied to, shall, if so requested by the proper party, include the amount due by way of interest up to the date of the grant of registration or exequatur. If the interest due on the claim up to the date of the judgment has been determined in the judgment of the original court and a certificate is produced emanating from the original court, specifying the date at which, in accordance with the law of the country of the original court, interest should be allowed as from that date upon the sum for which the judgment is given, the court applied to shall follow the indications so given in determining the amount of the interest. If this is not the case, the party claiming interest may prove what is the sum due under the law of the original court by way of interest on the claim which forms the subject of the judgment.

As from the date of registration or exequatur, interest shall be allowed at four per cent on the total sum (principal and interest) in respect of which registration or exequatur is granted.

Art. 9. Any difficulties which may arise in connexion with the interpretation of this Convention shall be settled through the diplomatic channel. It is, however, understood that the decisions of the respective courts of the territories of the High Contracting Parties cannot be reopened.

Art. 10. The present Convention, of which the English and French texts are equally authentic, shall be subject to ratification. Ratifications shall be exchanged in London.

The Convention shall come into force one month after the date on which ratifications are exchanged and shall remain in force for three years after the date of its coming into force. If neither of the High Contracting Parties shall have given notice through the diplomatic channel to the other not less than six months before the expiration of the said period of three years of his intention to terminate the Convention, it shall remain in force until the expiration of six months from the day on which either of the High Contracting Parties shall have given notice to terminate it.

Art. 11. (1) His Majesty the King and Emperor may at any time, while the Convention is in force under Article 10, and provided that an agreement has been first concluded by an exchange of notes on the points mentioned in paragraph (2) of this Article, by a notification given through His Ambassador at Brussels, extend the operation of this Convention to the Channel Islands, the Isle of Man, any of His Colonies, overseas territories, or Protectorates, or to any territories under His suzerainty, or to any mandated territories in respect of which the mandate is exercised by His Government in the United Kingdom.

(2) Prior to any notification of extension in respect of any territory under the preceding paragraph, an agreement shall be concluded between the High Contracting Parties by exchange of notes as to the courts of the territory concerned which shall be deemed to be "superior courts" for the purpose of the Convention, and the courts to which application for registration of any judgment shall be made.

(3) The date of the coming into force of any such extension shall be one month from the date of such notification.

(4) Either of the High Contracting Parties may, at any time after the expiry of three years from the coming into force of an extension of this

Convention to any of the territories referred to in paragraph (1) of this Article, terminate such extension on giving six months' notice of termination through the diplomatic channel.

(5) The termination of the Convention under Article 10 shall, unless otherwise expressly agreed to by both High Contracting Parties, ipso facto terminate it in respect of any territories to which it has been extended under paragraph (1) of this Article.

Art. 12. (1) His Majesty the King of the Belgians may at any time, while the Convention is in force under Article 10, and provided that an agreement has been concluded by an exchange of notes on the points mentioned in paragraph (2) of this Article, extend this Convention to the Belgian Congo or to the mandated territories administered by Belgium by a notification given through His Ambassador in London.

(2) Prior to any notification of extension in respect of any territory under the preceding paragraph, an agreement shall be concluded between the High Contracting Parties by exchange of notes as to the courts of the territory concerned which shall be deemed to be "superior courts" for the purposes of the present Convention, and the courts to which application for the grant of an exequatur in respect of any judgment shall be made.

(3) The provisions of paragraphs (3), (4) and (5) of Article 11 shall apply to any of the territories above mentioned to which this Convention has been extended.

Art. 13. (1) The High Contracting Parties agree that His Majesty the King and Emperor may, at any time, while the present Convention is in force, either under Article 10 or by virtue of any accession under this Article, and provided that an agreement has been concluded by an exchange of notes on the points mentioned in paragraph (2) of this Article, by a notification given through the diplomatic channel, accede to the present Convention in respect of any other member of the British Commonwealth of Nations whose Government may desire that such accession should be effected, provided that no notification of accession may be given at any time when His Majesty the King of the Belgians has given notice of termination in respect of all the territories of His Majesty the King and Emperor to which the Convention applies.

(2) Prior to any notification of accession under the preceding paragraph an agreement shall be concluded between the High Contracting Parties by an exchange of notes as to the courts in the country concerned which shall be deemed to be "superior courts" for the purposes of the present Convention, and the courts of which application for registration of any judgment shall be made.

(3) Any such accession shall take effect one month after the date of the notification.

(4) After the expiry of three years from the date of the coming into force of any accession under paragraph 1 of this Article, either of the High Contracting Parties may by giving a six months' notice of termination through the diplomatic channel, terminate the application of the Convention to any country in respect of which a notification of accession has been given. The termination of the Convention under Article 10 shall not affect its application to any such country.

(5) Any notification of accession under paragraph (1) of this Article may include any dependency or mandated territory administered by

the Government of the country in respect of which such notification of accession is given; and any notice of termination in respect of any such country under paragraph (4) shall apply to any dependency or mandated territory which was included in the notification of accession in respect of that country.

In witness whereof the undersigned have signed the present Convention, in English and French texts, and have affixed thereto their seals.

Done in duplicate at Brussels, this 2nd day of May, 1934.

Annex

(NB enthält nur Formeln)

Protocol

The undersigned Plenipotentiaries at the moment of signing the Convention between His Majesty the King of Great Britain, Ireland and the British Dominions beyond the Seas, Emperor of India, and His Majesty the King of the Belgians, relating to the Reciprocal Enforcement of Judgments, declare that it is understood that nothing in Art. 4 of the said Convention shall be deemed to oblige the Belgian courts to recognise the jurisdiction of a court in the territory of His Majesty the King and Emperor in cases relating to contracts of assurance where the assured are persons of Belgian nationality and exclusive jurisdiction is conferred on the Belgian courts by Article 1 of the Belgian law of the 20th April, 1920 (which Article is incorporated as Article 43 bis in the Belgian law of the 25th March, 1876, relating to the jurisdiction of the Belgian courts).

This Protocol shall be deemed to be an integral part of the Convention to which it relates.

Done in duplicate at Brussels, this 2nd day of May 1934, in English an French, both texts being equally authentic[1].

Belgien—Niederlande

Convention entre la Belgique et les Pays-Bas sur la compétence judiciaire territoriale, sur la faillite, ainsi que sur l'autorité et l'exécution des décisions judiciaires, des sentences arbitrales et des actes authentiques. Signée à Bruxelles, le 28 mars 1925. Textes officiels français et néerlandais. SdN. 93 (1929), S. 432.

Titre premier

De la compétence territoriale.

Art. 1. 1. En matière civile et en matière commerciale, les Belges dans les Pays-Bas et les Néerlandais en Belgique sont régis par les mêmes règles de compétence que les nationaux.

2. L'article 127 du Code de procédure civile néerlandais n'est pas applicable aux défendeurs belges et l'article 53 de la loi belge du 25 mars 1876 n'est pas applicable aux défendeurs néerlandais.

---

[1] Das vorstehende Abkommen ist in der englischen Fassung wiedergegeben, dafür das — ähnliche — französisch-britische Abkommen in der französischen Fassung.

Art. 2. Sous réserve pour chaque Etat d'apprécier la capacité d'agir devant ses tribunaux, les personnes civiles constituées conformément à la législation de l'un de deux Etats et y ayant leur siège, ainsi que les corporations, associations ou communautés qui, suivant la législation de l'une ou l'autre des Parties contractantes, ont le droit d'ester en justice, seront considérées pour l'application des règles de compétence territoriale comme ressortissants dudit Etat et y ayant leur domicile.

Art. 3. 1. Sauf les exceptions et modifications établies ou à établir par l'une des deux législations nationales, ainsi que par les conventions internationales, le défendeur sera assigné devant le juge de son domicile dans les Pays-Bas ou en Belgique ou, à défaut d'un tel domicile, devant le juge de sa résidence dans les Pays-Bas ou en Belgique.

2. Dans les Pays-Bas, le défendeur peut etre assigné devant le juge du demandeur, si en vertu des lois des deux pays, de la présente convention, ou des conventions internationales conclues par les Pays-Bas, il n'existe aucun autre tribunal compétent. En Belgique, le défendeur peut être assigné devant le juge du demandeur si en vertu des lois des deux pays, de la présente convention ou des conventions internationales conclues par la Belgique, il n'existe aucun autre tribunal compétent.

Art. 4. En matière mobilière (personnelle), civile ou commerciale, le demandeur peut saisir de la contestation le juge du lieu où l'obligation est née, a été ou doit être exécutée.

Art. 5. 1. Lorsqu'un domicile attributif de juridiction a été élu dans l'un des deux pays pour l'exécution d'un acte, les juges du lieu du domicile élu sont seuls compétents pour connaître des contestations relatives à cet acte, sauf les exceptions et modifications établies ou à établir par l'une des deux législations nationales ainsi que par les conventions internationales.

2. Si le domicile n'a été élu qu'en faveur de l'une des parties contractantes, celle-ci conserve le droit de saisir tout autre juge compétent.

3. Tout industriel ou commerçant, toute société civile ou commerciale de l'un des deux pays qui établit dans l'autre une succursale, une agence ou un établissement similaire, sera considéré, comme ayant élu domicile pour le jugement de toutes les contestations concernant la succursale, l'agence ou l'établissement, au lieu où ceux-ci out leur siège.

Art. 6. 1. Les tribunaux de l'un des Etats contractants renvoient, si l'une des parties le demande, devant les tribunaux de l'autre pays les contestations dont ils sont saisis, quand ces contestations y sont déjà pendantes ou quand elles sont connexes à d'autres contestations soumises à ces tribunaux. Ne peuvent être considérées comme connexes que les contestations qui procèdent de la même cause ou portent sur le même objet.

2. Le juge devant lequel la demande originaire est pendante connaît des demandes en garantie, des demandes en intervention et des demandes incidentes, ainsi que des demandes reconventionelles, à moins qu'il ne soit incompétent à raison de la matière.

Art. 7. Si, en cas de saisie-arrêt, la partie saisie n'a ni domicile, ni résidence dans aucun des deux pays, le tribunal du lieu de la saisie-arrêt est compétent pour connaître de l'existence de la créance, à moins qu'il ne soit incompétent à raison de la matière et sauf le cas de litispendance. Il l'est également pour statuer sur la demande en validité ou en mainlevée.

Art. 8. Les mesures provisoires ou conservatoires organisées par les législations néerlandaise ou belge peuvent, en cas d'urgence, être requises des autorités de chacun des deux pays, quel que soit le juge compétent pour connaître du fond.

Art. 9. 1. Les articles 1 à 8 s'appliquent à tous les cas où un ressortissant de l'un des Etats contractants agit ou est cité devant une juridiction de l'autre Etat, sous réserve, lorsque le défendeur n'est ni Belge, ni Néerlandais, des exceptions, résultant des conventions internationales.

2. Dans le cas où il y a plusieurs demandeurs ou défendeurs, ces articles s'appliquent même s'il n'y a qu'un seul demandeur ou défendeur qui est ressortissant de l'autre Etat.

3. Les demandes en intervention et les demandes incidentes n'exercent, en ce qui concerne la compétence, aucune influence sur le jugement de la demande principale.

Art. 10. Pour tous les cas où les articles précédents n'établissent ni règles de compétence commune, ni dérogation aux lois nationales, la compétence est réglée dans chaque Etat par la législation qui lui est propre.

Titre II.

De l'autorité et de l'exécution des décisions judiciaires, des sentences arbitrales et des actes authentiques.

Art. 11. 1. L'autorité des décisions judiciaires rendues en matière civile ou commerciale dans l'un des deux Etats sera reconnue dans l'autre, à la demande de toute partie intéressée, si elles réunissent les conditions suivantes:

1°. Que la décision ne contienne rien de contraire à l'ordre public ou aux principes du droit public du pays où elle est invoquée;

2°. Qu'elle soit susceptible d'exécution dans le pays où elle a été rendue, bien que des voies de recours y soient encore ouvertes contre elle;

3°. Que d'après les lois du pays où la décision a été rendue, l'expédition qui en est produite réunisse les conditions nécessaires à son authenticité;

4°. Que les parties aient été légalement représentées ou déclarées défaillantes, après avoir été légalement citées;

5°. Que les règles de compétence territoriale établies par la convention n'aient pas été méconnues.

2. Les règles relatives à la compétence, à la preuve et à la procédure ne concernent ni l'ordre public, ni les principes du droit public visés au 1° de l'alinéa précédent.

3. Le juge doit d'office examiner si la décision remplit à l'égard de toutes les parties, après qu'elles auront été légalement citées, les conditions énumerées à l'alinéa premier et le constater dans son jugement. Celui-ci a effet à cet égard envers toutes les parties et dans toute l'étendue du territoire.

Art. 12. 1. Les décisions judiciaires rendues dans l'un des deux Etats peuvent être mises à exécution dans l'autre Etat, tant sur les meubles que sur les immeubles, après y avoir été déclarées exécutoires.

2. L'exequatur est accordé par le tribunal civil de l'arrondissement où 'exécution doit etre poursuivie. Le jugement d'exequatur a effet envers toutes les parties et dans toute l'étendue du territoire.

3. L'examen du tribunal ne portera que sur les points énumérés dans l'article 11 et conformément à son alinéa 3.

Art. 13. En accordant l'exequatur, le juge ordonne, s'il y a lieu, les mesures nécessaires pour que la décision étrangère reçoive la même publicité que si elle avait été prononcée dans le ressort où elle est rendue exécutoire.

Art. 14. 1. Toute partie intéressée peut demander l'exequatur.

2. La procédure de la demande en exequatur est régie par la loi de l'Etat dans lequel l'exécution est requise.

3. Le jugement qui statue sur la demande en exequatur n'est pas susceptible d'opposition. Il peut toujours être attaqué par la voie de l'appel dans les quatorze jours après le jour du prononcé, si le jugement est contradictoire, et dans les quatorze jours après le jour de la signification s'il est par défaut.

4. Le juge peut exiger que la décision soit traduite dans la langue employée au lieu où il siège; cette traduction sera certifiée conforme par traducteur juré de son pays.

5. Une copie authentique dûment légalisée doit toujours être produite.

6. Le juge peut ordonner que l'exequatur sorte ses pleins et entiers effets, nonobstant recours, avec ou sans caution.

Art. 15. 1. Les sentences arbitrales rendues dans l'un des deux Etats seront reconnues dans l'autre et peuvent y être rendues exécutoires, si elles satisfont aux conditions exigées par les nos 1, 2, 3, et 4 de l'article 11.

2. L'exequatur est accordé par le président du tribunal civil de l'arrondissement dans lequel l'exécution est poursuivie.

Art. 16. 1. Les actes authentiques exécutoires dans l'un des deux pays peuvent être déclarés exécutoires dans l'autre par le président du tribunal civil de l'arrondissement où l'exécution est demandée.

2. Ce magistrat vérifie si les actes réunissent les conditions nécessaires pour leur authenticité dans le pays où ils ont été reçus et si les dispositions dont l'exécution est poursuivie n'ont rien de contraire à l'ordre public ou aux principes du droit public du pays où l'exequatur est requis.

Art. 17. 1. Les hypothèques terrestres conventionelles, consenties dans l'un des deux Etats, ne seront inscrites et ne produiront effet dans l'autre que lorsque les actes qui en contiennent la stipulation auront été rendus exécutoires par le président civil de l'arrondissement où les biens sont situés.

2. Ce magistrat vérifie si les actes et les procurations qui en sont le complément réunissent toutes les conditions nécessaires pour leur authenticité dans le pays où ils ont été reçus.

3. Les dispositions qui précèdent sont également applicables aux actes de consentement à radiation ou à réduction passés dans un des deux pays.

Art. 18. 1. Dans les cas prévus par les articles 15, 16, et 17, la décision du président a effet dans toute l'étendue du territoire.

2. La décision n'est pas susceptible d'opposition. Elle peut être attaquée par la voie de l'appel dans les quatorze jours après le jour du prononcé, si elle est contradictoire, et dans les quatorze jours après le jour de sa signification, si elle est par défaut.

3. Les formes de la requête, ainsi que la procédure d'appel, sont régies par les lois de l'Etat dans lequel l'exécution est requise.

Art. 19. Les dispositions du présent titre s'appliquent quelle que soit la nationalité des parties, sauf les exceptions résultant des conventions internationales.

Titre III.

De la faillite.

Titre IV.

Dispositions finales.

Art. 26. Les deux Etats contractants se communiqueront immédiatement toutes les modifications apportées aux lois et règles sur la compétence territoriale.

Art. 27. 1. La présente convention ne s'applique qu'au territoire européen de chacun des deux Etats et qu'aux décisions judiciaires rendues après son entrée en vigueur.

2. Le traité relatif à la procédure civile, conclu le 17 juillet 1905 à La Haye, reste également en vigueur pour les deux Etats.

Art. 28. 1. La présente convention sera ratifiée et entrera en vigueur simultanément dans les deux Etats au jour fixé par les Etats contractants.

2. L'échange des ratifications aura lieu le plus tôt possible à La Haye.

3. La Convention restera en vigueur pendant cinq ans, à partir du jour indiqué dans le premier alinéa.

4. Elle sera renouvelée tacitement de cinq en cinq ans, sauf dénonciation; la dénonciation pourra avoir lieu à tout moment et produira son effet six mois après qu'elle aura été notifiée.

En foi de quoi les plénipotentaires respectifs ont signé la présente convention en langues française et néerlandaise et y ont apposé leurs cachets.

Fait en double à Bruxelles, le 28 mars 1925.

Bolivien—Italien

Trattato di amicizia e di estradizione tra l'Italia e la Bolivia, 18 ottobre 1890. Raccolta ufficiale delle leggi 1901 I, S. 773.

XXV. Le sentenze e i giudizii arbitrali emanati in materie civili e commerciali in uno degli Stati contraenti avranno nel territorio dell'altro la stessa forza che hanno nel paese dove vennero emanati, quando riuniscano i seguenti requisiti:

a) Che la sentenza o lodo sia stato pronunziato in tribunale competente;

b) Che sia esecutorio o passato in autorità di cosa giudicata nello Stato in cui fu pronunziato;

c) Che la parte contro cui fu pronunziato sia stata legalmente citata e rappresentata o dichiarata contumace secondo la legge;

d) Che non si opponga alle leggi di ordine pubblico del paese in cui debba eseguirsi.

XXVI. I documenti richiesti per sollecitare l'esecuzione delle sentenze o lodi arbitrali sono:

a) Copia della sentenza o lodo;

b) Copia dei documenti necessari a stabilire che le parti vennero citate;

c) Copia autentica del documento in cui si dichiara che la sentenza o lodo è esecutorio o passato in autorità di cosa giudicata, sempre quando la copia della sentenza, o lodo, non contenga già detto documento.

L'esecuzione della sentenza o lodo potrà essere richiesta in via diplomatica, ovvero direttamente dalla parte interessata.

XXVII. La forza esecutiva o coercitiva delle sentenze o dei lodi arbitrali ed il giudizio a cui il loro adempimento dà luogo saranno quelli determinati dalle leggi di procedura dello Stato in cui si domanda l'esecuzione.

XXVIII. Gli atti di volontaria giurisdizione, come sono inventari, apertura di testamenti, stime e perizie, ed altri simili, praticati in uno Stato avranno nel territorio dell'altro la stessa validità come se fossero stati eseguiti nel suo stesso territorio, a condizione che riuniscano i requisiti stabiliti negli articoli antecedenti, in quanto è consentito dalla diversa indole loro.

XXIX. Le commissioni rogatorie che abbiano per oggetto di eseguire notificazioni, ricevere dichiarazioni o praticare qualsiasi altra incombenza di carattere giudiziario avranno esecuzione nel territorio dello stato richiesto in conformità delle sue leggi.

XXX. Gli interessati all'esecuzione degli atti giudiziari ai quali si riferiscono gli articoli anteriori potranno costituire procuratori e saranno a loro carico le spese occorrenti.

XXXI. I due Governi contraenti convengono che le controversie, le quali potessero sorgere intorno alla interpretazione ed alla esecuzione del presente trattato, ed alle conseguenze di qualche sua violazione, debbono assoggettarsi, quando siano esauriti i mezzi di comporle direttamente per amichevole accordo, alla decisione di commissioni arbitrali e che il risultato di simile arbitrato sarà obbligatorio per entrambi.

I componenti tali commissioni saranno scelti dai due Governi di commune consenso; ed in difetto di ciò, ognuna delle Parti nominerà il proprio arbitro od un numero eguale di arbitri, e gli arbitri nominati ne sceglieranno un ultimo.

La procedura arbitrale in ciascuno dei casi sarà determinata dalle Parti contraenti ed, in difetto, il collegio stesso degli arbitri s'intenderà autorizzato a preliminarmente determinarla.

XXXII. Il presente trattato durerà in vigore per dieci anni a decorrere dal giorno in cui si farà lo scambio delle ratifiche; ma se un anno prima dello spirare del termine niuna delle Parti contraenti avesse annunziato ufficialmente all'altra l'intenzione di farlo cessare, continuerà a rimanere in vigore sino ad un anno dopo che sia stata fatta la suddetta dichiarazione, qualunque sia l'epoca in cui abbia luogo.

XXXIII. Il presente trattato sarà approvato e ratificato da S. M. il Re d'Italia e da S. E. il Presidente costituzionale della repubblica di Bolivia, secondo la costituzione di ognuno dei due paesi, e le ratifiche saranno scambiate in Lima nel termine di un anno o prima se fosse possibile.

In fede di che i rispettivi plenipotenziari hanno firmato il presente trattato e vi hanno apposto il loro suggello.

Fatto in doppio originale a Lima, addì diciotto del mese di ottobre milleottocentonovanta.

Bulgarien—Jugoslawien

Convention relative à l'assistance judiciaire, conclue entre le Royaume de Bulgarie et le Royaume des Serbes, Croates et Slovènes, signée à Sofia le 26 novembre 1923. Traduction. SdN. 26 (1924), S. 102.

D. Exécution des jugements et transactions judiciaires en matière civile et commerciale.

Art. 11. En matière de juridiction contentieuse et gracieuse, les jugements, les ordres de paiement et autres arrêts rendus par les tribunaux civils ou commerciaux de chacune des Parties contractantes, ainsi que les transactions effectuées devant ces tribunaux, seront exécutoires sur les territoires de l'autre Partie contractante suivant les dispositions ci-après.

Les «certificats d'exécution» bulgares délivrés par les tribunaux bulgares en matière de lettres de change, conformément à l'article XIV de la loi sur l'exécution forcée, publiée dans le Journal Officiel N° 277 de 1897, auront, sur le territoire du Royaume des Serbes, Croates et Slovènes, la force d'un ordre de paiement.

Art. 12. L'exécution ne sera pas accordée lorsqu'il s'agit de droits de propriété ou d'autres droits réels sur des immeubles sis dans l'Etat auquel l'exécution est demandée.

Art. 13. L'exécution ne sera pas accordée au cas où elle servirait à faire valoir un rapport juridique ou une requête que, pour des raisons d'ordre public ou de morale, la loi du lieu de l'exécution ne reconnaît pas comme valables ou opérants.

Art. 14. L'exécution sur la base d'une décision judiciaire n'aura lieu qu'aux conditions suivantes:

1. Si le tribunal qui a statué sur la cause doit être considéré comme compétent aux termes de l'article 15 de la présente Convention;

2. Si la décision a acquis force de chose jugée et si aucune voie ordinaire de recours n'est plus admise.

Art. 15. La compétence du tribunal qui a statué sur la cause, sera considérée comme établie dans le sens de l'article 14, chiffre 1, si, d'après les lois de l'Etat requis, un tribunal de l'autre Partie contractante pouvait être saisi de l'affaire.

La compétence sera toujours considérée comme établie dans les cas suivants:

1. S'il s'agit d'une demande introduite par le porteur d'une lettre de change ou d'un chèque contre une personne obligée par la lettre de change ou le chèque, et s'il a été statué sur l'affaire par le tribunal du lieu considéré, d'après les lois appliquées par ce tribunal, comme lieu de paiement;

2. Si, sur une demande reconventionnelle, le tribunal devant lequel la demande initiale était pendante, a statué conformément aux lois valables pour ce tribunal;

3. Si les Parties en cause sont des commerçants et s'il a été statué sur une demande en exécution ou en résiliation d'un contrat ou en dommages-intérêts pour non-exécution ou exécution imparfaite, par le tribunal du lieu où le contrat doit être exécuté;

4. Si les parties s'étaient, d'un commun accord, soumises préalablement à la compétence du tribunal qui a statué sur l'affaire.

Art. 16. L'exécution sur la base d'une transaction judiciaire n'aura lieu que lorsque cette transaction sera exécutoire suivant les lois du lieu où elle a été passée.

Art. 17. L'exécution ne sera pas accordée, même dans les cas où les conditions stipulées par les articles 11 à 16 seraient remplies, si la Partie obligée invoque contre l'exécution une des raisons suivants:

1. La demande n'a pas été signifiée régulièrement au défendeur qui, pour cette raison, n'a pas pris part à la procédure sur laquelle est fondée la décision;
2. Par suite d'une autre irrégularité de procédure, la personne contre laquelle l'exécution doit être opérée, n'a pu prendre part à cette procédure;
3. D'après la législation du lieu où la décision a été rendue ou la transaction passée, cette décision ou transaction a cessé d'être exécutoire;
4. D'après la législation du lieu de l'exécution, l'exception de la chose jugée s'oppose à la requête qui donne lieu à l'exécution.

La signification ne sera considérée comme régulière aux termes du chiffre 1, que si la demande a été signifiée, en personne, au défendeur ou bien à son représentant autorisé à recevoir ladite demande. Sur le territoire de la Partie contractante dont les tribunaux ont été saisis de l'exécution, la signification doit avoir été effectuée par les voies judiciaires ou de la manière prévue au dernier alinéa de l'article 1er.

Art. 18. La demande d'exécution émanant du tribunal ou de la partie en cause, devra être accompagnée des pièces suivantes:

1. D'une expédition de la décision judiciaire, avec les considérants, ou d'une expédition de la transaction;
2. D'une déclaration officielle certifiant que la décision ou la transaction a acquis force de chose jugée et qu'aucune voie ordinaire de recours n'est plus admise.

Si la demande d'exécution est transmise par un tribunal, elle sera expédiée directement au tribunal de l'autre Etat où l'exécution devrait avoir lieu.

Si une Partie en cause expédie la demande d'exécution directement au tribunal de l'Etat où l'exécution d'une décision ou d'une transaction devrait être effectuée, les pièces énumérées aux chiffres 1 et 2 de cet article, devront être légalisées par l'administration judiciaire centrale de l'Etat d'où elles proviennent.

Art. 19. L'autorité compétente de l'Etat requis statuera sur l'admissibilité de l'exécution, sans entendre la Partie obligée. L'exécution sera accordée, si les conditions stipulées à cet égard par les articles 11 à 16 sont remplies, et le tribunal n'examinera pas d'office si l'exécution devrait être refusée pour des raisons énumérées à l'article 17. Il est interdit au tribunal requis d'entrer dans l'examen du fond de l'affaire.

En cas de besoin, le tribunal requis pourra demander des explications au tribunal qui a pris la décision dont l'exécution est demandée ou au tribunal qui a demandé l'exécution.

Art. 20. Lorsque la demande d'exécution est formulée par un tribunal, l'autorité qui procède à l'exécution désignera, pour la Partie poursuivante, un représentant et en avertira le tribunal requérant. Les frais occasionnés par la désignation du représentant seront à la charge du tribunal qui a demandé l'exécution.

Art. 21. Si l'exécution est accordée, les mesures nécessaires pour l'effectuer seront prises immédiatement et d'office. La Partie obligée pourra, sauf la faculté de recours reconnue par les lois du pays, s'opposer à l'exécution en invoquant que l'une des conditions stipulées par les articles 11 à 16, fait défaut ou en invoquant contre l'exécution, l'une des raisons énumérées à l'article 17. Sauf dans les cas prévus à l'article 13 et aux chiffres 3 et 4 de l'article 17, les raisons à faire valoir contre l'exécution devront être invoquées dans les deux semaines à dater de la signification du mandat d'exécution.

Le tribunal compétent d'après les lois du pays statuera sur la demande de la Partie obligée.

Si la Partie obligée s'est opposée à l'exécution, elle pourra demander qu'il soit sursis, jusqu'à la décision du tribunal, à toutes les mesures d'exécution ne se bornant pas à assurer le recouvrement.

Art. 22. En tant que cette Convention ne contient pas de dispositions spéciales, les lois de l'Etat requis devront être appliquées pour effectuer l'exécution.

Art. 23. Lorsque, à défaut des conditions requises, l'exécution est refusée, le demandeur sera libre de se pourvoir en recours.

La demande d'exécution pourra, toutefois, être renouvelée par le tribunal ou par la Partie intéressée, si les conditions stipulées par la présente Convention se trouvent être remplies ultérieurement.

Art. 24. Les frais de justice occasionnés par l'exécution des décisions et des transactions judiciaires seront à la charge des Parties en cause et devront être acquittés suivant les lois en vigueur dans le pays où l'exécution a lieu; ils seront, si la nécessité s'en présente, avancés par l'Etat requis.

Si le remboursement desdits frais ne peut être obtenu des Parties, ils seront supportés par l'Etat requérant.

Les taxes qu'il y aurait lieu d'acquitter lors de l'exécution seront fixées suivant les lois du pays où l'exécution doit être effectuée. L'exécution ne pourra, cependant, être retardée pour la raison que les taxes susmentionnées n'ont par été acquittées.

Art. 25. Les arrêts rendus et les transactions passées sur le territoire de l'une des Parties contractantes auront, sur le territoire de l'autre Partie, même force et effet que les décisions et transactions ayant leur origine dans le pays, en tant que l'exécution y est recevable en vertu de la présente Convention.

Art. 26. La contrainte par corps, soit comme moyen d'exécution, soit comme mesure simplement conservatoire, ne pourra, en matière civile ou commerciale, être appliquée aux étrangers, ressortissants de l'une des Parties contractantes, dans les cas où elle ne serait pas applicable aux ressortissants du pays. Un fait qui peut être invoqué par un ressortissant domicilié dans le pays, pour obtenir la levée de la contrainte par corps, doit déployer les mêmes effets au profit d'un ressortissant de l'autre Partie contractante, même si ce fait s'est produit à l'étranger.

E. Faillites. Art. 27—29 . . .

F. Dispositions finales.

Art. 30. La présente Convention entrera en vigueur le jour de l'échange des ratifications et elle conservera force obligatoire jusqu'à l'expiration d'un délai d'une année à courir du jour où l'une ou l'autre Partie contractante l'aura dénoncée.

En foi de quoi les Plénipotentiaires respectifs y ont apposé leurs signatures et l'ont revêtue de leurs sceaux.

Fait à Sofia en double exemplaire, en langues serbe et bulgare, le 26 novembre 1923.

Annexe

En vue de faciliter la liquidation des procès, en matière civile ou commerciale, pendants devant les tribunaux bulgares et dont les parties sont d'anciens ressortissants bulgares devenus, en vertu du Traité de Neuilly, ressortissants du Royaume des Serbes, Croates et Slovènes, les Parties contractantes sont convenues de ce qui suit:

Les procès pendants devant les tribunaux bulgares seront jugés par ces derniers; les parties en cause seront convoquées d'après les règles établies par la Convention relative à l'assistance judiciaire.

De même, les convocations devant les cours d'appel seront, outre la publication dans le Journal Officiel, signifiées séparément.

Les décisions obtenues des tribunaux bulgares au sujet de ces procès, seront exécutoires sur le territoire du Royaume des Serbes, Croates et Slovènes, dans les limites prescrites par la Convention relative à l'assistance judiciaire.

Fait à Sofia, le 26 novembre 1923, en double exemplaire, en langues serbe et bulgare.

Bulgarien—Österreich-Ungarn

Rechtshilfevertrag vom 31. Mai 1911 zwischen Österreich-Ungarn und dem Königreiche Bulgarien. Reichsgesetzblatt für die im Reichsrate vertretenen Königreiche und Länder 1912, S. 653.

D. Vollstreckung von Urteilen und gerichtlichen Vergleichen in Zivil- und Handelssachen.

Art. 11. Urteile, Zahlungsaufträge und andere Beschlüsse, die im streitigen oder außerstreitigen Verfahren von den Zivil- oder Handelsgerichten eines jeden der vertragschließenden Teile erlassen wurden, sowie die vor diesen Gerichten abgeschlossenen Vergleiche sind in den Gebieten des anderen Teiles nach Maßgabe der folgenden Bestimmungen vollstreckbar.

Art. 12. Eine Zwangsvollstreckung findet nur wegen vermögensrechtlicher Ansprüche und nur dann statt, wenn es sich nicht um streitige Eigentums- oder andere dingliche Rechte an unbeweglichen Gütern handelt, die in dem um Vollstreckung ersuchten Staate gelegen sind.

Die Bestimmung des Absatzes 1 schließt aber nicht aus, daß die unbeweglichen Güter, die in dem um Vollstreckung ersuchten Staate gelegen sind, der Zwangsvollstreckung unterworfen werden, wenn nur der Exekutionstitel (Artikel 11) nicht Eigentums- oder andere dingliche Rechte an unbeweglichen Gütern zum Gegenstande hat, die in dem Staate gelegen sind, wo die Vollstreckung durchgeführt werden soll.

Art. 13. Die Zwangsvollstreckung wird jedoch versagt, wenn dadurch ein Rechtsverhältnis zur Anerkennung oder ein Anspruch zur Verwirklichung gelangen soll, welchem durch das Gesetz des Ortes der Zwangsvollstreckung aus Rücksichten der öffentlichen Ordnung oder der Sittlichkeit die Gültigkeit oder Klagbarkeit versagt ist.

Art. 14. Auf Grund einer gerichtlichen Entscheidung findet die Zwangsvollstreckung nur unter folgenden Bedingungen statt:

1. Wenn die Zuständigkeit des Gerichtes, das in der Sache erkannt hat, gemäß Artikel 15 dieses Abkommens als begründet anzusehen ist;
2. wenn die Entscheidung rechtskräftig und vollstreckbar geworden ist.

Art. 15. Die Zuständigkeit des Gerichtes, das in der Sache erkannt hat, gilt im Sinne des Artikels 14, Ziffer 1, für begründet, wenn die Rechtssache nach den Gesetzen des ersuchten Staates bei einem Gerichte des anderen vertragschließenden Teiles anhängig gemacht werden konnte.

Unter allen Umständen gilt die Zuständigkeit in folgenden Fällen für begründet:

1. Wenn es sich um die Klage des Inhabers eines Wechsels oder eines Schecks gegen eine aus dem Wechsel oder dem Scheck verpflichtete Person handelt und das Gericht des Ortes erkannt hat, der nach den für das Gericht geltenden Gesetzen als Zahlungsort gilt;
2. wenn das Gericht, bei dem die Vorklage anhängig war, über eine Widerklage gemäß den für das Gericht geltenden Gesetzen erkannt hat;
3. wenn zwischen Streitteilen, die Handel- oder Gewerbetreibende sind, über Klagen auf Erfüllung oder Aufhebung eines Vertrages oder auf Entschädigung wegen Nichterfüllung oder wegen nicht gehöriger Erfüllung durch das Gericht des Ortes erkannt wurde, wo der Vertrag zu erfüllen ist;
4. wenn sich die Parteien durch eine vorherige Vereinbarung der Zuständigkeit des Gerichtes unterworfen haben, das in der Rechtssache erkannt hat.

Art. 16. Auf Grund eines gerichtlichen Vergleiches findet die Zwangsvollstreckung nur statt, wenn der Vergleich nach den Gesetzen des Ortes des Vergleichsabschlusses vollstreckbar ist.

Art. 17. Die Zwangsvollstreckung wird, selbst wenn die Bedingungen der Artikel 11—16 erfüllt sind, auf Grund eines von der verpflichteten Partei (Artikel 21) erhobenen Widerspruches abgelehnt:

1. Wenn die den Prozeß einleitende Verfügung dem Beklagten, der sich in dem die Grundlage der Entscheidung bildenden Verfahren auf den Streit nicht eingelassen hatte, nicht ordnungsmäßig zugestellt worden ist;
2. wenn infolge einer anderen Unregelmäßigkeit des Verfahrens der Person, wider welche die Zwangsvollstreckung geführt werden soll, die Möglichkeit, sich an dem Verfahren zu beteiligen, entzogen war;
3. wenn nach der Gesetzgebung des Ortes, wo die Entscheidung erlassen oder der Vergleich geschlossen wurde, deren Vollstreckbarkeit erloschen ist;
4. wenn nach der Gesetzgebung des Ortes der Zwangsvollstreckung dem Anspruche, wegen dessen die Zwangsvollstreckung stattfinden soll, die Einrede der entschiedenen Sache im Wege steht.

Die Zustellung hat als ordnungsmäßig im Sinne der Zahl 1 nur dann zu gelten, wenn die den Prozeß einleitende Verfügung dem Beklagten oder seinem zur Empfangnahme berechtigten Vertreter zu eigenen Handen zugestellt wurde. Hatte die Zustellung in den Gebieten jenes vertragschließenden Teiles, dessen Gerichte mit der Zwangsvollstreckung befaßt wurden, zu geschehen, so muß sie im Rechtshilfewege oder auf die im letzten Absatze des Artikels 1 vorgesehene Weise bewirkt worden sein.

Art. 18. Dem Ersuchen um Zwangsvollstreckung, das von dem Gerichte oder von der Prozeßpartei gestellt werden kann, sind folgende Beilagen anzuschließen:

1. Eine Ausfertigung der gerichtlichen Entscheidung, samt Gründen oder eine Ausfertigung des gerichtlichen Vergleiches;

2. eine amtliche Bestätigung, daß die Entscheidung rechtskräftig geworden ist und einen Exekutionstitel darstellt oder daß der gerichtliche Vergleich vollstreckbar geworden ist.

Wenn das Ersuchen von einem Gerichte ausgeht, finden die Bestimmungen des Artikels 1 über die Sprache und die Ausfertigung der Ersuchschreiben Anwendung. Ein derartiges Ersuchschreiben ist im diplomatischen Wege zu übermitteln.

Handelt es sich um ein Ersuchen der beteiligten Partei, das von dieser unmittelbar bei dem Gerichte des Landes eingebracht wurde, wo das Urteil oder der gerichtliche Vergleich vollstreckt werden soll, so müssen die in Ziffer 1 und 2 dieses Artikels erwähnten Aktenstücke von der obersten Justizverwaltung ihres Ursprungslandes beglaubigt und von einer Übersetzung in der Sprache des ersuchten Gerichtes begleitet sein. Die Richtigkeit der Übersetzung muß von dem diplomatischen oder konsularischen Vertreter des vertragschließenden Teiles, dessen Gericht das Urteil gefällt hat oder vor dessen Gerichte der Vergleich abgeschlossen wurde, oder von einem beeideten Übersetzer des ersuchten Staates bestätigt sein.

Art. 19. Über die Zulässigkeit der Zwangsvollstreckung entscheidet die zuständige Behörde des ersuchten Staates ohne Einvernehmung des Verpflichteten. Die Vollstreckung ist ohne amtswegige Prüfung, ob nicht einer der im Artikel 17 aufgezählten Ablehnungsgründe vorliegt, zu bewilligen, wenn die einschlägigen, durch die Artikel 11 bis 16 dieses Abkommens festgesetzten Bedingungen erfüllt sind. In eine Prüfung der Rechtssache selbst darf sich das ersuchte Gericht nicht einlassen.

Das ersuchte Gericht kann nötigenfalls von dem Gerichte, von dem der Exekutionstitel herrührt oder das um dessen Vollstreckung ersucht hat, Aufklärungen verlangen.

Art. 20. Wenn das Ersuchen um Zwangsvollstreckung von einem Gerichte ausgeht, so hat die zur Entscheidung berufene Behörde auf Verlangen des erwähnten Gerichtes für den betreibenden Gläubiger einen Vertreter zu bestellen und hiervon das ersuchende Gericht zu verständigen. Die Gebühren, die einem solchen Vertreter zu entrichten sind, fallen dem ersuchenden Gerichte zur Last.

Art. 21. Wurde die Zwangsvollstreckung bewilligt, so sind die nötigen Maßnahmen zu ihrem Vollzuge unverzüglich von Amts wegen zu treffen. Die verpflichtete Partei kann unbeschadet des durch das Gesetz des Landes eingeräumten Rekurses gegen die Zwangsvollstreckung Widerspruch erheben, wenn eine der in den Artikeln 11 bis 16 dieses Abkommens festgesetzten Bedingungen nicht gegeben ist oder wenn einer der im Artikel 17 aufgezählten Ablehnungsgründe vorliegt. Wenn der Widerspruch nicht auf die Bestimmungen der Artikel 13 und 17, Z. 3 und 4, gestützt ist, muß er innerhalb 14 Tagen nach Zustellung des Vollstreckungsbeschlusses vorgebracht werden.

Die Entscheidung über den Widerspruch ist dem nach den Gesetzen des Landes zuständigen Gerichte vorbehalten.

Wenn Widerspruch erhoben wurde, können auf Verlangen der verpflichteten Partei alle Maßnahmen der Zwangsvollstreckung, die über die Sicherung des Gläubigers hinausgehen, bis zur Entscheidung über den Widerspruch aufgeschoben werden.

Art. 22. Beim Vollzuge der Zwangsvollstreckung sind, sofern dieser Vertrag nicht besondere Bestimmungen enthält, die Gesetze des ersuchten Staates anzuwenden.

Art. 23. Wenn eine Zwangsvollstreckung wegen Mangels der geforderten Voraussetzungen abgelehnt wurde, hat der betreibende Gläubiger das Recht, Rekurs zu ergreifen.

Das Ersuchen um Vollstreckung kann übrigens von dem ersuchenden Gerichte oder von der beteiligten Partei erneuert werden, wenn die in diesem Vertrage festgesetzten Bedingungen nachträglich erfüllt werden.

Art. 24. Die Gerichtskosten, die durch die Vollstreckung von Entscheidungen und gerichtlichen Vergleichen verursacht werden, fallen den beteiligten Parteien zur Last und müssen entsprechend den im Vollstreckungsgebiete in Kraft stehenden Gesetzen bezahlt werden; sie werden nötigenfalls vom ersuchten Staate vorgestreckt.

Kann der Ersatz dieser Kosten nicht von den Parteien erlangt werden, so sind sie vom ersuchenden Staate zu tragen.

Sind anläßlich der Zwangsvollstreckung Gebühren zu bezahlen, so werden sie nach den Gesetzen des Landes, wo die Vollstreckung stattfinden soll, bemessen. Aus dem Grunde, daß die erwähnten Gebühren nicht bezahlt worden sind, darf aber die Vollstreckung nicht verzögert werden.

Art. 25. Die in den Gebieten eines der vertragschließenden Teile erflossenen Entscheidungen und die dort abgeschlossenen Vergleiche haben in den Gebieten des anderen Teiles die nämliche Kraft und nämliche Wirkung wie die inländischen Entscheidungen und Vergleiche, vorausgesetzt, daß sie daselbst auf Grund des gegenwärtigen Abkommens vollstreckbar wären.

Art. 26. Die Personalhaft, als Mittel zur Zwangsvollstreckung oder als bloßes Sicherungsmittel, kann in Zivil- oder Handelssachen gegen Ausländer, die Angehörige eines der Vertragsteile sind, in den Fällen nicht verhängt werden, in denen sie gegen Inländer unanwendbar wäre. Eine Tatsache, auf die sich ein im Lande wohnhafter Inländer berufen kann, um die Aufhebung der Personalhaft zu erlangen, soll in gleicher Weise dem Angehörigen des anderen Vertragsteiles zugute kommen, und zwar selbst dann, wenn sich diese Tatsache im Auslande ereignet hat.

E. Konkurse.

Art. 27—29 . . .

F. Schlußbestimmungen.

Art. 30. Das gegenwärtige Abkommen tritt gleichzeitig mit dem heute abgeschlossenen Konsularvertrage in Kraft und bleibt bis zum 31. Dezember 1917 in Geltung.

Falls keiner der vertragschließenden Teile zwölf Monate vor dem Ende dieses Zeitraumes seine Absicht, das Abkommen außer Kraft zu setzen, angezeigt haben sollte, bleibt es in Geltung bis zum Ablaufe eines Jahres von dem Tage ab, an dem es der eine oder der andere der vertragschließenden Teile gekündigt haben wird.

Art. 31. Das gegenwärtige Abkommen wird ratifiziert und die Ratifikationen werden in Sophia sobald als möglich ausgetauscht werden.

Urkund dessen haben die beiderseitigen Bevollmächtigten das Abkommen unterzeichnet und es mit ihren Siegeln versehen.

So geschehen in doppelter Urschrift in Sophia, am $\frac{\text{einunddreißigsten}}{\text{achtzehnten}}$ Mai eintausendneunhundertelf.

Schlußprotokoll.

Bei Vereinbarung des Rechtshilfevertrages heutigen Datums haben die unterzeichneten Bevollmächtigten folgende Erklärungen, die hinsichtlich ihrer Geltung und Wirksamkeitsdauer dem Vertrage selbst gleichstehen, abgegeben:

1. Entscheidungen, die von den österreichisch-ungarischen Konsularbehörden und von dem österreichischen und ungarischen Konsularobergerichte im Rahmen ihrer Zuständigkeit gefällt, und Vergleiche, die vor diesen Behörden abgeschlossen wurden, werden, wenn sie sich auf Zivil- und Handelssachen beziehen, mit denen die genannten Behörden vor dem Inkrafttreten des Vertrages befaßt waren, den im Artikel 11 des Vertrages erwähnten Entscheidungen und Vergleichen gleichgestellt.

Die Bestimmungen des Artikels 11 sind auch auf Entscheidungen, die vor dem Inkrafttreten des Vertrages von den österreichischen, ungarischen oder bulgarischen Gerichten gefällt wurden, sofern sie nicht infolge Versäumnisses der verpflichteten Partei ergangen sind, sowie auf Vergleiche anzuwenden, die vor jener Zeit vor den erwähnten Gerichten abgeschlossen wurden.

2. In Streitigkeiten zwischen Handels- oder Gewerbetreibenden wird als Vereinbarung über die Zuständigkeit des Gerichtes des Ortes, wo der Vertrag zu erfüllen ist (Artikel 15, Z. 3 und 4), die unbeanstandete Annahme einer Faktura angesehen, die zugleich mit der Ware oder schon vor ihrem Einlangen übersendet wurde und mit dem Vermerke versehen ist, daß die Zahlung an einem bestimmten Orte zu leisten ist und daß an diesem Orte die Klagen aus dem Geschäfte angebracht werden können.

3. Wenn in einem Streite zwischen Handelsleuten der Kläger eine Forderung auf Grund eines beglaubigten Auszuges aus seinen Handelsbüchern geltend macht, so wird das Gericht des Ortes, wo die Bücher geführt werden, als zuständig im Sinne des Artikels 15, Z. 3 angesehen.

Dieses Protokoll, welches ohne besondere Ratifikation bloß durch den Austausch der Ratifikationen zu dem bezüglichen Vertrage als von den vertragschließenden Teilen genehmigt und sanktioniert betrachtet wird, wurde in doppelter Urschrift am $\frac{\text{einunddreißigsten}}{\text{achtzehnten}}$ Mai 1911 in Sophia verfaßt.

Bulgarien—Österreich

Staatsvertrag zwischen der Republik Österreich und dem Königreich Bulgarien über Rechtshilfe, Auslieferung und Mitteilung von Zivilstandesurkunden. Vom 20. Oktober 1922.

Bundesgesetzblatt für die Republik Österreich 1924, S. 345.

Art. I. Der Rechtshilfevertrag, der Auslieferungsvertrag und die Vereinbarung über die wechselseitige Mitteilung der Zivilstandesurkunden der beiderseitigen Staatsangehörigen, die am 31. Mai 1911 zwischen der vormaligen österreichisch-ungarischen Monarchie und dem Königreiche Bulgarien abgeschlossen worden sind, werden von den Hohen Vertragschließenden Teilen angewendet werden.

Art. II. Der gegenwärtige Vertrag wird am Tage nach dem Austausche der Ratifikationsurkunden in Kraft treten. Er wird in Kraft bleiben, bis einer der Hohen Vertragschließenden Teile dem anderen sechs Monate vorher die Absicht, ihn außer Wirksamkeit treten zu lassen, mitgeteilt haben wird.

Art. III. Der gegenwärtige Vertrag wird sobald als möglich ratifiziert werden. Die Ratifikationsurkunden werden in Sofia ausgetauscht werden.

Urkund dessen haben die Bevollmächtigten ihre Unterschriften auf den gegenwärtigen Vertrag gesetzt.

Geschehen in Sofia in zweifacher Ausfertigung am 20. Oktober 1922.

Bulgarien—Rumänien

Convention judiciaire entre la Bulgarie et la Roumanie, signée à Bucarest, le 19 avril 1924. Texte officiel français. SdN. 33 (1925), S. 210.

Art. 12. Les jugements définitifs rendus en matière civile ou commerciale par les autorités judiciaires compétentes de l'une des Parties contractantes seront exécutés réciproquement sur le territoire de l'autre Partie contractante dans les conditions prévues par les lois des deux pays.

Art. 15. La présente Convention sera ratifée et les ratifications seront échangées à Bucarest aussitôt que faire se pourra.

Elle sera exécutoire trois mois après l'échange des ratifications et restera en vigueur jusqu'à une année à partir de la date de sa dénonciation par une des Parties contractantes.

En foi de quoi, les Plénipotentiaires respectifs ont apposé leurs signatures et leurs sceaux.

Fait à Bucarest, en double original, le 19 avril 1924.

Bulgarien—Tschechoslowakei

Convention entre la République Tchécoslovaque et le Royaume de Bulgarie relative à la protection et l'assistance judiciaire réciproques, en matière de droit civil et commercial. Signée à Sofia, le 15 mai 1926. Traduction. SdN. 60 (1927), S. 230.

Chapitre VIII.

Exécution réciproque des titres exécutoires.

Art. 21. 1. Chacune des Parties contractantes s'engage à autoriser et à poursuivre l'exécution, sur son territoire, des titres énumérés cidessous, émanant des autorités de l'autre Partie contractante et constituant des titres exécutoires aux termes des lois en vigueur sur le territoire de cette Partie.

2. Cette disposition ne s'applique pas aux décisions judiciaires prises en matière de droit de propriété, ou d'autres droits immobiliers, et concernant des biens situés sur le territoire de l'Etat requis.

Art. 22. 1. Seront considérés comme titres exécutoires:

a) Les sentences, les ordres (mandats de payer), les arrêts et autres décisions des tribunaux civils de toutes sortes, y compris les tribunaux de commerce, pour autant qu'ils sont certifiés conformes et que, d'après la législation de l'Etat requérant, ils ne sont plus sujets à aucune voie de recours ayant effet dilatoire; il en sera de même quant aux sentences rendues en matière pénale et concernant les dédommagements des parties lésées et les frais de procédure;

b) Les transactions conclues devant les tribunaux mentionnés ci-dessus, si elles sont certifiées conformes et munies d'une attestation du tribunal les déclarant exécutoires;

c) Les sentences et les décisions d'arbitres ou des tribunaux d'arbitrage, dans la mesure où, aux termes de la loi ou suivant un compromis écrit des parties, conclu dans les formes légales, l'arbitre ou le tribunal d'arbitrage sont autorisés à juger.

2. Ces sentences, décisions ou transactions devront être munies d'une attestation du tribunal de première instance dans le ressort duquel l'arbitre ou le tribunal d'arbitrage ont prononcé la sentence ou la décision, ou dans le ressort duquel la transaction a été conclue, le certifiant conforme et affirmant qu'aucune voie de recours avec effet dilatoire n'est plus recevable.

Art. 23. L'autorisation d'exécution et l'exécution elle-même seront réglées par les prescriptions en vigueur dans l'Etat où elles doivent avoir lieu, à moins que la présente convention n'y apporte des dérogations.

Art. 24. 1. La demande d'autorisation et d'exécution sera adressée par le demandeur au tribunal d'où émane le titre. Lorsqu'il s'agira de l'exécution d'un titre émanant d'un tribunal d'arbitrage ou d'un arbitre, la demande sera adressée au tribunal de première instance visé à l'article 22, alinéa 2.

2. Ces tribunaux transmettront sans retard, par la voie du Ministère de la Justice, au tribunal compétent la demande d'autorisation d'exécution, après l'avoir munie des attestations prévues à l'article 22 et y avoir joint les autres documents nécessaires.

3. La partie intéressée sera pourtant libre de saisir directement de sa demande d'autorisation et d'exécution le tribunal compétent de l'autre Etat contractant.

4. Le tribunal compétent examinera, sur la base des pièces reçues, si toutes les conditions sont remplies pour autoriser l'exécution. Cet examen, qui devra être terminé au plus tard dans un délai de trente jours à compter du jour où le tribunal a reçu les actes, devra avoir uniquement pour objet d'établir:

a) Si la compétence du tribunal qui a jugé l'affaire peut être considérée comme fondée d'après les lois de l'Etat où le titre exécutoire a été établi. Dans ce cas, il suffira que, d'après les prescriptions sur la compétence judiciaire en vigueur dans l'Etat saisi de la demande d'autorisation et d'exécution, aucun tribunal de l'Etat saisi n'ait été exclusivement compétent pour juger l'affaire en question;

b) S'il s'agit d'un titre exécutoire aux termes de l'article 22;

c) Si le défendeur a été, toutes les fois que la loi l'exige, dûment assigné pour prendre part à la procédure, et notamment si soit la demande ou la requête, soit la sentence, ou la décision formant le titre exécutoire, lui a été dûment signifiée; dans le cas où le jugement aurait été rendu par défaut, le tribunal devra, lorsque le défendeur le demande, constater si ce dernier n'a pas été mis dans l'impossibilité, par une irrégularité de procédure, de participer au procès ou de s'y faire représenter valablement. La Cour peut entendre sur ces points la partie contre laquelle la requête est dirigée, ou son représentant;

d) Si l'exécution n'a pas pour but un acte interdit d'après les lois en vigueur dans l'Etat requis, ou ne vise pas à faire connaître un état de droit ou à satisfaire à une réclamation contraires à la souveraineté de l'Etat requis ou aux bonnes moeurs, ou qui, d'après les lois de l'Etat requis, ne peuvent faire l'objet d'une action en justice ou sont inexécutables.

5. Ni le tribunal qui autorise l'exécution ni celui qui l'effectue, ne sont en droit d'examiner le fond de l'affaire.

Art. 25. 1. Le tribunal compétent pour autoriser l'exécution accordera, conformément à ses lois, les mesures provisoires (mesures de sûreté) nécessaires pour assurer les droits résultant du titre exécutoire à l'égard de la personne contre laquelle l'exécution est demandée, tant dans son propre ressort que dans celui d'autres tribunaux du même pays où se trouvent ses biens.

2. Ces mesures ne pourront être révoquées que si cette personne fournit une garantie suffisante pour satisfaire à tous les droits découlant du titre exécutoire.

Art. 26. Exécution conservatoire. Avant même que les titres prévus à l'article 22 soient devenus définitifs, ou que les délais prévus pour l'accomplissement soient écoulés, le tribunal compétent pour autoriser l'exécution pourra, sur demande faite dans la forme prescrite, accorder des mesures conservatoires conformément aux dispositions en vigueur dans l'Etat requis.

Art. 27. Mesures provisoires (conservatoires). Des mesures provisoires (conservatoires) seront accordées, même au cours du procès, à la demande de la partie dont les intérêts se trouvent menacés, même si un tribunal de l'autre Etat est compétent pour statuer dans l'affaire en question.

Chapitre IX.

Dispositions finales.

Art. 28. La présente convention, rédigée en langues tchécoslovaque et bulgare, les deux textes faisant également foi, sera ratifiée, et les ratifications seront échangées le plus tôt possible à Prague.

Elle entrera en vigueur un mois après l'échange des ratifications et restera en vigueur jusqu'à l'expiration d'un délai de six mois a compter du jour où elle aura été dénoncée par l'une des Parties contractantes.

En foi de quoi les plénipotentiaires ont signé la présente convention et l'ont revêtue de leurs sceaux.

Fait en double exemplaire, à Sofia, le 15 mai 1926.

Protocole additionnel

Les plénipotentiaires des Parties contractantes, en signant la Convention entre la République tchécoslovaque et le Royaume de Bulgarie relative à la protection et à l'assistance judiciaires réciproques, en matière de droit civil et commercial, déclarent s'être mis d'accord sur les points suivants:

1⁰ Au sens de la présente convention, le terme «tribunaux» comprend également les offices de tutelle et de curatelle («úřady poručenské» — «opatrovnické») en Slovaquie et en Russie sub-carpathique.

2⁰ Afin de faciliter la connaissance réciproque des circonscriptions judiciaires, les Parties contractantes se communiqueront la liste de leurs tribunaux d'appel, ainsi que des tribunaux de première instance qui en dépendent; une carte géographique indiquant le siège des tribunaux des diverses instances sera, autant que possible, jointe à la liste.

3⁰ Les Parties contractantes se mettront d'accord pour établir le formulaire — rédigé dans les langues officielles des deux Etats — accompagnant les demandes de signification d'actes.

4⁰ Les dispositions de l'article 15, alinéa 1, ne s'étendent pas aux actes rédigés, délivrés ou légalisés par les tribunaux écclésiastiques.

5⁰ Les «Izplnitelni listove» («lettres d'exécution») délivrés par les tribunaux bulgares conformément à la législation sur les lettres de change, seront compris dans la liste des titres exécutoires énoncés à l'article 22, alinéa 1a.

6⁰ Ce protocole fait partie intégrante de la présente convention. En foi de quoi les plénipotentiaires ont signé un protocole additionnel.

Fait en double à Sofia, le 15 mai 1926.

Columbien—Spanien

España—Colombia. Convenio para el cumplimiento de las sentencias civiles dictadas por los Tribunales de ambos países. Firmado en Madrid á 30 Mayo de 1908. Marqués de Olivart, Tratados y documentos internacionales de España, Madrid, IV 1912, S. 121

Art. I. Las sentencias civiles pronunciadas por los Tribunales comunes de una de las Altas Partes Contratantes, serán ejecutadas en la otra, siempre que reúnan los requisitos siguientes:

Primero. Que sean definitivas y que estén ejecutoriadas como en derecho se necesitaría para ejecutarlas en el país en que se hayan dictado.

Segundo. Que no se opongan á las leyes vigentes en el Estado en que se solicite su ejecución.

Art. II. La primera de las circunstancias á que se refiere el artículo anterior, se comprobará por un certificado expedido por el Ministro de Gobierno ó de Gracia y Justicia, siendo la firma de éstos legalizada por el correspondiente Ministro de Estado ó de Relaciones exteriores, y la de éste á su vez por el Agente diplomático respectivo, acreditada en el lugar de la legalización.

Art. III. Antes de ejecutarse la sentencia deberá oirse al Ministerio Público ó Fiscal, de acuerdo con las leyes de cada uno de los dos países contratantes; y contra el auto ó sentencia que dictare el Tribunal requerido, no podrá interponerse apelación.

Art. IV. El presente Convenio será ratificado conforme á las respectivas legislaciones, y las ratificaciones se canjearán en Madrid tan pronto como sea posible, permaneciendo en vigor hasta un año después del día en que una de las Altas Partes Contratantes lo denunciare en todo ó en parte.

En fe de lo cual, los infrascritos han firmado el presente Convenio, poniendo en él sus sellos.

Hecho por duplicado en Madrid á 30 de Mayo de 1908.

Costa-Rica—Italien

Convenzione fra l'Italia ed il Costarica, relativa alla nazionalità, all'assistenza giudiziaria gratuita, ecc. ecc. 6 maggio 1873. Raccolta ufficiale 44 (1875) S. 601.

Art. 7. Le sentenze ed ordinanze in materia civile e commerciale, emanate dai tribunali di una delle parti contraenti e debitamente legalizzate, avranno, sulla richiesta dei tribunali stessi, negli Stati dell'altra parte la stessa forza di quelle emanate dai tribunali locali, e saranno reciprocamente eseguite e produrranno gli stessi effetti ipotecarii sovra quei beni che ne saranno passibili secondo le leggi del paese, ed osservate le disposizioni delle leggi stesse in ordine all'iscrizione ed alle altre formalità.

Perché possano eseguirsi queste sentenze ed ordinanze, dovranno essere previamente dichiarate esecutorie dal tribunale superiore, nella cui giurisdizione o territorio dovrà aver luogo l'esecuzione, mediante un giudizio di deliberazione in cui, sentite le parti nella forma sommaria, si esaminerà:

1. Se la sentenza sia stata proferita da un'autorità giudiziaria competente;
2. Se sia stata pronunziata, citate regolarmente le parti;
3. Se le parti siano state legalmente rappresentate o legalmente contumaci;
4. Se la sentenza contenga disposizioni contrarie all'ordine pubblico o al diritto pubblico dello Stato.

Art. 8—9 . . .

Art. 10. La presente convenzione avrà la durata di cinque anni a contare dal giorno in cui avverrà lo scambio delle ratifiche. Nel caso in cui nessuno dei due Governi avesse notificato, sei mesi prima della fine dei cinque anni, la volontà di farne cessare gli effetti, la convenzione resterà obbligatoria per altri cinque anni, e cosi di seguito di cinque in cinque anni.

Art. 11. La presente convenzione sarà ratificata e le ratifiche saranno scambiate a Roma nel termine di dodici mesi, ed anche prima se sarà possibile.

In fede di che, i due plenipotenziari l'hanno firmata in doppio originale e vi hanno apposto il loro sigillo.

Fatto a Roma il sei maggio milleottocento settantatre.

Deutsches Reich—Italien

Abkommen zwischen dem Deutschen Reich und dem Königreich Italien über die Anerkennung und Vollstreckung gerichtlicher Entscheidungen in Zivil- und Handelssachen. Vom 9. März 1936. RGBl. 1937 II, S. 145

Art. 1. Den in Zivil- und Handelssachen ergangenen Entscheidungen der bürgerlichen Gerichte des einen Staates, die dort Rechtskraft erlangt haben, wird im Gebiet des anderen Staates dieselbe Wirkung zuerkannt, wenn für die Gerichte des Staates, in dem die Entscheidung gefällt wurde, eine Zuständigkeit nach Maßgabe der folgenden Artikel begründet war und nicht nach dem Recht des Staates, in dem die Entscheidung geltend gemacht wird, dessen eigene Gerichte oder die eines dritten Staates ausschließlich zuständig sind.

Das Verfahren, in dem die Anerkennung der Entscheidung nachzusuchen ist, bestimmt sich nach dem Recht des angerufenen Staates.

Art. 2. In vermögensrechtlichen Streitigkeiten sind die Gerichte des Staates, in dem die Entscheidung gefällt wurde, im Sinne des Artikels 1 zuständig, wenn die in einem zwischenstaatlichen Abkommen vorgesehenen Voraussetzungen gegeben sind oder eine der folgenden Voraussetzungen erfüllt ist:

1. wenn in dem Staate, in dem die Entscheidung erlassen worden ist, der Beklagte — oder einer der Beklagten, falls notwendige Streitgenossenschaft bestand — seinen Wohnsitz hatte und der Anspruch sich nicht auf den Besitz oder das Eigentum an einem Grundstück oder auf ein sonstiges Realrecht an einem Grundstück bezog;

2. wenn sich der Beklagte durch eine ausdrückliche Vereinbarung über Ansprüche aus bestimmt bezeichneten Rechtsverhältnissen der Zuständigkeit des Gerichts, das die Entscheidung gefällt hat, unterworfen oder sich vorbehaltlos auf den Rechtsstreit eingelassen hatte, es sei denn, daß beide Parteien Angehörige des Staates waren, in dem die Entscheidung geltend gemacht wird, und in diesem ihren Wohnsitz hatten;

3. wenn der Beklagte am Orte seiner geschäftlichen Niederlassung oder Zweigniederlassung für Ansprüche aus dem Betriebe dieser Niederlassung belangt worden ist;

4. wenn sich die Klage auf eine unerlaubte Handlung gründet, die in dem Staate begangen ist, in dem die Entscheidung gefällt wurde;

5. für eine Widerklage, wenn das Gericht für die Entscheidung über die Klage zuständig ist und der Gegenanspruch mit dem Klageanspruch oder mit einem vorgebrachten Verteidigungsmittel im Zusammenhang steht;

6. in Erbschaftsstreitigkeiten zwischen den Erben eines Angehörigen des Staates, in dem die Entscheidung gefällt wurde;

7. für eine dingliche Klage, die sich auf ein Grundstück im Gebiet des Staates bezieht, in dem die Entscheidung gefällt wurde.

Art. 3. In nicht vermögensrechtlichen Streitigkeiten sind die Gerichte des Staates, in dem die Entscheidung gefällt wurde, im Sinne des Artikels 1 zuständig, wenn die Parteien Angehörige dieses Staates waren oder dort ihren Wohnsitz hatten.

Art. 4. Die Anerkennung ist zu versagen, wenn die Entscheidung Bestimmungen enthält, die gegen die guten Sitten oder die öffentliche Ordnung verstoßen.

Sie ist ferner zu versagen, wenn in der Entscheidung hinsichtlich eines Angehörigen des angerufenen Staates bei Beurteilung der Handlungsfähigkeit oder der gesetzlichen Vertretung oder bei Beurteilung eines für den Anspruch maßgebenden familien- oder erbrechtlichen Verhältnisses oder der dafür maßgebenden Abwesenheits- oder Todeserklärung andere als die Gesetze zugrunde gelegt sind, die nach dem Rechte dieses Staates anzuwenden wären. Die Entscheidung ist jedoch anzuerkennen, wenn sie auch bei Anwendung dieser Gesetze begründet wäre.

Hat sich der Beklagte auf den Rechtsstreit nicht eingelassen, so ist die Anerkennung zu versagen, wenn die Zustellung der den Rechtsstreit einleitenden Ladung oder Verfügung an den Beklagten oder seinen zur Empfangnahme berechtigten Vertreter nicht rechtzeitig oder lediglich im Wege der öffentlichen Zustellung oder im Ausland auf einem anderen Wege als dem der gegenseitigen Rechtshilfe bewirkt worden ist.

Die Anerkennung ist auch zu versagen, wenn die Entscheidung mit einer über denselben Anspruch ergangenen Entscheidung eines Gerichts des angerufenen Staates im Widerspruch steht.

Art. 5. Das Gericht des Staates, in dem die Entscheidung geltend gemacht wird, ist bei der Prüfung der die Zuständigkeit eines Gerichts des anderen Staates begründenden Tatsachen und der Versagungsgründe an die tatsächlichen Feststellungen der Entscheidung nicht gebunden.

Im übrigen ist die Gesetzmäßigkeit der Entscheidung nicht zu prüfen.

Art. 6. Die in dem einen Staate ergangenen gerichtlichen Entscheidungen, die nach Maßgabe der vorstehenden Bestimmungen in dem anderen Staate anerkannt werden, werden dort auch vollstreckt, vorausgesetzt, daß sie in dem Staate, in dem sie ergangen sind, vollstreckbar sind.

Art. 7. Die Partei, die die Entscheidung geltend macht, hat beizubringen:

1. eine Ausfertigung der Entscheidung, die die für ihre Beweiskraft erforderlichen Voraussetzungen erfüllt;

2. die Urkunden, die dartun, daß die Entscheidung in dem Staat, in dem sie gefällt wurde, rechtskräftig ist und, gegebenenfalls, daß sie vollstreckbar ist;

3. die Urschrift oder eine beglaubigte Abschrift der Urkunden, aus denen sich ergibt, daß die den Rechtsstreit einleitende Ladung oder Verfügung der Partei, die sich auf den Rechtsstreit nicht eingelassen hatte, entsprechend der Vorschrift des Artikels 4 Abs. 3 zugestellt ist;

4. eine Übersetzung der vorerwähnten Urkunden; die Übersetzung muß von einem diplomatischen oder konsularischen Vertreter oder von einem beeidigten Dolmetscher eines der beiden Staaten als richtig bescheinigt sein.

Art. 8. Hinsichtlich der Anerkennung und Vollstreckung von Schiedssprüchen gilt im Verhältnis zwischen beiden Staaten das in Genf zur Zeichnung aufgelegte Abkommen zur Vollstreckung ausländischer Schiedssprüche vom 26. September 1927 mit der Maßgabe, daß es ohne Rücksicht auf die im Artikel 1 Abs. 1 daselbst enthaltenen Beschränkungen auf alle in einem der beiden Staaten ergangenen Schiedssprüche Anwendung findet.

Zum Nachweis, daß der Schiedsspruch eine endgültige Entscheidung im Sinne des Artikels 1 Abs. 2 lit. d des vorbezeichneten Abkommens darstellt, genügt eine Bescheinigung der zuständigen Behörden; die Zuständigkeit dieser Behörden ist durch das Justizministerium ihres Staates zu bestätigen.

Vor einem Schiedsgericht abgeschlossene Vergleiche stehen hinsichtlich ihrer Vollstreckbarkeit Schiedssprüchen gleich.

Art. 9. Vergleiche, die vor dem Gericht eines der beiden Staaten abgeschlossen sind und dort vollstreckbar sind, werden ebenso wie gerichtliche Entscheidungen behandelt, ohne daß es einer Prüfung der Zuständigkeit des Gerichts bedarf.

Art. 10. Der in dem einen der beiden Staaten zum Armenrecht zugelassenen Partei ist im anderen Staate in dem Verfahren, in dem sie die Anerkennung oder Vollstreckbarerklärung der zu ihren Gunsten ergangenen Entscheidung nachsucht, ebenfalls das Armenrecht zu bewilligen.

Art. 11. Die Gerichte jedes der beiden Staaten haben auf Antrag einer Partei die Entscheidung über Ansprüche abzulehnen, wegen deren vor einem nach diesem Abkommen zuständigen Gericht des anderen Staates bereits ein Verfahren anhängig ist.

Art. 12. Auf Arreste und andere einstweilige Verfügungen, auf die in einem Strafverfahren ergangenen Entscheidungen über privatrechtliche Ansprüche und auf Entscheidungen, die in einem Konkursverfahren oder in einem Vergleichsverfahren zur Abwendung des Konkurses ergangen sind, findet das Abkommen keine Anwendung.

Art. 13. Unter „Wohnsitz" im Sinne dieses Abkommens ist zu verstehen:

1. für den geschäftsfähigen Volljährigen, für den mündig erklärten, und für den Volljährigen, der bloß zur Vornahme gewisser Handlungen der Mitwirkung eines Beistandes bedarf, der Ort, an dem er sich in einem der beiden Staaten in der Absicht ständiger Niederlassung aufhält, oder in Ermangelung eines solchen Ortes der Ort in einem der beiden Staaten, an dem sich der hauptsächliche Sitz seiner Interessen befindet;
2. für eine Person, die unter elterlicher Gewalt oder unter Vormundschaft steht, der Ort des Wohnsitzes des gesetzlichen Vertreters;
3. für die Ehefrau der Ort des Wohnsitzes des Ehemannes; ist jedoch der Wohnsitz des Ehemannes unbekannt oder ist die Ehefrau von Tisch und Bett getrennt oder ist sie berechtigt, einen selbständigen Wohnsitz zu haben, so bestimmt sich der Wohnsitz der Ehefrau nach Maßgabe der Nr. 1;
4. für Gesellschaften und juristische Personen der in der Satzung bestimmte Sitz oder in Ermangelung eines solchen der Ort, an dem ihre Verwaltung geführt wird.

Art. 14. Die Vereinbarungen, die für besondere Rechtsgebiete über die Anerkennung und Vollstreckung von Entscheidungen zwischen beiden Staaten getroffen sind, werden durch dieses Abkommen nicht berührt.

Art. 15. Die im Artikel 18 Abs. 1 und 2 des Haager Abkommens über den Zivilprozeß vom 17. Juli 1905 genannten Kostenentscheidungen, die in einem der beiden Staaten ergangen sind, werden im Gebiete des anderen Staates auch auf unmittelbaren Antrag einer Partei kostenlos für vollstreckbar erklärt.

Art. 16. Vorbehaltlich der Vorschriften der Artikel 3 und 4 sind die Bestimmungen dieses Abkommens ohne Rücksicht auf die Staatsangehörigkeit der Parteien anzuwenden.

Art. 17. Die Hohen Vertragschließenden Teile behalten sich vor, durch eine mittels Notenwechsels zu treffende Vereinbarung das vorliegende Abkommen auf die italienischen Kolonien und Besitzungen auszudehnen.

Art. 18. Dieses Abkommen ist in deutscher und italienischer Sprache abgeschlossen. Beide Texte haben gleiche Kraft. Das Abkommen wird in zwei Stücken ausgefertigt; jedem der beiden Vertragsstaaten wird ein Stück ausgehändigt. Das Abkommen soll ratifiziert werden. Die Ratifikationsurkunden sollen so bald als möglich in Berlin ausgetauscht werden.

Das Abkommen tritt drei Monate nach dem Austausch der Ratifikationsurkunden in Kraft. Es findet keine Anwendung auf Entscheidungen, die vor seinem Inkrafttreten rechtskräftig geworden sind, und auf Vergleiche, die vor diesem Zeitpunkt zustande gekommen sind.

Das Abkommen kann von jedem der vertragschließenden Staaten gekündigt werden. Es bleibt jedoch nach erfolgter Kündigung noch sechs Monate in Kraft.

Zu Urkund dessen haben die Bevollmächtigten dieses Abkommen unterzeichnet.

Geschehen in Rom, am 9. März 1936.

Deutsches Reich—Österreich

Vertrag über Rechtsschutz und Rechtshilfe zwischen dem Deutschen Reiche und der Republik Österreich. Vom 21. Juni 1923. Deutsches RGBl. 1924 II, S. 55.

III. Abschnitt

Zwangsvollstreckung

Art. 19. (1) Rechtskräftige Entscheidungen der bürgerlichen Gerichte des einen Staates sind ohne Unterschied ihrer Benennung (Urteile, Beschlüsse, Zahlungsbefehle, Zahlungsaufträge, Vollstreckungsbefehle) im Gebiete des anderen Staates nach Maßgabe der nachstehenden Bestimmungen vollstreckbar. Ausgenommen bleiben Arreste und einstweilige Verfügungen.

(2) Als bürgerliche Gerichte gelten auch die Sondergerichte und diejenigen Schiedsgerichte, die ohne Rücksicht auf einen Schiedsvertrag vermöge einer besonderen staatlichen Anordnung zur Entscheidung privatrechtlicher Ansprüche zuständig sind.

Art. 20. Zur Entscheidung über die Bewilligung der Zwangsvollstreckung sind im Deutschen Reiche die Amtsgerichte, in Österreich die Bezirksgerichte zuständig. Örtlich zuständig ist das Gericht, bei dem der Verpflichtete seinen allgemeinen Gerichtsstand hat und in Ermangelung eines solchen das Gericht, in dessen Bezirk sich Vermögen des Verpflichteten befindet oder die Vollstreckungshandlung vorzunehmen ist.

Art. 21. (1) Der Antrag des Gläubigers auf Bewilligung der Zwangsvollstreckung hat zu enthalten:

1. die genaue Bezeichnung des Gläubigers und des Verpflichteten sowie ihrer gesetzlichen Vertreter;
2. die Angabe der Umstände, die für die Zuständigkeit des angerufenen Gerichts wesentlich sind;
3. die bestimmte Bezeichnung des zu vollstreckenden Anspruchs und der vollstreckbaren Entscheidung;
4. soweit nach dem Rechte des Staates, in dessen Gebiete die Zwangsvollstreckung stattfinden soll, deren Vollzug von Amts wegen stattfindet, die Bezeichnung der anzuwendenden Zwangsmittel und bei Vollstreckung in das Vermögen des Verpflichteten die Bezeichnung der Vermögensteile, auf welche die Zwangsvollstreckung gerichtet werden soll, sowie des Ortes, an dem sie sich befinden, ferner nach Beschaffenheit des Falles alle weiteren Angaben, die für den Vollzug der Zwangsvollstreckung von Wichtigkeit sind.

(2) Dem Antrag soll für jeden Antragsgegner eine Abschrift beigefügt sein.

Art. 22. Dem Antrag ist eine vollständige Ausfertigung der Entscheidung beizufügen, auf Grund deren die Zwangsvollstreckung gegen den Verpflichteten erfolgen soll. Die Rechtskraft der Entscheidung ist, soweit sie sich nicht schon aus der Ausfertigung ergibt, durch öffentliche Urkunden nachzuweisen.

Art. 23. Hängt die Vollstreckung der Entscheidung nach deren Inhalt von dem Ablauf einer Frist oder von dem Eintritt einer anderen Tatsache ab oder wird die Bewilligung der Zwangsvollstreckung zugunsten eines anderen als des in der Entscheidung bezeichneten Gläubigers oder gegen einen anderen als den dort bezeichneten Verpflichteten nachgesucht, so bestimmt sich die Frage, inwieweit die Bewilligung der Zwangsvollstreckung von dem Nachweis besonderer Voraussetzungen abhängig ist oder ob die Entscheidung für oder gegen den anderen vollstreckbar ist, nach dem Rechte des Staates, dessen Gericht die Entscheidung erlassen hat. Die nach den maßgebenden Vorschriften erforderlichen Nachweise sind, sofern nicht die nachzuweisenden Tatsachen bei dem über die Bewilligung der Zwangsvollstreckung entscheidenden Gericht offenkundig sind, durch öffentliche oder öffentlich beglaubigte Urkunden zu führen. Kann ein solcher Nachweis nicht erbracht werden, so ist nach Artikel 24 Abs. 2, Satz 2 zu verfahren.

Art. 24. (1) Über den Antrag auf Bewilligung der Zwangsvollstreckung wird durch Beschluß entschieden. Entspricht der Antrag nicht den Bestimmungen der Artikel 20 bis 22 oder ergeben sich Anhaltspunkte für das Vorliegen eines Versagungsgrundes (Artikel 25), so hat das Gericht zunächst dem Antragsteller die Beseitigung der Mängel aufzugeben. Es kann dem Antragsteller hiezu eine Ausschlußfrist bestimmen. Das Gericht kann auch das Gericht, das die zu vollstreckende Entscheidung erlassen hat, um Aufklärung ersuchen.

(2) Das Gericht kann, soweit ihm dies zur Behebung von Zweifeln sachgemäß erscheint, den Verpflichteten unter Mitteilung einer Abschrift des Antrags hören. In dieser Abschrift sind dem Schuldner die in Artikel 21 Abs. 1, Zahl 4 vorgeschriebenen Angaben nicht mitzuteilen. Das Gericht kann auch eine mündliche Verhandlung anordnen. Eine solche muß angeordnet werden, wenn im Falle des Artikel 23 die er-

forderlichen Nachweise für Tatsachen, die bei dem Gerichte nicht offenkundig sind, durch öffentliche oder öffentlich beglaubigte Urkunden nicht geführt werden können.

Art. 25. (1) Die Zwangsvollstreckung ist zu versagen, wenn die Mängel des Antrags nicht innerhalb der im Artikel 24 bestimmten Ausschlußfrist behoben sind.

(2) Sie ist ferner zu versagen,

1. wenn nach den Gesetzen des Vollstreckungsstaats in diesem Staate ein ausschließlicher Gerichtsstand für die Rechtsstreitigkeit besteht;

2. wenn durch die Zwangsvollstreckung ein Rechtsverhältnis zur Anerkennung oder ein Anspruch zur Verwirklichung gelangen soll, dem im Gebiete des Vollstreckungsstaats aus Rücksichten der öffentlichen Ordnung oder der Sittlichkeit die Gültigkeit, Verfolgbarkeit oder Klagbarkeit versagt ist.

(3) Sie ist außerdem zugunsten eines inländischen Beteiligten zu versagen,

1. wenn in der Entscheidung bei Beurteilung seiner Handlungs- oder Prozeßfähigkeit oder seiner gesetzlichen Vertretung oder bei Beurteilung eines für den Anspruch maßgebenden familien- oder erbrechtlichen Verhältnisses oder der dafür maßgebenden Feststellung des Todes einer Person zu seinem Nachteil andere als die nach dem Rechte des Vollstreckungsstaats anzuwendenden Gesetze zugrunde gelegt sind;

2. wenn er sich auf den Rechtsstreit nicht eingelassen hatte und ihm die Ladung oder die Verfügung, durch die das Verfahren eingeleitet worden war, lediglich im Wege der Ersatzzustellung oder der öffentlichen Zustellung (deutsche Zivilprozeßordnung §§ 181 bis 184, 203 bis 206, österreichische Zivilprozeßordnung §§ 102 bis 105, 115) zugestellt war. Dies gilt jedoch nur, wenn er bereits bei Einleitung des Verfahrens die inländische Staatsangehörigkeit besessen hat;

3. wenn für die Entscheidung des erkennenden Gerichts lediglich der Gerichtsstand des Vermögens (deutsche Zivilprozeßordnung § 23, österreichische Jurisdiktionsnorm § 99) oder der Gerichtsstand des § 88, Abs. 2 der österreichischen Jurisdiktionsnorm gegeben war, es sei denn, daß sich in letzterem Falle der Beklagte auf den Rechtsstreit eingelassen hatte.

(4) Das Gericht ist bei Prüfung der Versagungsgründe an die tatsächlichen Feststellungen der Entscheidung nicht gebunden. Eine weitere Nachprüfung der Gesetzmäßigkeit der zu vollstreckenden Entscheidung findet nicht statt.

Art. 26. (1) Gegen den Beschluß durch den über den Antrag auf Bewilligung der Zwangsvollstreckung entschieden wird, findet im Deutschen Reiche die sofortige Beschwerde, in Österreich der Rekurs statt.

(2) Gegen die Bewilligung der Zwangsvollstreckung findet außerdem der Widerspruch statt, wenn ein Grund zur Versagung der Zwangsvollstreckung vorliegt, der nicht bereits gemäß Abs. 1 geltend gemacht worden ist. Sofern der Widerspruch nicht auf die Versagungsgründe des Artikel 25, Abs. 2 oder Abs. 3, Zahl 1 gestützt wird, ist er binnen 14 Tagen nach Zustellung des die Zwangsvollstreckung bewilligenden Beschlusses zu erheben.

Art. 27. Im Wege der sofortigen Beschwerde (des Rekurses) oder des Widerspruchs kann der Schuldner ferner geltend machen Einwendungen gegen den Anspruch im Sinne des § 767 der deutschen Zivilprozeßordnung und des § 35 der österreichischen Exekutionsordnung, sowie Einwendungen, welche die in den §§ 732, 768 der deutschen Zivilprozeßordnung und im § 36 der österreichischen Exekutionsordnung bezeichneten Voraussetzungen der Vollstreckbarkeit betreffen. Derartige Einwendungen können auch in den in diesen Vorschriften bezeichneten besonderen Verfahren geltend gemacht werden.

Art. 28. (1) Über den Widerspruch ist nach mündlicher Verhandlung durch Urteil zu entscheiden.

(2) Ist Widerspruch erhoben, so kann das Gericht auf Antrag oder von Amts wegen anordnen, daß die Zwangsvollstreckung gegen oder ohne Sicherheitsleistung einstweilen eingestellt (aufgeschoben) werde oder nur gegen Sicherheitsleistung stattfinde oder daß die erfolgten Vollstreckungsmaßregeln gegen Sicherheitsleistung aufzuheben seien.

Art. 29. Für die Verkündung und Zustellung des über den Antrag auf Bewilligung der Zwangsvollstreckung ergehenden Beschlusses gelten im Deutschen Reiche die Vorschriften des § 329, Abs. 1 und 3, der Zivilprozeßordnung, in Österreich die Vorschriften des § 64 der Exekutionsordnung. Die Zustellung des die Zwangsvollstreckung bewilligenden Beschlusses an den Schuldner erfolgt indessen im Deutschen Reiche in jedem Falle auf Betreiben des Gläubigers.

Art. 30. (1) Soweit nach den Gesetzen des Vollstreckungsstaats die Zwangsvollstreckung von Amts wegen erfolgt, ist ihr Vollzug unverzüglich einzuleiten, es sei denn, daß sich der Gläubiger vorbehalten hat, wegen der Vornahme des Vollzugs noch besonders einzuschreiten.

(2) Findet ein Vollzug von Amts wegen nicht statt, so erfolgt die Zwangsvollstreckung auf Betreiben des Gläubigers auf Grund einer mit der Vollstreckungsklausel versehenen Ausfertigung (vollstreckbare Ausfertigung) des Beschlusses über die Bewilligung der Zwangsvollstreckung, die der Gerichtsschreiber unverzüglich dem Gläubiger von Amts wegen zu erteilen hat.

(3) Die Zwangsvollstreckung auf Betreiben des Gläubigers darf nur beginnen, wenn der Bewilligungsbeschluß dem Verpflichteten bereits zugestellt ist oder gleichzeitig zugestellt wird. Soweit nach dem Recht des Vollstreckungsstaats der Beginn der Zwangsvollstreckung aus inländischen gleichartigen Vollstreckungstiteln von dem Ablauf gewisser Fristen seit der Zustellung abhängig ist, müssen diese Fristen seit Zustellung des Bewilligungsbeschlusses verstrichen sein.

Art. 31. (1) Soweit dieser Vertrag nicht besondere Bestimmungen enthält, sind die in dem Gebiete des Vollstreckungsstaats geltenden Vorschriften über das Verfahren, insbesondere die Vorschriften über die Aufschiebung und Einstellung der Zwangsvollstreckung sowie über den Widerspruch und sonstige Rechte Dritter ihr gegenüber auch auf die Zwangsvollstreckungen anzuwenden, die nach diesem Vertrage bewilligt werden. Soweit nach diesen Vorschriften das Prozeßgericht erster Instanz für Vollstreckungshandlungen oder für die eine Zwangsvollstreckung betreffenden Klagen zuständig ist, tritt an seine Stelle das Gericht, welches die Zwangsvollstreckung bewilligt hat.

(2) Wird in dem Gebiete des Staates, dessen Gericht die zu vollstreckende Entscheidung erlassen hat, im Nichtigkeits- oder Wieder-

aufnahmeverfahren die Aufschiebung oder Einstellung der Zwangsvollstreckung angeordnet, so ist auch das Verfahren in dem Vollstreckungsstaat aufzuschieben oder einzustellen.

Art. 32. Die Bestimmungen der Artikel 19 bis 31 finden entsprechende Anwendung

1. auf die vor einem bürgerlichen Gericht im streitigen Verfahren abgeschlossenen Vergleiche und auf die gerichtlich bestätigten Vermögensauseinandersetzungen und Dispachen;

2. auf die gerichtlichen und notariellen Urkunden, in denen sich der Verpflichtete der Zwangsvollstreckung unterworfen hat.

Art. 33. Bei der Bewilligung der Zwangsvollstreckung auf Grund von Akten der im Artikel 32 bezeichneten Art dürfen keine höheren Gebühren eingehoben werden, als bei der Bewilligung der Zwangsvollstreckung auf Grund einer ausländischen gerichtlichen Entscheidung.

IV. Abschnitt

Anerkennung gerichtlicher Entscheidungen

Art. 34. Rechtskräftige Entscheidungen, denen keiner der im Artikel 25 angeführten Gründe entgegensteht, werden unbeschadet der Bestimmungen des Artikels 36, Abs. 2, Zahl 1, auch im Gebiete des anderen Staates als wirksam anerkannt.

V. Abschnitt

Übergangs- und Schlußbestimmungen

Art. 35. Die Bestimmungen der Artikel 2 bis 18 treten im Verhältnis zwischen den vertragschließenden Staaten an die Stelle der Vorschriften des Haager Abkommens über den Zivilprozeß vom 17. Juli 1905.

Art. 36. (1) Von dem Tage des Inkrafttretens dieses Vertrags an treten für die Rechtsbeziehungen zwischen den vertragschließenden Staaten frühere Staatsverträge, Vereinbarungen und Regierungserklärungen über Fragen, die durch den vorstehenden Vertrag geregelt sind, außer Kraft.

(2) Unberührt bleiben

1. die in den beiden vertragschließenden Staaten geltenden Vorschriften über Ehesachen, über Rechtsstreitigkeiten, welche die Feststellung des Rechtsverhältnisses zwischen Eltern und Kindern betreffen, sowie über das Konkursverfahren und die Todeserklärung;

2. die Bestimmungen der Artikel 2 und 24 des deutschösterreichischen Wirtschaftsabkommens vom 1. September 1920;

3. die internationalen Kollektivverträge, an denen beide vertragschließende Staaten beteiligt sind.

Art. 37. Dieser Vertrag tritt drei Monate nach dem Austausch der Ratifikationsurkunden in Kraft. Der Vertrag kann von jedem der vertragschließenden Staaten gekündigt werden. Er bleibt jedoch nach erfolgter Kündigung noch sechs Monate in Kraft.

Art. 38. Dieser Vertrag wird ratifiziert und die Ratifikationsurkunden werden sobald wie möglich in Berlin ausgetauscht werden.

Urkund dessen haben die Bevollmächtigten den Vertrag in doppelter Ausfertigung unterzeichnet und mit ihren Siegeln versehen.

So geschehen in doppelter Urschrift in Wien, am 21. Juni 1923.

Deutsches Reich—Schweiz

Abkommen zwischen dem Deutschen Reich und der Schweizerischen Eidgenossenschaft über die gegenseitige Anerkennung und Vollstreckung von gerichtlichen Entscheidungen und Schiedssprüchen. Vom 2. November 1929. RGBl. 1930 II S. 1066.

Art. 1. Die im Prozeßverfahren über vermögensrechtliche Ansprüche ergangenen rechtskräftigen Entscheidungen der bürgerlichen Gerichte des einen Staates werden ohne Unterschied ihrer Benennung (Urteile, Beschlüsse, Vollstreckungsbefehle), jedoch mit Ausnahme der Arreste und einstweiligen Verfügungen, und ohne Rücksicht auf die Staatsangehörigkeit der an dem Rechtsstreit beteiligten Parteien im Gebiete des andern Staates anerkannt, wenn für die Gerichte des Staates, in dessen Gebiet die Entscheidung gefällt wurde, eine Zuständigkeit nach Maßgabe des Artikel 2 begründet war und nicht nach dem Rechte des Staates, in dessen Gebiet die Entscheidung geltend gemacht wird, für dessen Gerichte eine ausschließliche Zuständigkeit besteht.

Art. 2. Die Zuständigkeit der Gerichte des Staates, in dem die Entscheidung gefällt wurde, ist im Sinne des Artikel 1 begründet, wenn sie in einer staatsvertraglichen Bestimmung vorgesehen oder eine der folgenden Voraussetzungen erfüllt ist:

1. wenn der Beklagte zur Zeit der Klageerhebung oder zur Zeit der Erlassung der Entscheidung seinen Wohnsitz oder die beklagte juristische Person ihren Sitz in diesem Staate hatte;
2. wenn sich der Beklagte durch eine ausdrückliche Vereinbarung der Zuständigkeit des Gerichts, das die Entscheidung gefällt hat, unterworfen hatte;
3. wenn der Beklagte sich vorbehaltlos auf den Rechtsstreit eingelassen hatte;
4. wenn der Beklagte am Orte seiner geschäftlichen Niederlassung oder Zweigniederlassung für Ansprüche aus dem Betriebe dieser Niederlassung belangt worden ist;
5. für eine Widerklage, wenn der Gegenanspruch mit dem in der Klage geltend gemachten Anspruch oder mit den gegen diesen vorgebrachten Verteidigungsmitteln in rechtlichem Zusammenhange steht.

Art. 3. Die in nicht vermögensrechtlichen Streitigkeiten zwischen Angehörigen eines der beiden Staaten oder beider Staaten ergangenen rechtskräftigen Entscheidungen der bürgerlichen Gerichte des einen Staates werden im Gebiete des anderen Staates anerkannt, es sei denn, daß an dem Rechtsstreit ein Angehöriger des Staates, in dem die Entscheidung geltend gemacht wird, beteiligt war und nach dem Rechte dieses Staates die Zuständigkeit eines Gerichts des anderen Staates nicht begründet war. Dies gilt auch insoweit, als die in einer nichtvermögensrechtlichen Streitigkeit ergangene Entscheidung sich auf einen vermögensrechtlichen Anspruch mit erstreckt, der von dem in ihr festgestellten Rechtsverhältnis abhängt.

Art. 4. Die Anerkennung ist zu versagen, wenn durch die Entscheidung ein Rechtsverhältnis zur Verwirklichung gelangen soll, dem im Gebiete des Staates, wo die Entscheidung geltend gemacht wird, aus

Rücksichten der öffentlichen Ordnung oder der Sittlichkeit die Gültigkeit, Verfolgbarkeit oder Klagbarkeit versagt ist.

Sie ist ferner zugunsten eines inländischen Beteiligten zu versagen, wenn in der Entscheidung bei Beurteilung seiner Handlungsfähigkeit oder seiner gesetzlichen Vertretung oder bei Beurteilung eines für den Anspruch maßgebenden familien- oder erbrechtlichen Verhältnisses oder der dafür maßgebenden Feststellungen des Todes einer Person zu seinem Nachteil andere als die nach dem Rechte des Staates, wo die Entscheidung geltend gemacht wird, anzuwendenden Gesetze zugrunde gelegt sind.

Hat sich der Beklagte auf den Rechtsstreit nicht eingelassen, so ist die Anerkennung zu versagen, wenn die Zustellung der den Rechtsstreit einleitenden Ladung oder Verfügung an den Beklagten oder seinen zur Empfangnahme berechtigten Vertreter nicht rechtzeitig oder lediglich im Wege der öffentlichen Zustellung oder im Auslande auf einem anderen Wege als dem der Rechtshilfe bewirkt worden ist.

Art. 5. Das Gericht des Staates, wo die Entscheidung geltend gemacht wird, ist bei der Prüfung der die Zuständigkeit eines Gerichts des anderen Staates begründenden Tatsachen und der Versagungsgründe an die tatsächlichen Feststellungen der Entscheidung nicht gebunden. Eine weitere Nachprüfung der Gesetzmäßigkeit der Entscheidung findet nicht statt.

Art. 6. Die Entscheidungen der Gerichte des einen Staates, die nach den vorstehenden Bestimmungen im Gebiete des anderen Staates anzuerkennen sind, werden auf Antrag einer Partei von der zuständigen Behörde dieses Staates für vollstreckbar erklärt. Vor der Entscheidung ist der Gegner zu hören. Die Vollstreckbarerklärung hat in einem möglichst einfachen und schleunigen Verfahren zu erfolgen.

Die Vollziehung der für vollstreckbar erklärten Entscheidung bestimmt sich nach dem Rechte des Staates, in dem die Vollstreckung beantragt wird.

Art. 7. Die Partei, die für eine Entscheidung die Vollstreckbarerklärung nachsucht, hat beizubringen:

1. eine vollständige Ausfertigung der Entscheidung; die Rechtskraft der Entscheidung ist, soweit sie sich nicht schon aus der Ausfertigung ergibt, durch öffentliche Urkunden nachzuweisen;
2. die Urschrift oder eine beglaubigte Abschrift der Urkunden, aus denen sich die der Vorschrift des Artikel 4 Abs. 3 entsprechende Ladung der nicht erschienenen Partei ergibt.

Auf Verlangen der Behörde, bei der die Vollstreckbarerklärung beantragt wird, ist eine Übersetzung der im Abs. 1 bezeichneten Urkunden in die amtliche Sprache dieser Behörde beizubringen. Diese Übersetzung muß von einem diplomatischen oder konsularischen Vertreter oder einem beeidigten Dolmetscher eines der beiden Staaten als richtig bescheinigt sein.

Art. 8. Die in einem gerichtlichen Güteverfahren (Sühneverfahren) oder nach Erhebung der Klage vor einem bürgerlichen Gericht abgeschlossenen oder von einem solchen bestätigten Vergleiche stehen, vorbehaltlich der Bestimmung des Artikel 4 Abs. 1, hinsichtlich ihrer Vollstreckbarkeit anzuerkennenden gerichtlichen Entscheidungen im Sinne der Artikel 6 und 7 gleich.

Art. 9. Hinsichtlich der Anerkennung und Vollstreckung von Schiedssprüchen gilt im Verhältnis zwischen den beiden Staaten das in Genf zur Zeichnung aufgelegte Abkommen zur Vollstreckung ausländischer Schiedssprüche vom 26. September 1927 mit der Maßgabe, daß es ohne Rücksicht auf die im Artikel 1 Abs. 1 daselbst enthaltenen Beschränkungen auf alle in einem der beiden Staaten ergangenen Schiedssprüche Anwendung findet.

Zum Nachweis, daß der Schiedsspruch eine endgültige Entscheidung im Sinne des Artikel 1 Abs. 2 lit. d des vorbezeichneten Abkommens darstellt, genügt in Deutschland eine Bescheinigung der Geschäftsstelle des Gerichts, bei dem der Schiedsspruch niedergelegt ist, in der Schweiz eine Bescheinigung der zuständigen Behörde des Kantons, in dem der Schiedsspruch ergangen ist.

Vor einem Schiedsgericht abgeschlossene Vergleiche werden in derselben Weise wie Schiedssprüche vollstreckt.

Art. 10. Dieses Abkommen soll ratifiziert werden. Die Ratifikationsurkunden sollen sobald als möglich in Berlin ausgetauscht werden.

Das Abkommen tritt drei Monate nach dem Austausch der Ratifikationsurkunden in Kraft. Es findet keine Anwendung auf Entscheidungen, die vor seinem Inkrafttreten rechtskräftig geworden sind, und auf Vergleiche, die vor diesem Zeitpunkt zustandegekommen sind.

Das Abkommen kann von jedem der vertragschließenden Staaten gekündigt werden. Es bleibt jedoch nach erfolgter Kündigung noch sechs Monate in Kraft.

Zu Urkund dessen haben die Bevollmächtigten dieses Abkommen unterzeichnet.

Ausgefertigt in doppelter Urschrift in Bern, am 2. November 1929.

Dominikanische Republik—Italien

Trattato di navigazione e di commercio tra l'Italia e la Repubblica di San Domingo. 18 ottobre 1886. Raccolta ufficiale delle leggi 98 (1890), S. 3333.

Art. 22. Le sentenze ed ordinanze in materia civile e commerciale emanate dai tribunali di una delle parti contraenti, e debitamente legalizzate, ancorchè pronunziate prima della conclusione del presente trattato, avranno, negli Stati dell'altra parte, la stessa forza di quelle emanate dai tribunali locali, e saranno reciprocamente eseguite e produrranno gli stessi effetti ipotecarii sovra quei beni che ne saranno passibili, secondo le leggi del paese ed osservate le disposizioni delle leggi stesse in ordine alla iscrizione od alle altre formalità.

Perchè possano eseguirsi, queste sentenze ed ordinanze dovranno essere previamente dichiarate esecutorie dal tribunale superiore nella cui giurisdizione o territorio dovrà aver luogo la esecuzione mediante un giudizio di delibazione in cui, sentite le parti nella forma sommaria, si esaminerà:

1° Se la sentenza sia stata proferita da un'autorità giudiziaria competente;

2° Se sia stata pronunciata, citate regolarmente le parti;

3° Se le parti sieno state legalmente rappresentate o legalmente contumaci;

4° Se la sentenza non contenga disposizioni contrarie all'ordine pubblico o al diritto pubblico dello Stato.

L'esecutorietà della sentenza potrà essere richiesta in via diplomatica ovvero direttamente dalla parte interessata.

Quando è chiesta in via diplomatica, se la parte interessata non ha, ad un tempo, costituito un procuratore, questi gli verrà deputato d'ufficio dal tribunale che deve dichiarare esecutoria la sentenza.

La parte istante dovrà soddisfare al procuratore deputato d'ufficio, il pagamento d'ogni legittima sua competenza.

Art. 26. Le due Parti contraenti si concedono reciprocamente, tutti i diritti e favori in materia di commercio, di navigazione e consolare che sono concessi, o potranno esserlo, in seguito, alla nazione più favorita.

Art. 28. I due Governi contraenti convengono che le controversie, le quali possano sorgere intorno alla interpretazione e alla esecuzione del presente trattato o alle conseguenze di qualche sua violazione, debbano assoggettarsi, quando siano esauriti i mezzi di comporle direttamente per amichevole accordo, alla decisione di commissioni arbitrali, e che il risultato di simile arbitrato sia obbligatorio per entrambi.

I componenti di tali commissioni saranno scelti dai due Governi di comune consenso; in difetto di ciò, ognuno dei paesi nominerà il proprio arbitro o un numero eguale di arbitri, e gli arbitri nominati ne sceglieranno un ultimo.

La procedura arbitrale sarà, in ciascuno dei casi determinata dalle Parti contraenti, e in difetto, il collegio stesso degli arbitri si intenderà autorizzato a preliminarmente determinarla.

Art. 29. Il presente trattato sarà in vigore per dieci anni da decorrere dal giorno in cui si farà lo scambio delle ratifiche, ma, se un anno prima dello spirare del termine, niuna delle Parti contraenti avesse annunciata ufficialmente all'altra l'intenzione di farne cessare gli effetti, continuerà a rimanere in vigore per ambe le Parti sino ad un anno dopo che siasi fatta la suddetta dichiarazione, qualunque sia l'epoca in cui abbia luogo.

Art. 30. Il presente trattato sarà approvato e ratificato da Sua Maestà il Re d'Italia e da S. E. il presidente della Repubblica di San Domingo, secondo la costituzione di ognuno dei due paesi, e le ratifiche ne saranno scambiate a San Domingo nel termine di un anno dal giorno della firma od anche più presto se ciò sarà possibile.

In fede di che i rispettivi plenipotenziari hanno firmato il presente trattato e vi hanno apposto il sigillo delle loro armi.

Fatto in San Domingo capitale della Repubblica di San Domingo, addì 18 ottobre dell'anno di N. S. 1886.

Frankreich—Großbritannien

Convention entre la Grande-Bretagne et l'Irlande du Nord et la France pour l'exécution reciproque des jugements en matière civile et commerciale. Signée à Paris, le 18 janvier 1934. Textes officiels anglais et français. SdN. 171 (1936) S. 185.

Titre I.
Dispositions générales.

Art. 1. Dans la présente convention:

§ 1. Les mots «Sa Majesté» désignent Sa Majesté le Roi de Grande-Bretagne, d'Irlande et des Dominions britanniques au delà des mers, Empereur des Indes.

§ 2. Les mots «Territoires de l'une (ou de l'autre) Haute Partie contractante» designent:

a) En ce qui concerne Sa Majesté, le Royaume-Uni (l'Angleterre, le Pays de Galles, l'Ecosse et l'Irlande du Nord) ainsi que tout territoire sur lequel la convention sera étendue par application des dispositions des articles 11 ou 13; et

b) En ce qui concerne la République française, le territoire métropolitain de la France, y compris la Corse et les îles adjacentes, et tout territoire auquel la convention aura été étendue par application des dispositions de l'article 12.

§ 3. Les mots «tribunaux supérieurs» désignent:

a) Pour le Royaume-Uni the House of Lords, et pour l'Angleterre et le Pays de Galles the Supreme Court of Judicature (Court of Appeal and High Court of Justice), the Courts of Chancery of the Counties Palatine of Lancaster and Durham; pour l'Ecosse the Court of Session et pour l'Irlande du Nord the Supreme Court of Judicature; et

b) Pour la France: la Cour de cassation, les Cours d'appel, les Tribunaux de première instance et les Tribunaux de commerce et, en cas de condamnation à des réparations au profit des parties civiles par les juridictions criminelles, les Tribunaux correctionnels et les Cours d'assises. Tous les autres tribunaux seront, au sens de la présente convention, des «tribunaux inférieurs».

§ 4. Le mot «jugement» désigne toute décision d'un tribunal quelle que soit son appellation (jugement, arrêt, ordonnance, etc.) fixant les droits des parties sur le fond même du procès, à l'exclusion notamment de tous jugements provisoires, préparatoires ou interlocutoires.

§ 5. Les mots «tribunal d'origine» désignent le tribunal qui a rendu le jugement. Les mots «tribunal requis» désignent le tribunal auquel on demande de reconnaître au jugement l'autorité de la chose jugée ou auquel est soumise une demande d'enregistrement ou d'exequatur.

§ 6. Les mots «partie perdante» désignent toute personne contre laquelle le jugement a été rendu par le tribunal d'origine, et comprennent, le cas échéant, toute autre personne contre laquelle le jugement peut être exécuté; les mots «partie gagnante» désignent toute personne au profit de laquelle le jugement a été rendu par le tribunal d'origine, et comprennent, le cas échéant, toute autre personne qui peut se prévaloir du jugement.

Art. 2. § 1. Les Hautes Parties contractantes conviennent que les jugements rendus, après la date de la mise en vigueur de la présente convention, par les tribunaux supérieurs siégeant sur le territoire de l'une d'elles, seront sur le territoire de l'autre, quelle que soit la nationalité de la partie perdante ou de la partie gagnante, reconnus comme ayant l'autorité de la chose jugée et rendus exécutoires dans les cas et sous les conditions indiquées aux articles 3—8 de la présente convention.

§ 2. Les dispositions de la présente convention s'appliquent exclusivement aux jugements rendus en matières civile ou commerciale et aux jugements en matière criminelle condamnant au payement d'une somme d'argent au profit d'une partie civile pour réparation d'un préjudice.

§ 3. Toutefois les dispositions de la présente convention ne s'appliquent pas:

a) Aux décisions rendues sur appel des jugements des tribunaux inférieurs;

b) Aux jugements rendus en matière de statut personnel (état et capacité de personnes), de droit de famille (y compris les jugements en matière matrimoniale ou relatifs aux rapports pécuniaires entre époux), de successions et testaments, de faillites, de liquidations de sociétés, associations ou autres personnes morales.

§ 4. Il est entendu que rien dans la présente convention ne doit être interprété comme interdisant de reconnaître l'autorité de la chose jugée ou d'accorder la force exécutoire sur le territoire de l'une des Hautes Parties contractantes conformément aux dispositions de la loi en vigueur sur ce territoire à des jugements prononcés par les tribunaux de l'autre, et non visés par la présente convention ou pour lesquels on ne peut invoquer les dispositions de la présente convention.

Titre II.

Reconnaissance de l'autorité de la chose jugée.

Art. 3. § 1. Les jugements visés à l'article 2 rendus par les tribunaux de l'une des Hautes Parties contractantes seront reconnus comme ayant l'autorité de la chose jugée par les tribunaux de l'autre dans les cas où l'on ne pourrait opposer à ces jugements des moyens tirés des dispositions suivantes:

a) Le tribunal d'origine n'était pas compétent, d'après les règles du droit international privé en vigueur dans le pays du tribunal requis;

b) Le jugement a été rendu par défaut et la partie perdante prouve que le défendeur devant le tribunal d'origine n'a pas eu connaissance de l'action intentée contre lui en temps utile pour pouvoir y répondre, même si la procédure suivie a été légale et valable d'après la loi du pays du tribunal d'origine;

c) Le jugement est contraire à l'ordre public dans le pays du tribunal requis; il en sera ainsi notamment dans les cas suivants:

(i) Le jugement se rapporte à un litige qui a déjà fait l'objet entre les mêmes parties d'un jugement ayant dans le pays du tribunal requis l'autorité de la chose jugée;

(ii) Le tribunal requis estime que le jugement a été obtenu par des manoeuvres frauduleuses de l'une ou l'autre partie;

(iii) Le tribunal requis estime que la partie perdante défenderesse devant le tribunal d'origine n'était pas d'après les règles du droit international public justiciable du tribunal d'origine et n'avait pas accepté sa juridiction;

(iv) La partie perdante n'est pas, d'après les règles du droit international public, justiciable du tribunal requis.

d) La partie perdante prouve qu'il a été fait appel ou opposition ou qu'il a été introduit un recours contre le jugement dans le pays du tribunal d'origine. Il est entendu que si les délais impartis par la loi du pays du tribunal d'origine pour engager ces procédures ne sont pas expirés, le tribunal requis, s'il le juge opportun, peut ne pas reconnaître immédiatement au jugement l'autorité de la chose jugée et donner à la partie perdante un délai raisonnable pour engager les procédures d'appel, opposition ou autres recours.

§ 2. Il est entendu que la reconnaissance de l'autorité de la chose jugée ne sera pas refusée pour le seul motif que le tribunal d'origine, pour déterminer la loi applicable dans l'espèce, a appliqué des règles de droit international privé autres que celles suivies dans le pays du tribunal requis.

§ 3. Il est entendu que la reconnaissance de l'autorité de la chose jugée au sens de la présente convention signifie que le dispositif du jugement a valeur obligatoire entre les parties (partie gagnante et partie perdante) et peut être opposé par elles comme une exception à toute nouvelle action intentée entre les mêmes parties sur le même objet et pour la même cause.

Art. 4. § 1. Nonobstant les dispositions de l'article 3, § 1 a), et sous réserve des dispositions des paragraphes 2 et 3 du présent article, le tribunal d'origine sera considéré comme compétent dans les cas suivants:

a) Si la partie perdante était demanderesse principale, reconventionnelle ou par intervention devant le tribunal d'origine;

b) Si la partie perdante défenderesse devant le tribunal d'origine a comparu volontairement devant ce tribunal. Il est entendu que les mots «comparu volontairement» ne visent pas le cas où la comparution a eu pour unique objet de s'opposer à la saisie de biens ou d'obtenir la mainlevée de cette saisie ou pour contester la compétence du tribunal d'origine;

c) Si la partie perdante défenderesse devant le tribunal d'origine avait, avant que l'action ne fût entamée, valablement souscrit un engagement tendant à soumettre la contestation objet du procès aux tribunaux du pays du tribunal d'origine ou à ce tribunal lui-même;

d) Si la partie perdante défenderesse devant le tribunal d'origine avait, au moment où l'action a été intentée, une résidence habituelle dans le pays du tribunal d'origine, ou lorsqu'il s'agit d'une société, si elle avait son siège social effectif dans ce pays;

e) Si la partie perdante défenderesse devant le tribunal d'origine avait dans le pays de ce tribunal soit un établissement d'affaires ou de commerce, soit une succursale, et si la contestation concerne une affaire traitée à cet établissement ou succursale ou par son intermédiaire.

Toutefois, la compétence du tribunal d'origine ne sera pas reconnue dans les cas indiqués aux paragraphes d) et e) ci-dessus si la partie perdante prouve au tribunal requis que l'action a été entamée devant le tribunal d'origine contrairement à un engagement valable spécifiant entre les parties un autre mode de règlement de la contestation.

§ 2. Les dispositions du paragraphe 1 du présent article ne s'appliquent pas aux jugements en matière de propriété immobilière ou aux jugements «in rem» relatifs à la propriété mobilière. Toutefois, dans ces cas, la compétence du tribunal d'origine sera reconnue si les biens immobiliers ou mobiliers se trouvaient situés dans le pays de ce tribunal au moment où l'action a été engagée.

§ 3. On ne pourra contester la compétence du tribunal d'origine pour le motif qu'il était incompétent d'après la loi de son pays, si d'après cette dernière loi, le jugement a l'autorité de la chose jugée.

Titre III.

Exécution des jugements.

Art. 5. § 1. Seront sur le territoire de l'une des Hautes Parties contractantes rendus exécutoires de la manière indiquée aux articles 6 à 8 du présent titre les jugements émanant des tribunaux de l'autre Haute Partie contractante visés à l'article 2:

a) S'ils sont susceptibles d'exécution dans le pays du tribunal d'origine;

b) S'ils condamnent au payement d'une somme d'argent déterminée, à l'exception des jugements condamnant au payement d'impôts, d'Etat ou autres, ou d'amendes;

c) S'ils sont susceptibles d'obtenir la reconnaissance de la chose jugée conformément aux dispositions du titre précédent.

§ 2. En accordant force exécutoire à un jugement, le tribunal requis donnera, à la demande de la partie gagnante, force exécutoire à la condamnation aux dépens prononcée par le tribunal d'origine; toutefois il pourra, à la demande de la partie perdante, limiter le montant de cette condamnation à 10 pour cent de la somme pour laquelle force exécutoire est accordée au jugement.

Art 6. § 1. Pour obtenir l'exécution dans le Royaume-Uni d'un jugement émanant d'un tribunal supérieur français, il faut présenter une demande en vue de l'«enregistrement» (registration) de ce jugement accompagnée de la copie intégrale certifiée conforme de ce document. Cette copie, délivrée par le tribunal d'origine, contiendra toutes indications sur la procédure suivie et reproduira les motifs de la décision. La demande doit être présentée dans les formes exigées devant le tribunal requis:

a) Pour L'Angleterre et le Pays de Galles à la «High Court of Justice»;

b) Pour l'Ecosse à la «Court of Session»;

c) Pour l'Irlande du Nord à la «Supreme Court of Judicature».

§ 2. Un jugement revêtu de la formule exécutoire conformément aux prescriptions de la loi française, est, en l'absence de preuve contraire, considéré comme susceptible d'exécution dans le pays où il a été rendu au sens de l'article 5 § 1 a). La formule actuellement employée est celle reproduite en annexe à la présente convention.

§ 3. Quand une demande aura été introduite au sujet d'un jugement remplissant les conditions prévues à l'article 5, l'enregistrement sera accordé, sauf dans les cas suivants:

a) Si les obligations pécuniaires résultant du jugement sont complètement éteintes;

b) Si la personne qui demande l'enregistrement n'a pas qualité pour le faire.

Art. 7. § 1. Pour obtenir l'exécution en France d'un jugement émanant d'un tribunal supérieur d'un territoire de Sa Majesté il faut introduire une demande, accompagnée d'une copie certifiée du jugement; cette copie délivrée par le tribunal d'origine contiendra toutes indications sur la procédure suivie et reproduira les motifs de la décision. La demande sera introduite dans les formes exigées par la loi française devant le tribunal de première instance du lieu du domicile de la partie perdante ou devant tout autre tribunal compétent d'après la loi française.

§ 2. Tout jugement dont une copie certifiée conforme a été délivrée par le tribunal d'origine sera considérée comme un jugement susceptible d'exécution dans le pays du tribunal d'origine à la date où la copie a été délivrée.

§ 3. Quand une demande aura été introduite au sujet d'un jugement remplissant les conditions prévues à l'article 5, l'exequatur sera accordé sauf dans les cas suivants:

a) Si les obligations pécuniaires résultant du jugement sont complètement éteintes;

b) Si la personne qui demande l'exequatur n'a pas qualité pour le faire.

Art. 8. § 1. Quand un jugement a été enregistré conformément aux dispositions de l'article 6 ou a été revêtu de l'exequatur conformément aux dispositions de l'article 7, il produira à partir de la date de l'enregistrement ou de l'obtention de l'exequatur, et en ce qui concerne les mesures d'exécution, les mêmes effets que s'il avait été rendu par le tribunal requis à la date de l'enregistrement ou de l'obtention de l'exequatur. Ce dernier tribunal aura compétence pour exercer tout contrôle sur l'exécution du jugement comme il peut le faire sur les jugements émanant de lui.

§ 2. Toute copie certifiée conforme par le tribunal d'origine et munie de son sceau ou de son cachet sera dispensée de législation.

Une traduction des documents produits devant le tribunal requis et certifiée conforme selon les prescriptions de la loi du pays de ce tribunal peut être exigée par lui.

§ 3. Bien que les procédures visées aux articles 6 et 7 soient réglées par la loi du tribunal requis, il est dans l'intention des Hautes Parties contractantes que ces procédures soient aussi simples et aussi rapides que possible.

Aucun dépôt pour garantir le remboursement des frais ni caution judicatum solvi ne pourra être exigé en cas de demande d'enregistrement ou d'exequatur.

§ 4. La demande d'enregistrement ou d'exequatur à moins que la loi du pays requis n'accorde des délais plus longs pourra être faite pendant un délai minimum de six ans commençant soit du jour où le jugement a été rendu, soit du jour où a été rendu l'arrêt mettant fin à toute procédure dans le cas où un recours aurait été introduit contre la décision de première instance.

§ 5. Il est entendu:

(i) Que si les obligations pécuniaires résultant du jugement pour lequel on demande l'enregistrement en vertu de l'article 6 ou l'exequatur en vertu de l'article 7 ne sont que partiellement éteintes, l'enregistrement ou l'exequatur sera accordé pour les sommes qui seraient encore dues et sous réserve que le jugement remplira les conditions indiquées dans la présente convention;

(ii) Que si le jugement dont l'enregistrement ou l'exequatur sont demandés en vertu des articles 6 ou 7 condamne au payement de sommes d'argent dues à divers titres et que pour certains chefs de condamnation il y a des motifs obligeant à refuser l'enregistrement ou l'exequatur le tribunal requis devra accorder l'enregistrement ou l'exequatur à l'égard des chefs de condamnations contre lesquels on ne peut invoquer des exceptions tirées des dispositions de la présente convention.

(iii) Que si, d'après le jugement, la somme d'argent à payer est exprimée dans une monnaie autre que celle du pays du tribunal requis, la loi de ce pays déterminera si, et de quelle façon, cette somme sera convertie dans la monnaie du pays du tribunal requis de manière à satisfaire aux obligations résultant du jugement.

§ 6. Dans le jugement accordant l'enregistrement ou l'exequatur, le tribunal requis, sur la demande d'une des parties, comprendra la somme due à titre d'intérêt jusqu'à la date de l'octroi de l'enregistrement ou de l'exequatur. Si le tribunal d'origine a lui-même déjà fixé les intérêts dus jusqu'à la date de son jugement, et, s'il est produit un certificat émanant de lui, indiquant à quel taux les intérêts doivent être calculés depuis cette date d'après la loi de son pays, le tribunal requis sera tenu par ces déclarations pour la fixation du montant des intérêts. Dans le cas contraire la partie, qui réclame les intérêts, devra prouver quelle somme est due à ce titre d'après la loi du pays du tribunal d'origine.

A partir de la date de l'enregistrement ou de l'exequatur, la totalité (principal et intérêts), des sommes déterminées dans le jugement accordant l'enregistrement ou l'exequatur portera intérêt de droit à 4 pour cent.

Titre IV.

Dispositions finales.

Art. 9. Les Hautes Parties contractantes conviennent que toutes les difficultés qui s'élèveront entre elles au sujet de l'interprétation ou de l'application de la présente convention seront réglées par la voie diplomatique. Il est entendu qu'il ne pourra être portée atteinte aux décisions des tribunaux des deux Hautes Parties contractantes.

Art. 10. La présente convention, dont les textes anglais et français font également foi, sera soumise à ratification. Les ratifications seront échangées à Paris. La convention produira effet un mois après la date de l'échange des ratifications et restera en vigueur pendant trois ans. Si aucune des Hautes Parties contractantes n'a avisé l'autre par la voie diplomatique, au moins six mois avant l'expiration de ladite période de trois ans, de son intention de mettre fin à la convention, celle-ci restera en vigueur jusqu' à l'expiration d'un délai de six mois à compter du jour où l'une des Hautes Parties contractantes aura fait connaître son intention d'y mettre fin.

Art. 11. § 1. Sa Majesté pourra, en tout temps, tant que la convention sera en vigueur en vertu de l'article 10, et à condition qu'un accord ait été préalablement conclu par un échange de notes au sujet des points mentionnés au paragraphe 2 du présent article, étendre, par une notification donnée par l'entremise de son Ambassadeur à Paris, l'application de la présente convention aux îles de la Manche, à l'île de Man, à ses colonies, territoires d'outre-mer, protectorats ou territoires sous sa suzeraineté ou territoires sous mandat dont le mandat est exercé par son gouvernement dans le Royaume-Uni.

§ 2. Avant qu'il soit procédé à la notification de l'extension à un territoire en vertu du paragraphe précédent, les Hautes Parties contractantes concluront un arrangement par échange des notes indiquant les tribunaux du territoire qui seront considérés comme tribunaux supérieurs au sens de la présente convention et ceux auxquels devront être adressées les demandes d'enregistrement.

§ 3. La convention entrera en vigueur sur le nouveau territoire trois mois après la date de la notification indiquée au paragraphe 1.

§ 4. Chacune des Hautes Parties contractantes pourra, à tout moment après l'expiration d'un délai de trois ans à partir de l'entrée en vigueur de l'extension de la présente convention à l'un quelconque des territoires visés au paragraphe 1 du présent article, mettre fin à cette extension en donnant par la voie diplomatique un préavis de dénonciation de six mois.

§ 5. Sauf convention contraire et expresse entre les deux Hautes Parties contractantes, la dénonciation de la convention, conformément à l'article 10, y mettra fin ipso facto, en ce qui concerne tous territoires auxquels son application aura été étendu conformément au paragraphe 1 du présent article.

Art. 12. § 1. Le Gouvernement français peut, à tout moment, par une notification donnée par l'entremise de l'Ambassadeur de la République française à Londres pendant la durée de la convention, et à condition qu'un accord ait été préalablement conclu par un échange de notes au sujet des points mentionnés au paragraphe 2 du présent article, étendre l'application de la présente convention à l'Algérie, aux colonies, aux pays sous protectorat français ou sous mandat administrés par le Gouvernement français.

§ 2. Avant qu'il soit procédé à la notification de l'extension à un des territoires désignés au paragraphe précédent, les Hautes Parties contractantes devront conclure un arrangement par échange de notes pour déterminer quels tribunaux du territoire seront considérés comme supérieurs au sens de la présente convention et ceux devant lesquels devront être introduites les demandes d'exequatur.

§ 3. Les dispositions des paragraphes 3, 4 et 5 de l'article précédent s'appliquent aux territoires auxquels la présente convention a été étendu en vertu du paragraphe 1 du présent article.

Art. 13. § 1. Tant que la présente convention sera en vigueur, soit en vertu de l'article 10, soit en vertu d'une adhésion donnée conformément au présent article, et à condition qu'un accord ait été préalablement conclu par un échange de notes au sujet des points mentionnés au paragraphe 2 du présent article, Sa Majesté pourra, à tout moment, adhérer, par une notification donnée par la voie diplomatique, à la présente convention pour l'un des membres du Commonwealth britannique dont le gouvernement désire cette accession, mais aucune notification d'adhésion ne pourra être donnée à aucun moment lorsque le Président de la République française aura notifié la dénonciation pour tous les territoires de Sa Majesté auxquels la convention s'applique.

§ 2. Avant qu'il soit procédé à la notification d'une adhésion conformément aux dispositions du paragraphe précédent, les Hautes Parties contractantes devront conclure un arrangement par échange de notes déterminant quels tribunaux du pays seront considérés comme tribunaux supérieurs au sens de la présente convention et ceux auxquels devront être adressées les demandes d'enregistrement.

§ 3. L'accession prendra effet trois mois après la date de sa notification.

§ 4. Après l'expiration d'un délai de trois ans, à compter de la date de l'entrée en vigueur d'une adhésion donnée en vertu du paragraphe 1 du présent article, chacune des Hautes Parties contractantes pourra, en donnant par la voie diplomatique un préavis de dénonciation de six mois, mettre fin à l'application de la présente convention en ce qui concerne chaque pays pour lequel une notification d'adhésion aura été donnée. La dénonciation de la convention en vertu de l'article 10 ne produira pas effet à l'égard des pays visés au présent article.

§ 5. Toute notification d'adhésion en vertu du paragraphe 1 du présent article pourra comprendre toute dépendance ou tout territoire sous mandat administré par le gouvernement du pays pour lequel cette notification d'adhésion est donnée, et toute notification de dénonciation pour ce pays, faite en vertu du paragraphe 4, s'appliquera à toute dépendance ou tout territoire sous mandat qui aura été compris dans la notification d'adhésion pour ce pays.

En foi de quoi les soussignés ont signé la présente convention dont les textes français et anglais ont la même valeur[1] et y ont apposé leurs cachets.

Fait à Paris en double exemplaire le 18 janvier 1934.

Annexe

(Voir article 6, § 2.)

Formule exécutoire.

Décret du 2 septembre 1871.

Art. 2. Les expéditions des jugements, arrêts, mandats de justice ainsi que les grosses et expéditions des contrats et de tous autres actes susceptibles d'exécution forcée, seront intitulées ainsi qu'il suit:

„République française. Au nom du peuple français."

Et terminées par la formule suivante:

„En conséquence, le Président de la République française mande et ordonne à tous huissiers sur ce requis de mettre ledit arrêt (ou ledit jugement, etc.) à exécution, aux procureurs généraux et aux procureurs de la République près les tribunaux de première instance d'y tenir la main, à tous commandants et officiers de la force publique de prêter main-forte lorsqu'ils en seront légalement requis.

„En foi de quoi le présent arrêt (ou jugement, etc.) a été signé par . . . .".

Protocole

Les plénipotentiaires soussignés, au moment de signer la convention entre Sa Majesté le Roi de Grande-Bretagne, d' Irlande et des Dominions britanniques au delà des mers, Empereur des Indes, et le Président de la République française, concernant l'exécution réciproque des jugements, déclarent qu'il est entendu que rien dans l'article 4 de ladite convention ne sera considéré comme obligeant les tribunaux français à reconnaître la compétence d'un tribunal du territoire de Sa Majesté dans des affaires relatives à des contrats d'assurance, dans les cas visés:

1. A la loi du 2 janvier 1902, relative à la compétence en matière d'assurances.

2. Aux articles 3 et 84 de la loi du 13 juillet 1930, relative au contrat d'assurance.

Le présent protocole fait partie intégrante de la convention à laquelle il se rapporte.

Fait à Paris, le 18 janvier 1934.

---

[1] Das vorstehende Abkommen ist in der französischen Fassung wiedergegeben, dafür das — ähnliche — belgisch-britische Abkommen in der englischen Fassung.

Frankreich—Italien

Convention entre la France et l'Italie sur l'exécution des jugements en matière civile et commerciale. Signée à Rome, le 3 juin 1930.

Texte officiel français.

SdN. 153 (1934) S. 136.

Titre Premier

De l'autorité de la chose jugée et de l'exécution forcée.

Art. 1. Les décisions rendues en matière civile et commerciale par les juridictions de l'une des Hautes Parties contractantes ont de plein droit l'autorité de la chose jugée sur le territoire de l'autre Partie, si elles réunissent les conditions suivantes:

1° Que la décision émane d'une juridiction compétente selon les règles du titre II de la présente convention autant qu'elles sont applicables ou, à défaut, selon les règles admises en la matière par la législation du pays où la décision est invoquée;

2° Que la décision ne contienne rien de contraire à l'ordre public ou aux principes de droit public du pays où elle est invoquée;

3° Que la décision soit passée en force de chose jugée et susceptible d'exécution d'après la loi du pays où elle a été rendue;

4° Que les parties aient été légalement citées, représentées ou déclarées défaillantes et, en cas de décision par défaut, que la citation ait atteint en temps utile la partie défaillante;

5° Que la décision ne soit pas en contradiction avec une autre décision déjà prononcée sur le même objet par une juridiction du pays où elle est invoquée, ou que le même litige n'ait pas été porté par les mêmes parties devant une juridiction de ce même pays avant que la décision invoquée ait été rendue.

Art. 2. Les décisions rendues en matière civile ou commerciale par les juridictions de l'une des Hautes Parties contractantes ne peuvent donner lieu à aucune exécution forcée par les autorités de l'autre Partie, ni faire l'objet de la part de ces autorités d'aucune formalité publique, telle que l'inscription ou transcription sur les registres publics, qu'après y avoir été déclarées exécutoires.

Les décisions des juridictions d'un des Etats rendues exécutoires sur le territoire de l'autre Etat y entraîneront hypothèque judiciaire dans les mêmes conditions que les décisions émanant des juridictions nationales.

Art. 3. L'exequatur est accordé à la demande de toute partie intéressée par l'autorité compétente d'après la loi du pays où il est requis.

Cette autorité doit se borner à vérifier si les conditions prévues à l'article premier sont remplies: elle procédera d'office à cet examen et devra en constater le résultat dans son jugement. Celui-ci a effet entre toutes les parties à l'instance en exequatur et dans toute l'étendue du territoire.

L'exequatur peut être accordé partiellement pour l'un ou l'autre seulement des chefs de la décision étrangère.

En accordant l'exequatur, le jugement ordonne, s'il y a lieu, les mesures nécessaires pour que la décision étrangère reçoive la même publicité que si elle avait été prononcée dans le ressort où elle a été rendue exécutoire.

La procédure de la demande en exequatur est régie par la loi du pays dans lequel l'exécution est demandée.

Art. 4. La partie qui invoque l'autorité d'une décision judiciaire, ou qui en demande l'exécution, doit produire:

1° Une expédition de la décision réunissant les conditions nécessaires à son authenticité;

2° L'original de l'exploit de signification de la décision ou de tout autre acte qui tient lieu de signification;

3° Les pièces de nature à établir que la décision est passée en force de chose jugée et est devenue exécutoire;

4° Une copie authentique de la citation de la partie qui a fait défaut à l'instance et toutes pièces de nature à établir que cette citation l'a atteinte en temps utile;

5° Une traduction des pièces énumérées ci-dessus, certifiée conforme d'après les règles admises par les lois du pays où la décision est invoquée, ou par les traités, sauf dispense de la part de l'autorité judiciaire compétente.

Art. 5. Les sentences arbitrales rendues valablement dans l'un des deux Etats sont reconnues dans l'autre et peuvent y être déclarées exécutoires si elles satisfont aux conditions indiquées à l'article premier, autant que ces conditions sont applicables.

L'exequatur est accordé par l'autorité compétente d'après la loi du pays où il est requis.

Art. 6. Les actes authentiques exécutoires dans l'un des deux pays peuvent être déclarés exécutoires dans l'autre par l'autorité compétente d'après la loi du pays où l'exécution est demandée.

Cette autorité vérifie seulement si les actes réunissent les conditions nécessaires pour leur authenticité dans le pays où ils ont été reçus et si les dispositions dont l'exécution est poursuivie n'ont rien de contraire à l'ordre public ou aux principes du droit public du pays où l'exequatur est requis.

Art. 7. Les hypothèques terrestres conventionelles, consenties dans l'un des deux Etats, seront inscrites et produiront effet dans l'autre seulement lorsque les actes qui en contiennent la stipulation auront été rendus exécutoires par l'autorité compétente, d'après la loi du pays où l'inscription est demandée. Cette autorité vérifie seulement si les actes et les procurations, qui en sont le complément, réunissent toutes les conditions nécessaires pour leur validité dans le pays où ils ont été reçus.

Les dispositions qui précèdent sont également applicables aux actes de consentement à radiation ou à réduction passés dans un des deux pays.

Art. 8. Les dispositions du présent titre s'appliquent quelle que soit la nationalité des parties.

Art. 9. Les décisions rendues par les juridictions de l'un des deux Etats en faveur d'une partie admise au bénéfice de l'assistance judiciaire gratuite seront déclarées exécutoires gratuitement sur le territoire de l'autre Etat, sans que la partie qui en demande l'exécution soit tenue d'obtenir à nouveau, à cet effet, l'admission au bénéfice de l'assistance judiciaire gratuite.

Titre II.

De la compétence judiciaire et de la faillite.

Art. 10. Les règles de compétence du présent titre n'ont pour objet que l'application du n° 1 de l'article premier.

Art. 11. En matière personnelle ou mobilière, dans les contestations entre Français et Italiens sont compétentes les juridictions de celui des deux pays où le défendeur a son domicile, ou, à défaut de domicile dans l'un des deux pays, sa résidence habituelle.

Si dans les contestations prévues au paragraphe précédent il y a plusieurs défendeurs, le demandeur peut, à son choix, porter son action devant les juridictions du pays du domicile, ou, à défaut de domicile dans l'un des deux pays, devant les juridictions du pays de la résidence habituelle de l'un d'eux.

Art. 12. Dans les contestations entre Français et Italiens, lorsqu'un domicile attributif de juridiction a été élu dans celui des deux pays où un contrat a été conclu ou doit recevoir son exécution, les juridictions du pays du domicile élu sont compétentes pour connaître des contestations relatives au contrat. L'élection de domicile doit avoir été acceptée expressément par les parties et spécialement pour chaque contrat. Si le domicile n'a été élu qu'en faveur d'une des parties, celle-ci conserve le droit de saisir tout juge compétent.

Art. 13. Le Français ou l'Italien qui possède soit un établissement commercial, industriel ou autre, soit une succursale dans l'un ou l'autre des deux pays est réputé faire élection de domicile dans le pays où est situé l'établissement ou la succursale pour le jugement de toute contestation concernant les contrats directement conclus par l'établissement ou par la succursale.

Art. 14. Si l'action a pour objet un contrat considéré comme matière commerciale par la loi du pays où cette action est portée, le demandeur français ou italien peut saisir les juridictions de celui des deux pays où le contrat a été conclu ou de celui où il doit recevoir exécution.

Art. 15. L'action en réparation du dommage causé par un délit ou quasi-délit peut être portée devant les juridictions de celui des deux pays où le fait dommageable s'est produit.

Art. 16. Les juridictions de celui des deux pays où est situé l'immeuble sont compétentes pour toutes les contestations concernant la possession ou la propriété de cet immeuble et pour celles qui concernent les droits réels sur cet immeuble.

Les contestations concernant les contrats relatifs à l'immeuble et devant être exécutés dans le lieu où est situé cet immeuble peuvent être portées devant les mêmes juridictions.

Art. 17. En cas de contestation entre Français et Italiens, les juridictions de celui des deux pays où le défunt avait son domicile pourront connaître, quelle que soit la nature mobilière ou immobilière des biens composant la succession:

1° Jusqu'au partage, des actions en pétition d'hérédité, des actions en partage et de toutes autres actions entre cohéritiers et des actions contre l'exécuteur testamentaire;

2° Jusqu'à l'expiration d'un délai de deux ans à partir du jour du décès, des actions en nullité ou en rescision du partage, des actions en garantie des lots et des actions des légataires et des créanciers contre les héritiers.

Art. 18. Les juridictions du pays où une demande est portée conformément aux règles du présent titre pourront connaître des demandes en compensation, des demandes incidentes ou accessoires et des demandes reconventionnelles.

Art. 19. Les juridictions de l'un des Etats contractants doivent, si l'une des parties le demande, se dessaisir des contestations portées devant elles quand ces contestations sont déjà pendantes devant les juridictions de l'autre pays, ou quand elles sont connexes à d'autres contestations déjà pendantes entre les mêmes parties devant ces juridictions, sous réserve que celles-ci soient compétentes selon les règles du présent titre.

Ne peuvent être considérées comme connexes que les contestations qui procèdent de la même cause ou portent sur le même objet.

Art. 20—27 (faillite).

Art. 28. Le mot domicile, tel qu'il est employé dans la présent titre, désigne:

1° Pour les majeurs jouissant de leur capacité, les mineurs émancipés, les majeurs auxquels est seulement imposée l'assistance d'un conseil pour l'accomplissement de certains actes, le lieu où se trouve le siège principal de leurs affaires;

2° Pour les mineurs, le lieu du domicile du représentant légal;

3° Pour le majeur n'ayant pas l'administration de ses biens et le mineur non émancipé, orphelin de père et de mère, le lieu où l'administrateur des biens ou le tuteur a son propre domicile;

4° Pour la femme mariée, le lieu du domicile de son mari et, si le domicile du mari est inconnu ou si la femme est séparée de corps ou autorisée à avoir un domicile séparé, le lieu où se trouve le siège principal de ses affaires;

5° Pour les sociétés, le lieu où est établi le siège social.

Titre III

Dispositions diverses.

Art. 29. En matière civile et commerciale, dans les instances portées devant les juridictions françaises par un Italien et devant les juridictions italiennes par un Français, les juges ne peuvent se déclarer incompétents en raison de l'extranéité des parties.

Art. 30. Les règles par lesquelles la législation d'un des deux Etats déclare ses juridictions compétentes en raison uniquement de la nationalité du demandeur et sans autre titre de compétence en ce qui concerne les contestations relatives à des obligations nées d'un contrat ou quasi-contrat ou d'un délit ou quasi-délit, ne seront pas applicables aux ressortissant de l'autre Etat dans les cas suivants:

1° Lorsque le défendeur a son domicile ou sa résidence dans le pays dont il est ressortissant;

2° Lorsque l'obligation est née ou doit être exécutée dans le pays dont le défendeur est ressortissant.

La disposition qui précède devra être appliquée d'office par les juridictions de chacun des deux pays.

Art. 31. Aucun dépôt ni caution, sous quelque dénomination que ce soit, ne peut être imposé, à raison soit de leur qualité d'étrangers, soit de défaut de domicile ou résidence dans le pays, aux ressortissants de l'un des deux Etats qui seront demandeurs ou intervenants devant les juridictions de l'autre Etat.

Art. 32. Les mesures provisoires ou conservatoires organisées par la législation d'un des deux pays peuvent en cas d'urgence être requises des autorités de ce pays quelle que soit la juridiction compétente pour connaître du fond.

Art. 33. Toutes les dispositions de la présente convention s'appliquent aux sociétés commerciales constituées selon les lois de l'un des deux pays et ayant leur siège social dans ce pays, ainsi qu'à celles qui sont visées au protocole annexé à la Convention d'établissement du 3 juin 1930, *ad* article 6.

Art. 34. Lorsqu'un Français domicilié en France sera partie dans une action portée devant les juridictions italiennes ou devra accomplir une formalité en Italie et lorsqu'un Italien domicilié en Italie sera partie dans une action portée devant les juridictions françaises ou devra accomplir une formalité en France, les délais prévus par les lois de procédure seront augmentés d'un mois, à moins que ces lois elles-mêmes n'accordent un délai plus long.

Art. 35. Le changement de nationalité en cours d'instance ne modifie pas la compétence d'une autorité régulièrement saisie.

Art. 36. Les stipulations de la présente convention ne dérogent pas aux dispositions des autres accords réglant la compétence judiciaire et l'exécution des jugements au sujet de matières spéciales.

Titre IV

Application, interprétation, durée de la convention.

Art. 37. Toutes les contestations qui s'élèveraient entre les Hautes Parties contractantes relativement à l'interprétation ou à l'application de la présente convention, pourront être soumises à l'arbitrage à la demande de l'une ou de l'autre de ces Parties.

Dans ce cas chacune des Parties contractantes nommera un arbitre et les deux arbitres ainsi désignés choisiront un sur-arbitre qui sera président. Les deux Parties rédigeront un compromis précisant les questions de principe que les arbitres devront trancher au sujet de l'interprétation ou de l'application de la convention.

Les arbitres se réuniront sur le territoire de celui des Etats qui a demandé l'arbitrage.

La sentence arbitrale sera définitive et obligatoire.

Elle ne pourra porter atteinte à des droits acquis en vertu de décisions judiciaires passées en force de chose jugée.

Art. 38. La présente convention sera applicable sur le territoire métropolitain des deux Parties et sur le territoire de l'Algérie.

Les Hautes Parties contractantes se réservent d'appliquer d'un commun accord, par échange de notes, la présente convention aux colonies, pays de protectorat et autres territoires soumis à leur souveraineté ou à leur autorité.

La présente convention abroge et remplace l'article 22 du Traité[1] du 24 mars 1760 entre la France et la Sardaigne et la Déclaration[2] échangée le 11 septembre 1860 entre la France et la Sardaigne.

Art. 39. La présente convention sera ratifiée et les ratifications en seront échangées à Rome aussitôt que faire se pourra.

Elle entrera en vigueur un mois après l'échange des ratifications.

Elle aura une durée de trois ans et restera en vigueur après ce terme tant que l'une des Hautes Parties contractantes n'aura pas notifié par un préavis de six mois son intention d'en faire cesser les effets.

En foi de quoi les plénipotentiaires ont signé la présente convention et y ont apposé leur sceau.

Fait à Rome, en double exemplaire, le 3 juin 1930.

Frankreich—Schweiz

Vertrag

zwischen

der Schweiz und Frankreich über den Gerichtsstand und die Vollziehung von Urtheilen in Civilsachen. Abgeschlossen am 15. Juni 1869. Amtliche Sammlung der Bundesgesetze und Verordnungen der schweizerischen Eidgenossenschaft, IX 1869, S. 1002.

I.

Klage und Gerichtsstand.

Art. 1. In Streitigkeiten zwischen Schweizern und Franzosen, oder zwischen Franzosen und Schweizern, über bewegliche Sachen und persönliche Ansprüche, mögen sie aus dem bürgerlichen oder aus dem Handelsverkehr entsprungen sein, ist der Kläger verpflichtet, seine Klage bei dem natürlichen Richter des Beklagten anhängig zu machen. Es gilt dies auch für Regreßklagen, welches immer das Gericht sein mag, bei welchem die ursprüngliche Klage anhängig ist.

Hat der Beklagte, sei er Schweizer oder Franzose, weder in der Schweiz noch in Frankreich einen bekannten Wohnsiz oder Aufenthaltsort, so kann er vor dem Gerichte des Wohnortes des Klägers belangt werden.

Wenn jedoch die Klage auf Erfüllung eines Vertrages geht, der vom Beklagten entweder in der Schweiz oder in Frankreich, aber außerhalb des Bereiches des erwähnten natürlichen Richters eingegangen worden ist, so kann dieselbe bei dem Richter des Ortes angehoben werden, wo der Vertrag abgeschlossen wurde, insofern die Parteien zur Zeit, wo der Prozeß anhängig gemacht wird, daselbst ihren Aufenthalt haben.

Art. 2. In Streitigkeiten zwischen Schweizern, die sämtlich in Frankreich, oder zwischen Franzosen, die sämtlich in der Schweiz ihren Wohnsitz oder ein kaufmännisches Etablissement haben, kann der Kläger seine Klage auch bei dem Gerichte des Wohnortes des Beklagten oder des Ortes, wo das Etablissement desselben sich befindet, anhängig machen, und es darf dieses Gericht nicht aus dem Grunde, daß die Parteien Ausländer seien, die Annahme der Klage verweigern.

---

[1] Wenck, Codex juris gentium recentissimi, Tome III, page 218.

[2] de Martens, Nouveau Recueil général de Traités, tome XVII, partie II, page 49.

Dieselbe Bestimmung findet auch dann Anwendung, wenn ein Schweizer einen in Frankreich wohnhaften oder sich daselbst aufhaltenden Fremden vor einem französischen Gerichte, und umgekehrt, wenn ein Franzose einen in der Schweiz wohnhaften oder sich daselbst aufhaltenden Fremden vor einem schweizerischen Gerichte belangt.

Art. 3. Ist an einem anderen Orte als an dem Wohnsize des Beklagten Domizil gewählt worden, so ist der Richter des gewählten Domizils allein kompetent, über Streitigkeiten, zu welchen die Erfüllung des Vertrages Anlaß gibt, zu urtheilen.

Art. 4. Dingliche Klagen auf Immobilien sind bei dem Richter der gelegenen Sache anzuheben.

Dasselbe gilt auch von persönlichen Klagen, wenn sie mit dem Eigenthum oder mit einem Benuzungsrechte an Immobilien zusammenhängen.

Art. 5. Jede Klage betreffend Liquidation oder Theilung einer Erbschaft, sei es in Folge von Testament oder Intestaterbrecht, und betreffend die Abrechnung zwischen Erben und Legataren, ist vor dem Gerichte des Ortes geltend zu machen, wo die Erbschaft eröffnet worden ist, und zwar, wenn es sich um die Verlassenschaft eines Franzosen handelt, der in der Schweiz verstorben ist, vor dem Gerichte seines lezten Wohnortes in Frankreich, und wenn es sich um die Verlassenschaft eines Schweizers handelt, der in Frankreich verstorben ist, vor dem Gerichte seines Heimatortes. Immerhin müssen für die Theilung und für die Veräußerung von Immobilien die Geseze des Landes, wo dieselben liegen, beobachtet werden.

Wenn bei der Theilung von Erbschaften, zu denen gleichzeitig mit Einheimischen auch Fremde berufen sind, die Gesezgebung eines der beiden Länder den eigenen Angehörigen besondere Rechte und Vortheile auf das in diesem Lande befindliche Vermögen einräumt, so können die Angehörigen des andern Landes in analogen Fällen ebenfalls die Rechte und Vortheile ansprechen, welche die Gesezgebung des Staates, dem sie angehören, gewährt.

Es versteht sich jedoch von selbst, daß in Erbschaftssachen die von den betreffenden Gerichten erlassenen Urtheile, wofern sie nur eigene Staatsangehörige betreffen, im anderen Staate vollziehbar sein sollen, welche Geseze auch in diesem leztern in Kraft sein mögen.

Art. 6. Der Konkurs über einen Franzosen, der in der Schweiz ein Handelsgeschäft hat, kann von dem Gerichte seines Wohnortes in der Schweiz, und umgekehrt kann der Konkurs über einen Schweizer, der in Frankreich ein Handelsgeschäft hat, von dem Gerichte seines Wohnortes in Frankreich ausgesprochen werden.

Nachdem ein solches Urtheil gemäß den Bestimmungen des nachstehenden Art. 16 auch für das andere Land vollziehbar erklärt worden ist, hat der Vertreter der Masse (Syndic) die Befugniß, durch Produktion des Urtheils die Ausdehnung des Konkurses auf das bewegliche und unbewegliche Vermögen, das der Gemeinschuldner in dem andern Lande besizt, zu verlangen.

In diesem Falle kann der Vertreter der Masse die Guthaben des Gemeinschuldners bei dessen Schuldnern eintreiben und zum Verkauf der dem Gemeinschuldner angehörigen beweglichen und unbeweglichen Vermögensstüke schreiten; er soll jedoch bei diesem Verkaufe die Geseze beobachten, welche an dem Orte bestehen, wo die Vermögensstüke liegen.

Die Beträge, welche der Vertreter der Masse in dem Lande der Heimat des Gemeinschuldners, sei es aus dem Verkaufe von beweglichem Gut, sei es aus der Einziehung von Forderungen bezogen hat, sollen in die gemeine Masse am Orte des Konkurses eingeworfen und mit den übrigen Aktiven der Masse nach Vorschrift der am Konkursorte geltenden Geseze unter sämmtliche Gläubiger, ohne Rüksicht auf ihre Herkunft, vertheilt werden.

Was den Erlös aus den Immobilien betrifft, so soll derselbe unter die Berechtigten nach den Gesezen des Landes, wo die Immobilien liegen, vertheilt werden. Es sind daher die Gläubiger, seien sie Franzosen oder Schweizer, welche sich für Wahrung ihrer Privilegien oder Hypotheken nach den Gesezen des Landes der gelegenen Sache gerichtet haben, bezüglich dieses Erlöses, ohne Rüksicht auf ihre Nationalität, in diejenige Klasse zu verweisen (kolloziren), in die sie gesezlich gehören.

Art. 7. Klagen, welche auf Schadenersaz, oder auf eine Restitution, oder auf das Wiedereinwerfen von Vermögensstüken, oder auf die Nichtigkeit eines Rechtsgeschäftes abzielen, und ebenso alle Klagen, die in Folge der Falliterklärung selbst oder in Folge eines Urtheils, das die Fallimentserklärung auf einen andern Zeitpunkt festsezt, als er ursprünglich fixirt war, oder Klagen, die aus irgendwelchen andern Gründen gegen Gläubiger oder gegen Dritte angehoben werden, sind bei dem Gerichte des Wohnsizes des Beklagten anhängig zu machen, es wäre denn, daß sich der Rechtsstreit auf dingliche Rechte an Immobilien beziehen würde.

Art. 8. Im Falle ein Akkommodement zu Stande gekommen ist, so haben alle Bestimmungen des Akkommodements, und zwar insbesondere auch die Abtretung des in seinem Heimatlande gelegenen Vermögens von Seite des Schuldners, die gleichen Wirkungen, wie in dem Lande, in welchem der Konkurs eröffnet worden ist, unter der Voraussezung jedoch, daß das Urtheil, welches das Akkommodement bestätigt (Homologationsurtheil), gemäß der Vorschriften des Art. 16 vollziehbar erklärt worden ist.

Art. 9. Ist in der Schweiz oder in Frankreich über einen in dem einen oder andern Lande niedergelassenen Fremden, welcher schweizerische und französische Kreditoren hat und in Frankreich oder in der Schweiz Vermögen besizt, Konkurs eröffnet worden, so sind auch auf diesen Konkurs die Vorschriften der Artikel 7 und 8 anwendbar.

Art. 10. Für minderjährige und bevormundete Schweizer, die in Frankreich wohnen, gilt die vormundschaftliche Gesetzgebung ihrer Heimatkantone, und in gleicher Weise gilt für minderjährige und bevormundete Franzosen, die in der Schweiz wohnen, das französische Gesez. Es sollen daher Streitigkeiten über die Einsezung einer Vormundschaft oder über die Verwaltung des Vermögens von Minderjährigen und Bevormundeten vor die kompetente Behörde des Heimatlandes gebracht werden, mit Ausschluß jedoch von Streitigkeiten über Immobilien, bei welchen die Geseze der gelegenen Sache ihre Anwendung finden, so weit nicht konservatorische Maßregeln nothwendig werden, welch' leztere dem Richter des Wohnortes zustehen.

Art. 11. Wird bei einem schweizerischen oder bei einem französischen Gerichte eine Klage anhängig gemacht, die nach Inhalt der vorhergehenden Artikel nicht in seine Kompetenz fällt, so soll es von Amtes wegen, und zwar selbst in Abwesenheit des Beklagten, die Parteien an den kompetenten Richter verweisen.

Art. 12. Gegen ein Kontumazialurtheil kann nur bei den Behörden des Landes, in welchem dieses Urtheil erlassen worden ist, Opposition eingelegt werden.

Art. 13. Von Franzosen, die in der Schweiz eine Klage anheben, kann keine andere Gebühr, Kaution oder Hinterlage verlangt werden als eine solche, die nach den Gesezen des Kantons, wo die Klage angehoben wird, auch von schweizerischen Angehörigen anderer Kantone gefordert werden darf.

In gleicher Weise kann auch von Schweizern, die in Frankreich eine Klage vor Gericht geltend machen, keine Gebühr, Kaution oder Hinterlage gefordert werden, denen die Franzosen gemäß den französischen Gesezen nicht auch unterworfen sind.

Art. 14. Die Schweizer in Frankreich und die Franzosen in der Schweiz haben Anspruch auf gerichtliche Verbeiständung in Gemäßheit der Geseze des Landes, in welchem sie die Verbeiständung verlangen. Jedoch soll neben den Förmlichkeiten, welche jene Geseze vorschreiben, die Armuth noch außerdem durch Urkunden der kompetenten Behörden der Heimat der betreffenden Partei konstatirt werden.

Diese Urkunden hat der diplomatische Agent des andern Landes zu legalisiren und seiner Regierung zu übermitteln.

II.

Vollziehung der Urtheile.

Art. 15. Urtheile oder definitive Erkenntnisse in Zivil- oder Handelssachen, die durch Gerichte oder Schiedsgerichte in dem einen der beiden kontrahirenden Staaten ausgefällt worden und in Rechtskraft erwachsen sind, sollen in dem andern Staate nach den Formen und unter den Voraussezungen des Art. 16 vollziehbar sein.

Art. 16. Die Partei, zu deren Gunsten in einem der beiden Staaten die Vollziehung eines Urtheils oder eines richterlichen Erkenntnisses verlangt wird, muß dem Gerichte oder einer andern kompetenten Behörde des Ortes oder eines der Orte, wo die Vollziehung stattfinden soll, folgende Aktenstüke vorlegen:

1. das Urtheil oder das Erkenntniß in einer durch den Gesandten oder, in Ermangelung eines solchen, durch die Behörden des betreffenden Landes legalisirten Ausfertigung;
2. das Original des Aktes über die Notifikation des genannten Urtheils oder Erkenntnisses, oder irgend einen andern Akt, welcher im betreffenden Lande die Stelle der Notifikation gültig vertritt;
3. eine durch den Gerichtsschreiber des urtheilenden Gerichtes ausgestellte Bescheinigung, daß keinerlei Opposition, Appellation oder ein anderes Rechtsmittel vorliege.

Auf die Vorweisung dieser drei Aktenstüke hin soll über das Begehren um Vollziehung entschieden werden. Dies geschieht in Frankreich durch das als Kammer für Justizgeschäfte versammelte Gericht, und zwar auf den Bericht eines durch den Präsidenten hiezu bezeichneten Richters und auf den Antrag der Staatsanwaltschaft. In der Schweiz geschieht die Entscheidung durch die kompetente Behörde in der gesezlich bestimmten Form. In beiden Ländern soll jedoch eine Entscheidung nicht gefaßt werden, bevor der Partei, gegen welche die Vollziehung verlangt wird, mittelst Notifikation der Tag und die Stunde des Entscheides zur Kenntniß gebracht worden ist.

Art. 17. Die Behörde, welche über das Vollziehungsbegehren zu entscheiden hat, soll in keiner Weise in die materielle Würdigung der Prozeßsache eintreten. Eine Vollziehung kann nur in den folgenden Fällen verweigert werden:

1. wenn der Entscheid von einer inkompetenten Behörde gefällt worden ist;
2. wenn ein kontradiktorisches Urtheil erlassen worden ist, ohne daß die Parteien gehörig zitirt worden sind und gesezlich vertreten waren, oder wenn ein Kontumazialurtheil erlassen worden ist, ohne daß die Parteien gehörig zitirt worden sind;
3. wenn die Normen des öffentlichen Rechtes oder die Interessen der öffentlichen Ordnung des Landes, wo die Vollziehung verlangt wird, einer Vollziehung des Entscheides der fremden richterlichen Behörde entgegenstehen.

Ein Urtheil, durch welches die Vollziehung entweder gestattet oder verweigert wird, ist wegen Nichterscheinens einer Partei nicht anfechtbar, wohl aber kann gegen dasselbe inner der Frist und nach den gesezlichen Formen des Landes, wo es ausgefällt wurde, an die kompetente Behörde rekurrirt werden.

Art. 18. Wenn das Urtheil persönliche Haft nach sich zieht, so kann das Gericht diesen Theil des Entscheides nicht vollziehen, wenn die Gesezgebung des Landes die persönliche Haft in dem Falle, um den es sich in dem Urtheil handelt, nicht zuläßt.

Jedenfalls kann die persönliche Haft nur inner den Grenzen und in der Form vollzogen werden, die das Gesez des Landes, in welchem die Vollziehung verlangt wird, vorschreibt.

Art. 19. Wenn über die gemäß Art. 15, 16 und 17 bewilligte Vollziehung von Urtheilen und Entscheiden Anstände entstehen, so sind sie bei derjenigen Behörde anzubringen, welche über das Vollziehungsbegehren selbst geurtheilt hat.

III.

Zustellung von Gerichtsbefehlen und von andern gerichtlichen und außergerichtlichen Aktenstüken. Requisitorien.

Art. 20. Gerichtsbefehle, Zitationen, Notifikationen, Aufforderungen und andere Prozeßakten, die in der Schweiz ausgestellt und für Personen bestimmt sind, die in Frankreich ihren Wohnsitz oder ihren Aufenthalt haben, sollen durch den Bundesrath direkt demjenigen schweizerischen diplomatischen oder Konsularagenten zugestellt werden, welcher dem kaiserlichen Prokurator, der sie an den Bestimmungsort vermitteln soll, am nächsten ist.

Der diplomatische oder Konsularagent stellt sie diesem Beamten der Staatsanwaltschaft zu, und dieser schikt ihm die Empfangsbescheinigung derjenigen Person zurük, welcher die Aktenstüke zugekommen sind.

In gleicher Weise überschikt die französische Regierung alle Gerichtsbefehle und Aktenstüke, die in Frankreich ausgestellt und für Personen bestimmt sind, die in der Schweiz ihren Wohnsiz oder Aufenthalt haben, an den französischen diplomatischen oder Konsularagenten in der Schweiz, welcher der mit der Zustellung beauftragten schweizerischen Behörde am nächsten wohnt. Die Behörde, welcher die Aktenstüke zugestellt sind, hat einen Empfangschein zu erheben und dem Agenten zurükzusenden.

Art. 21. Die beiden vertragschließenden Regierungen verpflichten sich, die Requisitorien, welche durch die Gerichtsbeamten der beiden Länder für die Instruktion von Prozessen in Zivil- und Handelssachen erlassen worden sind, auf ihren resp. Gebieten auszuführen, insoweit als die Geseze des Landes, wo die Vollziehung stattfinden soll, der Ausführung nicht entgegenstehen.

Die Zustellung der genannten Requisitorien soll immer auf dem diplomatischen Wege und in keiner andern Weise stattfinden. Die aus den Requisitorien erwachsenden Kosten fallen demjenigen Staate zur Last, der sie vollziehen soll.

Art. 22. Der gegenwärtige Staatsvertrag ist abgeschlossen für zehn Jahre, von dem Tage an gerechnet, an welchem die Ratifikationsurkunden ausgewechselt werden. Für den Fall, daß keiner der kontrahirenden Staaten ein Jahr vor dem Ablaufe dieses Termins seine Absicht angezeigt hat, die Wirkung desselben aufhören zu machen, bleibt der Vertrag noch für ein Jahr in Kraft, und so weiter, von Jahr zu Jahr, bis zum Schlusse eines Jahres von dem Tage an gerechnet, an welchem einer der kontrahirenden Theile ihn gekündigt haben wird.

Der Zeitpunkt, mit welchem der gegenwärtige Staatsvertrag in Kraft tritt, wird im Protokoll über die Auswechslung der Ratifikationen angegeben werden.

Die Bestimmungen des Vertrages vom 18. Juli 1828 über die Gerichtsbarkeit und Vollziehung von Urtheilen sind und bleiben hiemit abgeschafft.

Zur Beglaubigung des Vorstehenden haben die Bevollmächtigten den gegenwärtigen Vertrag unterzeichnet und demselben ihre Siegel beigedrukt.

So geschehen in Paris, den 15. Juni 1869.

Zusatzakte zum Vertrage zwischen der Schweiz und Frankreich über den Gerichtsstand und die Vollziehung von Urteilen in Zivilsachen. Unterzeichnet in Paris am 4. Oktober 1935.

Eidgenössische Gesetzsammlung 52 (1936), S. 442.

Art. 1. Dem Artikel 1 des Vertrages vom 15. Juni 1869 wird, in Abweichung vom Abs. 1, folgender Absatz beigefügt:

„Die Streitigkeiten betreffend Schäden aus Unfällen, die durch den Verkehr mit Straßenfahrzeugen verursacht worden sind, können nach Wahl des Klägers entweder vor den Richter des Ortes, wo der Schaden verursacht worden ist, oder vor den in Absatz 1 genannten Richter gebracht werden."

Art. 2. Nach Artikel 2 des Vertrages vom 15. Juni 1869 wird folgender Artikel eingefügt:

„Art. 2 bis. Die in der Gesetzgebung eines der beiden Staaten vorgesehenen vorläufigen oder sichernden Maßnahmen können bei den Behörden dieses Staates nachgesucht werden, welches immer auch die Gerichtszuständigkeit zur Entscheidung über die Sache selbst sei."

Art. 3. Die gegenwärtige Zusatzakte soll ratifiziert werden. Die Ratifikationsurkunden sollen sobald als möglich in Paris ausgetauscht werden.

Diese Akte tritt einen Monat nach dem Austausch der Ratifikationsurkunden in Kraft.

So geschehen in Paris am 4. Oktober 1935.

Frankreich/Tunis—Italien

Convention consulaire et d'établissement entre l'Italie et la Tunisie. 28 septembre 1896. Raccolta ufficiale delle leggi 1897 I, S. 259.

Art. 11. Les jugements et arrêts en matière civile et commerciale prononcés en Italie par les tribunaux italiens et dûment légalisés auront en Tunisie, et ceux prononcés en Tunisie par les tribunaux français et dûment légalisés auront en Italie, lorsqu'ils auront acquis la force de chose jugée, la même valeur que les jugements et arrêts prononcés par les tribunaux du pays. Néanmoins, les dits jugements et arrêts ne pourront être exécutés, qu'après que le tribunal compétent du pays où ils doivent recevoir leur exécution les aura déclarés excécutoires à la suite d'un jugement prononcé dans la forme sommaire et dans lequel il sera constaté qu'ils ont été prononcés par une autorité judiciaire compétente, les parties dûment citées et régulièrement représentées, ou légalement déclarées défaillantes, et qu'ils ne contiennent aucune disposition contraire à l'ordre public et au droit public de l'Etat.

Art. 34. La présente convention restera en vigueur jusqu'au 1er octobre 1905. Dans le cas où aucune des Hautes Parties contractantes n'aurait notifié, douze mois avant ladite date, son intention d'en faire cesser les effets, elle demeurera obligatoire jusqu'à l'expiration d'une année à partir du jour où l'une ou l'autre des Parties contractantes l'aura dénoncée.

Art. 35. La présente convention sera soumise à la ratification de Sa Majesté le Roi d'Italie et de M. le Président de la République française et les ratifications en seront échangées à Paris le plus tôt que faire se pourra.

Elle entrera en vigueur immédiatement après l'échange des ratifications.

En foi de quoi, les plénipotentiaires respectifs ont signé la présente convention et y ont apposé leurs cachets.

Fait en double exemplaire, à Paris, le 28 septembre 1896.

Griechenland—Tschechoslowakei

Convention entre la République Tchécoslovaque et la République Hellénique relative à la reconnaissance et à l'exécution de décisions judiciaires. Signée à Athènes, le 7 avril 1927. Texte officiel français. SdN. 88 (1929), S. 212.

Art. 1. Seront considérées comme des décisions judiciaires, au sens de la convention, les décisions rendues en matière civile ou commerciale, dans la procédure soit contentieuse soit non contentieuse, par les tribunaux ordinaires, les tribunaux spéciaux, les tribunaux arbitraux ou els autorités de tutelle (curatelle).

Les décisions rendues, dans un procès pénal, sur conclusion de la partie civile, et les décisions prononçant la faillite ou homologuant un concordat ne seront pas considérées comme des décisions judiciaires en matière civile ou commerciale au sens de la convention.

Art. 2. L'autorité des décisions judiciaires au sens de l'article 1er rendues dans l'un des Etats contractants sera reconnue dans l'autre Etat si elles remplissent les conditions suivantes:

1⁰ Que, pour l'affaire en question, les règles de compétence judiciaire internationale admises par le droit de l'Etat dans lequel la décision est invoquée, n'excluent pas la juridiction de l'autre Etat.

2⁰ Que la reconnaissance de la décision ne soit pas contraire à l'ordre public ou aux principes du droit public de l'Etat où la décision est invoquée.

3⁰ Que, d'après la loi de l'Etat où la décision a été rendue, celle-ci soit passée en force de chose jugée.

4⁰ Qu'en cas de jugement par défaut, la partie défaillante contre laquelle la décision est invoquée ait été régulièrement citée, conformément à la loi de l'Etat où la décision a été rendue, et que la citation l'ait atteinte en temps utile.

L'examen par les autorités de l'Etat où la décision est invoquée ne portera que sur les conditions énumérées sous chiffres 1 à 4. Ces autorités devront examiner d'office si lesdites conditions sont remplies. Cet examen devra être terminé au plus tard dans les deux mois à compter du jour où l'autorité compétente a reçu les actes.

Art. 3. Les décisions judiciaires rendues dans l'un des Etats contractants pourront être mises à exécution dans l'autre Etat si elles sont exécutoires dans l'Etat où elles ont été rendues et si elles remplissent les conditions énumérées dans l'article 2, chiffres 1 à 4.

L'examen par les autorités de l'Etat où l'exécution est demandée ne portera que sur les exigences indiquées au précédent alinéa. Ces autorités devront examiner d'office s'il est satisfait auxdites exigences. Cet examen devra être terminé au plus tard dans les deux mois à compter du jour où l'autorité compétente a reçu les actes.

Art. 4. La partie qui invoque la décision ou qui en demande l'exécution devra produire:

1⁰ Une expédition de la décision remplissant les conditions nécessaires à son authenticité.

2⁰ Les pièces de nature à établir que la décision est passée en force de chose jugée et, s'il y a lieu, qu'elle est devenue exécutoire.

3⁰ Une copie authentique de l'assignation de la partie qui a fait défaut à l'instance et l'attestation que la citation l'a atteinte en temps utile.

4⁰ Une traduction des pièces énumérées ci-dessus certifiée conforme d'après les presciptions de l'un ou l'autre Etat; la traduction sera produite en Tchécoslovaquie en langue tchécoslovaque, en Grèce dans la langue grecque.

Art. 5. Les sentences arbitrales rendues dans l'un des Etats contractants et y ayant acquis la même autorité que les décisions judiciaires seront reconnues et mises à exécution dans l'autre Etat si elles satisfont aux prescriptions des articles précédents, en tant que celles-ci sont applicables.

Il en sera de même pour les transactions judiciaires et pour les transactions conclues devant des arbitres ou des tribunaux arbitraux.

Art. 6. La loi de l'Etat requis régira la compétence et la procédure en matière d'exécution. Il en sera de même quant aux mesures prévues aux articles 8 à 10.

Art. 7. Les dispositions de la présente convention s'appliqueront, quelle que soit la nationalité des parties.

Art. 8. Le tribunal compétent à autoriser l'exécution accordera à la demande de la Partie, conformément à ses lois, la prise des mesures de sûreté pour assurer les droits résultant du titre exécutoire à l'égard du débiteur. Le tribunal révoquera éventuellement ces mesures, conformément à ses lois.

Art. 9. Avant même que les décisions indiquées aux articles 1 et 5 soient passées en force de chose jugée, ou que le délai prévu dans la décision pour l'accomplissement se soit écoulé, le tribunal compétent à autoriser l'exécution pourra, sur la demande faite dans sa forme prescrite, accorder la prise de mesures conservatoires d'après les dispositions en vigueur dans L'Etat requis.

Art. 10. Des mesures provisoires seront accordées déjà avant le procès ou au cours du procès sur la demande de la partie dont les intérêts se trouvent menacés, même si un tribunal de l'autre Etat est compétent pour statuer dans l'affaire en question.

Art. 11. La présente convention sera ratifiée et les ratifications en seront échangées à Athènes.

Cette convention entrera en vigueur un mois après l'échange des ratifications et produira ses effets encore un an après la dénonciation qui pourra avoir lieu en tout temps.

En foi de quoi les plénipotentiaires ont signé la présente convention en deux exemplaires.

Fait à Athènes, le 7 avril 1927.

Honduras—Italien

Trattato di commercio e navigazione tra l'Italia e l'Honduras. 31 dicembre 1868. Raccolta ufficiale delle leggi 46 (1875), S. 3512.

Art. 20. Le sentenze ed ordinanze in materia civile e commerciale, emanate dai tribunali di una delle parti contraenti e debitamente legalizzate, avranno, sulla richiesta dei tribunali stessi, negli Stati dell' altra parte la stessa forza di quelle emanate dai tribunali locali, e saranno reciprocamente eseguite e produrranno gli stessi effetti ipotecari sovra quei beni che ne saranno passibili secondo le leggi del paese, ed osservate le disposizioni delle leggi stesse in ordine all'iscrizione ed alle altre formalità.

Perchè possano eseguirsi queste sentenze ed ordinanze dovranno essere previamente dichiarate esecutorie dal tribunale superiore, nella cui giurisdizione o territorio dovrà aver luogo l'esecuzione, mediante un giudizio di delibazione, in cui, sentite le parti nella forma sommaria, si esaminerà:

1. Se la sentenza sia stata proferita da un'autorità giudiziaria competente;

2. Se sia stata pronunziata, citate regolarmente le parti;

3. Se le parti sieno state legalmente rappresentate o legalmente contumaci;

4. Se la sentenza contenga disposizioni contrarie all'ordine pubblico o al diritto pubblico dello Stato.

La esecutorietà della sentenza potrà essere richiesta in via diplomatica, ovvero direttamente dalla parte interessata.

Quando è chiesta in via diplomatica, se la parte interessata non ha ad un tempo costituito un procuratore, questi gli verrà deputato d'ufficio dal tribunale che deve dichiarare esecutoria la sentenza.

La parte istante dovrà soddisfare al procuratore deputato di ufficio il pagamento d'ogni legittima sua competenza.

Art. 21. Gli atti notarili di qualunque specie, ancorchè stipulati prima della conclusione del presente trattato, avranno rispettivamente nei due paesi la stessa forza e valore di quelli emanati e ricevuti dalle autorità locali e dai notari esercenti sul luogo, quando questi sieno stati sottoposti a tutte le formalità ed al pagamento dei relativi diritti stabiliti nei rispettivi Stati.

Gli atti notarili però non potranno avere la forza esecutiva che la legge loro accorda, se questa non fu prima loro impartita dal tribunale del circondario in cui vuol farsi l'esecuzione, previo sommario giudizio, in cui si compiranno le formalità stabilite dall'articolo precedente in quanto vi sono applicabili.

Art. 23. Se una delle parti contraenti accordasse nell'avvenire ad un altro Stato qualche particolare favore o concessione in materia di commercio, die navigazione e di qualunque altro oggetto contemplato nella presente convenzione, questo s'intenderà ipso facto e di pieno diritto concesso all'altra parte.

Art. 24. Il presente trattato sarà in vigore per dieci anni, da decorrere dal giorno in cui si farà lo scambio delle ratifiche; ma se un anno prima dello spirare del termine niuna delle parti contraenti avesse annunziata ufficialmente all'altra l'intenzione di farne cessare gli effetti, continuerà a rimanere in vigore per ambe le parti sino ad un anno dopo che siasi fatta la dichiarazione, qualunque sia l'epoca in cui abbia luogo.

Art. 25. Il presente trattato sarà approvato e ratificato da S. M. il Re d'Italia e da S. E. il Presidente di Honduras, secondo la costituzione di ognuno dei due paesi, e le ratifiche saranno scambiate a Guatemala nel termine di un anno dal giorno della firma, o anche più presto se ciò sarà possibile.

In fede di che i rispettivi plenipotenziari hanno firmato il presente trattato e vi hanno apposto il sigillo delle loro armi.

Fatto a Guatemala addì 31 di dicembre 1868.

Italien—Jugoslawien

Accordo fra l'Italia e il Regno Serbo-Croato-Sloveno per l'esecutorietà delle sentenze in materia civile e commerciale. 6 aprile 1922.

Raccolta ufficiale delle leggi 1923 XI, S. 9985.

(Stimmt wörtlich mit dem italienisch-tschechoslowakischen Vertrag vom gleichen Tage überein, doch heißt es

im Art. 4, Zeile 1, „osservate" statt „conservate";

im Art. 8, Abs. 1, „La presente convenzione sarà ratificata" statt „Il presente Accordo sarà ratificato";

am Schluß „in italiano e in francese" statt „in italiano e in cecoslovacco".)

Italien—Nicaragua

Trattato di amicizia, commercio e navigazione tra l'Italia e la Repubblica di Nicaragua, 25 gennaio (Januar) 1906. Raccolta ufficiale delle leggi 1906 V, S. 4252.

Art. 21. Le sentenze ed ordinanze in materia civile e commerciale emanate dai tribunali di una delle Parti contraenti, e debitamente legalizzate, avranno, sulla richiesta dei tribunali stessi, negli Stati dell'altra Parte, la stessa forza di quelle emanate dai tribunali locali e saranno reciprocamente eseguite e produrranno gli stessi effetti ipotecari sovra quei beni che ne saranno passibili, secondo le leggi del paese ed osservate le disposizioni delle leggi stesse in ordine alla inscrizione ed alle altre formalità.

Perchè possano eseguirsi queste sentenze ed ordinanze dovranno essere previamente dichiarate esecutorie dal tribunale superiore nella cui giurisdizione o territorio dovrà aver luogo la esecuzione, mediante un giudizio di delibazione, in cui, citate le parti in via sommaria, si esaminerà:

1° se la sentenza sia stata proferita da un'autorità giudiziaria competente;

2° se sia stata pronunziata citate regolarmente le parti;

3° se le parti sieno state legalmente rappresentate o legalmente contumaci;

4° se la sentenza contenga disposizioni contrarie all'ordine pubblico o al diritto pubblico interno dello Stato.

L'esecutorietà della sentenza potrà essere richiesta in via diplomatica, ovvero direttamente dalla parte interessata.

Quando è chiesta in via diplomatica, se la parte interessata non ha allo stesso tempo costituito un procuratore, questi gli verrà deputato d'ufficio dal tribunale che deve dichiarare esecutoria la sentenza.

La parte istante dovrà soddisfare al procuratore deputato d'ufficio il pagamento de' suoi onorari e delle spese che gli sono dovute.

Art. 25. Se una delle Parti contraenti accordasse nell'avvenire ad un altro Stato qualche particolare favore o concessione in materia di commercio, di navigazione o di altro oggetto contemplato nel presente trattato, questo si intenderà ipso facto concesso all'altra Parte.

Art. 26. I due Governi contraenti convengono che le controversie le quali possano sorgere intorno alla interpretazione o alla esecuzione del presente trattato, od alle conseguenze di qualche sua violazione, debbano assoggettarsi, quando sieno esauriti i mezzi di comporle direttamente per amichevole accordo, alla decisione di commissioni arbitrali, e che il risultato di simile arbitrato sarà obbligatorio per entrambi.

I componenti di tali commissioni saranno scelti dai due Governi di comune consenso; in difetto di ciò, ognuna delle Parti nominerà il proprio arbitro o un numero eguale di arbitri, e gli arbitri nominati ne sceglieranno un ultimo.

La procedura arbitrale sarà in ciascuno dei casi determinata dalle parti contraenti, e, in difetto, il collegio stesso degli arbitri si intenderà autorizzato previamente a determinarla.

Art. 27. Il presente trattato starà in vigore per dieci anni, a decorrere dal giorno in cui si farà lo scambio delle ratifiche, ma, se un anno prima dello spirare del termine, niuna delle Parti contraenti avesse annunciato ufficialmente all'altra l'intenzione di farne cessare gli effetti, continuerà in vigore per ambe le Parti sino ad un anno dopo che siasi fatta la suddetta dichiarazione, qualunque sia l'epoca in cui abbia luogo.

Art. 28. Il presente trattato sarà approvato e ratificato da S. M. il Re d'Italia e dall'Eccellentissimo signor Presidente della Repubblica di Nicaragua, secondo la costituzione di ognuno dei due Paesi, e le ratifiche ne saranno scambiate a Parigi nel termine di un anno dal giorno della firma, od anche più presto, se ciò sarà possibile.

In fede di che, i rispettivi plenipotenziari hanno firmato il presente trattato e vi hanno apposto il sigillo delle loro armi.

Fatto, in due esemplari dello stesso tenore, nella città di Managua il venticinque di gennaio dell'anno mille novecento sei.

Italien—Niederlande

(noch nicht ratifiziert)

Convention entre l'Italie et les Pays-Bas sur la reconnaissance et l'exécution des décisions judiciaires en matière civile et commerciale. 7 mars 1935. Gazzetta ufficiale del Regno d'Italia 1935 XIII, S. 3534.

Art. 1. Les décisions rendues en matière civile et commerciale par les juridictions de l'un des deux Etats ont l'autorité de la chose jugée sur le territoire de l'autre Etat, si elles réunissent les conditions suivantes:

1. que la décision émane d'une juridiction compétente selon l'art. 2 de la présente convention;

2. que la reconnaissance de la décision ne soit pas contraire à l'ordre public ou aux principes du droit public de l'Etat où la décision est invoquée;

3. que la décision ne soit pas en contradiction avec une décision déjà rendue sur la même contestation par une juridiction de l'Etat requis;

4. que la décision soit passée en force de chose jugée d'après la loi de l'Etat où elle a été rendue;

5. qu'en cas de jugement par défaut, la citation qui a introduit l'instance ait été remise en temps utile à la partie défaillante.

L'autorité de la chose jugée peut être invoquée par toute partie intéressée selon les règles de procédure en vigueur dans l'Etat requis.

Art. 2. La compétence des juridictions de l'Etat où la décision a été rendue est fondée au sens de l'article premier, n. 1, si elle est prévue par une autre Convention entre les Hautes Parties contractantes, où dans les cas mentionnés ci-après:

1. lorsque dans l'Etat où la décision a été rendue se trouvait le domicile du défendeur ou de l'un des défendeurs, s'il y en avait plusieurs dans la même contestation;

2. lorsque, par une convention expresse en vue de contestations déterminées, le défendeur s'était soumis à la compétence du tribunal qui a rendu la décision, sauf si toutes les parties avaient leur domicile dans l'Etat où la décision est invoquée.

Il en est de même si, au cours de la procédure, le défendeur a expressément déclaré se soumettre à la compétence du tribunal qui a rendu la décision;

3. lorsque le défendeur, ayant un établissement commercial ou industriel ou une succursale sur le territoire de l'Etat où la décision a été rendue, y a été cité pour des contestations ayant trait à l'exploitation de l'établissement ou de la succursale;

4. lorsque, la compétence étant fondée en ce qui concerne la demande principale, il s'agit d'une demande accessoire, ou d'une demande en garantie, ou bien d'une demande reconventionelle en connexité avec la demande principale ou avec les moyens de défense invoqués contre celle-ci;

5. en matière d'état, de capacité ou de droit de famille des ressortissants de l'Etat où la décision a été rendue;

6. lorsqu'il s'agit de contestations concernant la possession ou la propriété d'un immeuble situé dans l'Etat où la décision a été rendue, ou bien concernant les droits réels sur un tel immeuble;

7. en matière successorale, si le défunt avait son domicile dans l'Etat où la décision a été rendue, et quelle que soit la nature mobilière ou immobilière des biens composant la succession:

a) pour les actions en pétition d'hérédité, les actions en partage et toutes autres actions entre cohéritiers, jusqu'au partage;

b) pour les actions en nullité ou en rescision du partage et les actions en garantie des lots, jusqu'à l'expiration d'un délai de deux ans à partir du jour du partage;

c) pour les actions contre l'exécuteur testamentaire jusqu'au partage, et, si le partage n'est pas nécessaire, jusqu'à l'expiration d'un délai de deux ans à partir du jour du décès;

d) pour les actions de légataire et des créanciers, n'exerçant pas des droits réels sur des immeubles, dans les limites indiquées à la lettre précédente.

Les dispositions qui précèdent ne s'appliquent pas aux contestations pour lesquelles le droit de l'Etat requis reconnaît comme exclusivement compétentes ses propres juridictions ou celles d'un Etat tiers.

Art. 3. Les décisions judiciaires rendues par les juridictions de l'un des deux Etats et qui réunissent les conditions énumérées à l'article premier pourront, après avoir été déclarées exécutoires à la demande de toute partie intéressée, donner lieu à l'exécution forcée dans l'autre Etat, tant sur les meubles que sur les immeubles, ou y faire l'objet de formalités telles que l'inscription ou la transcription sur les registres publics.

Ne seront déclarées exécutoires dans l'Etat requis que les décisions qui sont susceptibles d'exécution dans l'Etat où elles ont été rendues.

L'autorité judiciaire compétente de l'Etat requis procédera d'office à l'examen des conditions prévues à l'art. 1 et à l'alinéa précédent, et devra en constater le résultat dans son jugement. Celui-ci a effet entre toutes les parties à l'instance en exequatur et dans toute l'étendue du territoire de l'Etat requis.

L'exequatur peut être accordé partiellement pour l'un ou l'autre seulement des chefs de la décision étrangère.

La procédure de la demande en exequatur est réglée par la loi de l'Etat dans lequel l'exécution est demandée.

Art. 4. Les juridictions de l'Etat dans lequel la décision est invoquée ne sont pas liées, lors de l'examen des faits qui déterminent la compétence des juridictions de l'autre Etat, par les constatations rapportées dans la décision.

Elles ne procèdent pas à un nouvel examen du fond de la décision.

Art. 5. La partie qui invoque la décision doit produire:

1. une expédition de la décision réunissant les conditions nécessaires à son authenticité;

2. les pièces de nature à établir que la décision est passée en force de chose jugée et, s'il y a lieu, qu'elle est exécutoire;

3. l'original ou une copie certifiée conforme de la citation de la partie qui a fait défaut à l'instance et toutes les pièces de nature à établir que cette citation l'a atteinte en temps utile;

4. une traduction des pièces énumérées ci-dessus, certifiée conforme d'après les règles admises par les lois de l'Etat où la décision est invoquée ou par les traités, sauf dispense de la part de l'autorité judiciaire compétente.

Si ces documents sont dressés, délivrés ou légalisés par un tribunal de l'une des Hautes Parties Contractantes, ils n'ont besoin d'aucune légalisation pour être utilisés sur le territoire de l'autre Partie, pourvu qu'ils soient munis du sceau ou du timbre dudit tribunal.

Art. 6. La partie admise à l'assistance judiciaire gratuite dans l'un des deux Etats en bénéficiera de plein droit dans la procédure tendant à faire reconnaître ou déclarer exécutoire sur le territoire de l'autre Etat la décision qui a été rendue en sa faveur.

Art. 7. En ce qui concerne la reconnaissance et l'exécution des sentences arbitrales, la Convention pour l'exécution des sentences arbitrales étrangères, déposée à Genève pour la signature le 26 septembre 1927, règle les relations entre les deux Etats, en ce sens qu'elle s'applique à toutes les sentences arbitrales rendues dans l'un des deux Etats, sans égard aux restrictions prévues à son article premier alinéa.

Art. 8. Les actes authentiques exécutoires dans l'un des deux Etats peuvent être déclarés exécutoires dans l'autre Etat par l'autorité compétente d'après la loi de ce dernier.

Ladite autorité vérifie seulement si les actes réunissent les conditions nécessaires pour leur authenticité dans l'Etat où ils ont été reçus, s'ils y sont exécutoires, et si les dispositions dont l'exécution est poursuivie n'ont rien de contraire à l'ordre public ou aux principes du droit public de l'Etat où l'exequatur est requis.

Les dispositions qui précèdent s'appliquent aux transactions et aux accords conclus devant les autorités judiciaires et certifiés ou confirmés par celles-ci.

Art. 9. Les juridictions de l'un des deux Etats doivent, si l'une des parties le demande, se dessaisir des contestations portées devant elles puand ces contestations sont déjà pendantes devant les juridictions de l'autre Etat, sous réserve que celles-ci soient compétentes conformément aux règles de la présente Convention.

La disposition qui précède ne s'applique pas, lorsqu'une action en validation ou en mainlevée d'une saisie conservatoire effectuée dans l'un des deux Etats est portée devant les juridictions de cet Etat. En ce cas, la compétence desdites juridictions pour statuer, d'après leur loi interne, sur le fond de la contestation, reste entière, nonobstant le fait que celle-ci se trouve déjà pendante devant les juridictions de l'autre Etat.

Art. 10. La qrésente Convention ne s'applique pas aux décisions ordonnant un sépuestre ou toute autre mesure provisoire, ni aux décisions rendues dans un procès pénal sur conclusions de la partie civile, ni aux décisions rendues en matière de sursis et de faillite.

Art. 11. Le mot domicile désigne aux effets de la présente Convention:

1. pour le majeur jouissant de sa capacité, le mineur émancipé, le majeur auquel est seulement imposée l'assistance d'un conseil pour l'accomplissement de certains actes, le lieu où il a, dans l'un des deux Etats, sa résidence ou, à défaut d'un tel lieu, le lieu où se trouve dans l'un des deux Etats le siège principal de ses intérêts;

2. pour les personnes sous puissance paternelle ou sous tutelle, le lieu du domicile du représentant légal;

3. pour la femme mariée, le lieu du domicile de son mari. Toutefois si le domicile du mari est inconnu ou si la femme est séparée de corps ou autorisée à avoir un domicile séparé, le domicile de la femme est déterminé par le n. 1;

4. pour les sociétés et pour les personnes morales autres que les sociétés, même pendant leur liquidation, le lieu où est établi le siège social.

Art. 12. La présente Convention ne déroge pas aux dispositions des accords réglant la compétence judiciaire, la reconnaissance et l'exécution des jugements au sujet de matières spéciales.

Art. 13. Les décisions relatives aux frais et dépens visées à l'art. 18, 1er et 2e alinéas, de la Convention sur la procédure civile conclue à La Haye le 17 juillet 1905, et rendues dans l'un des deux Etats, seront déclarées exécutoires sur le territoire de l'autre Etat, non seulement sur une demande faite par la voie diplomatique, mais aussi à la requête directe de la partie intéressée.

Art. 14. Les dispositions de la présente Convention s'appliquent quelle que soit la nationalité des parties, sauf les exceptions résultant des Conventions internationales.

Art. 15. La présente Convention sera applicable sur le territoire métropolitain des deux Hautes Parties Contractantes.

Art. 16. La présente Convention sera ratifiée. Les ratifications en seront échangées à la Haye aussitôt que faire se pourra.

Cette Convention entrera en vigueur un mois après l'échange des ratifications. Elle ne s'appliquera qu'aux décisions judiciaires ou aux sentences arbitrales passées en force de chose jugée après son entrée en vigueur ainsi qu'aux actes visés à l'art. 8 intervenus après ledit moment.

Cette Convention pourra être dénoncée par chacun des deux Etats. Toutefois, elle demeurera en vigueur encore un an après la dénonciation.

Fait à Rome, en double exemplaire, le 7 mars 1935.

Italien—Paraguay

Trattato di amicizia e commercio tra l'Italia e il Paraguay. 22 agosto 1893. Raccolta ufficiale delle leggi 1894 III, S. 3457.

Art. 18. Le sentenze ed ordinanze in materia civile e commerciale emanate dai tribunali di una delle Parti contraenti, e debitamente legalizzate, avranno, sulla richiesta dei tribunali stessi, negli Stati dell'altra Parte, la stessa forza di quelle emanate dai tribunali locali e saranno reciprocamente eseguite e produrranno gli stessi effetti ipotecari sovra quei beni che ne saranno passibili, secondo le leggi del paese ed osservate le disposizioni delle leggi stesse in ordine alla iscrizione ed alle altre formalità.

Perchè possano eseguirsi queste sentenze ed ordinanze dovranno essere previamente dichiarate esecutorie dal tribunale superiore nella cui giurisdizione o territorio dovrà aver luogo la esecuzione, mediante un giudizio di delibazione, in cui, citate le parti in via sommaria, si esaminerà:

1⁰ se la sentenza sia stata proferita da una autorità giudiziaria competente;

2⁰ se sia stata pronunziata citate regolarmente le parti;

3⁰ se la parti sieno state legalmente rappresentate o legalmente contumaci;

4⁰ se la sentenza contenga disposizioni contrarie all'ordine pubblico o al diritto pubblico interno dello Stato.

L'esecutorietà della sentenza potrà essere richiesta in via diplomatica, ovvero direttamente dalla parte interessata.

Quando è chiesta in via diplomatica, se la parte interessata non ha allo stesso tempo costituito un procuratore, questi gli verrà deputato d'ufficio dal tribunale che deve dichiarare esecutoria la sentenza.

La parte istante dovrà soddisfare al procuratore deputato d'ufficio il pagamento dei suoi onorari e delle spese che gli sono dovute.

Art. 21. Se una delle Parti contraenti accordasse nell'avvenire ad un altro Stato qualche particolare favore o concessione in materia di commercio, di navigazione o di altro oggetto contemplato nel presente trattato, questo si intenderà ipso facto e di pien diritto concesso all'altra Parte.

Art. 23. I due Governi contraenti convengono che le controversie, le quali possono sorgere intorno alla interpretazione o alla esecuzione del presente trattato, od alle conseguenze di qualche sua violazione, debbano assoggettarsi, quando sieno esauriti i mezzi di comporle direttamente per amichevole accordo, alla decisione di commissioni arbitrali, e che il risultato di simile arbitrato sarà obbligatorio per entrambi.

I componenti di tali commissioni saranno scelti dai due Governi di comune consenso; in difetto di ciò, ognuna delle Parti nominerà il proprio arbitro o un numero eguale di arbitri, e gli arbitri nominati ne sceglieranno un ultimo.

La procedura arbitrale sarà in ciascuno dei casi determinata dalle Parti contraenti, e, in difetto, il collegio stesso degli arbitri si intenderà autorizzato previamente a determinarla.

Art. 24. Il presente trattato starà in vigore per quattro anni, a decorrere dal giorno in cui si farà lo scambio delle ratifiche, ma, se un anno prima dello spirare del termine, niuna delle parti contraenti avesse annunciato ufficialmente all'altra l'intenzione di farne cessare gli effetti, continuerà in vigore per ambe le Parti sino ad un anno dopo che siasi fatta la suddetta dichiarazione, qualunque sia l'epoca in cui abbia luogo.

Art. 25. Il presente trattato sarà approvato e ratificato da S. M. il Re d'Italia e dall'eccellentissimo signor Presidente della Repubblica del Paraguay secondo la costituzione di ognuno dei due Paesi, e le ratifiche ne saranno scambiate in questa capitale nel termine di un anno dal giorno della firma, od anche più presto, se ciò sarà possibile.

In fede di che, i rispettivi plenipotenziari hanno firmato il presente trattato e vi hanno apposto il sigillo delle loro armi.

Fatto all'Assunzione, capitale della Repubblica del Paraguay, addì ventidue del mese di agosto dell'anno di N. S. mille ottocento novantatre.

Italien—Peru

Trattato di commercio e di navigazione tra il Regno d'Italia e la Repubblica del Perù. 23 dicembre 1874. Raccolta ufficiale delle leggi 55 (1878), S. 2604.

Art. 18. Le sentenze ed ordinanze in materia civile e commerciale emanate dai tribunali di una delle parti contraenti, che siano debitamente legalizzate, avranno, a richiesta dei tribunali stessi, negli Stati dell'altra parte, la medesima forza di quelle che sono emanate dai tribunali locali, e saranno reciprocamente eseguite e produrranno i medesimi effetti ipotecari sopra quei beni che ne saranno passibili, secondo le leggi del paese, e saranno osservate le disposizioni delle leggi stesse in ordine alla iscrizione e alle altre formalità.

Perchè possano eseguirsi queste sentenze ed ordinanze, dovranno previamente essere dichiarate esecutorie dal tribunale superiore nella cui giurisdizione o territorio dovrà aver luogo l'esecuzione, mediante un giudizio di delibazione, in cui sentite le parti nella forma sommaria, si esaminerà:

1° Se la sentenza è stata proferita da un'autorità giudiziaria competente;

2° Se sia stata pronunziata, citate regolarmente le parti;

3° Se le parti sieno state legalmente citate o legalmente contumaci;

4° Se la sentenza contenga disposizioni contrarie all'ordine pubblico dello Stato od al suo diritto pubblico.

La forza esecutoria della sentenza potrà essere richiesta in via diplomatica ovvero direttamente dalla parte interessata. Se la parte interessata non ha opportunamente costituito un procuratore, questo le verrà deputato d'ufficio dal tribunale che deve dichiarare esecutoria la sentenza.

La parte instante dovrà soddisfare al procuratore deputato d'ufficio il pagamento d'ogni legittima sua competenza.

Art. 20. Se una delle parti contraenti accordasse nell'avvenire ad un altro Stato qualche particolare favore o concessione in materia di commercio, di navigazione o di qualunque altro oggetto contemplato nella presente convenzione, questo s'intenderà ipso facto e di pieno diritto concesso all'altra parte.

Art. 21. Il presente trattato sarà in vigore per dieci anni, da decorrere dal giorno in cui si farà lo scambio delle ratifiche; ma se un anno prima dello spirare del termine niuna delle parti contraenti avesse annunziato all'altra l'intenzione di farne cessare gli effetti, continuerà a rimanere in vigore per ambo le parti sino ad un anno dopo che siasi fatta la suddetta dichiarazione qualunque sia l'epoca in cui abbia luogo.

Art. 22. Il presente trattato sarà approvato e ratificato da S. M. il Re d'Italia e da S. E. il Presidente della repubblica del Perù, secondo la costituzione di ognuno dei due paesi, e le ratifiche saranno scambiate in Roma o in Lima nel termine di diciotto mesi dal giorno della firma, ed anche più presto se ciò sarà possibile.

Italien—Rumänien

Convention consulaire et d'établissement entre l'Italie et la Roumanie. 17/5 août 1880. Raccolta ufficiale delle leggi 62 (1881), S. 577.

Art. 11. Les arrêts (sententiæ) en matière civile et commerciale prononcés par les tribunaux de l'un des deux Etats contractants et dûment légalisés auront, dans le territoire de l'autre, lorsqu'ils auront acquis la force de chose jugée, la même force que les arrêts prononcés par les tribunaux du pays. Néanmoins les dits arrêts ne pourront être exécutés, et ne produiront leurs effets, quant aux hypothèques, qu'après que le tribunal compétent du pays où ils doivent recevoir leur exécution les aura déclarés exécutoires à la suite d'un jugement prononcé dans la forme sommaire et dans lequel il sera constaté:

1° que l'arrêt a été prononcé par une autorité judiciaire compétente;

2° que la citation des parties a été faite régulièrement;

3° que les parties ont été légalement représentées ou légalement déclarées défaillantes;

4° que l'arrêt ne contient aucune disposition contraire à l'ordre public et au droit public de l'Etat.

Les arrêts dont il est parlé ci-dessus devront être accompagnés d'une traduction dûment légalisée dans la langue du pays où ils devront recevoir leur exécution, ou en français.

La partie intéressée, soit directement, soit par l'entremise du tribunal qui a prononcé l'arrêt, pourra demander qu'il lui soit donné force exécutoire.

La lettre rogatoire qu'on expédiera à cet effet pourra être transmise même par la voie diplomatique.

Dans ce dernier cas, si la partie intéressée ne nomme pas le procureur chargé de demander qu'il soit donné force exécutoire à l'arrêt, le dit procureur sera nommé d'office par le tribunal saisi de la demande.

Il demeure entendu que les frais de procès devront, en tout cas, rester à la charge des parties intéressées.

Art. 32. Les deux Hautes Parties contractantes sont convenues que les différences qui pourraient se produire touchant l'interprétation ou l'exécution de la présente convention, ou les conséquences de l'infraction d'une de ses stipulations, devront être soumises, lorsque les moyens de les arranger directement par un accord amiable auront été épuisés, au jugement de commissions arbitrales, et le résultat d'un tel arbitrage sera obligatoire pour les deux Gouvernements.

Les membres des dites commissions seront choisis par les deux Gouvernements d'un commun accord; en défaut de quoi, chacune des parties nommera son propre arbitre ou un nombre égal d'arbitres, et les arbitres nommés en nommeront un autre de leur choix.

La procédure arbitrale sera, dans chaque cas spécial, déterminée par les parties; en défaut de quoi, le collège même des arbitres aura la faculté de la déterminer préalablement.

Art. 33. La présente convention sera en vigueur pendant cinq années, a dater du jour de l'échange des ratifications; si aucune des Hautes Parties contractantes ne notifie à l'autre une année avant l'expiration de ce terme son intention d'en faire cesser les effets, elle continuera à rester en vigueur pendant une année encore, à partir du jour où l'une ou l'autre des Hautes Parties contractantes l'aura dénoncée.

Les stipulations qui précèdent seront exécutoires dans les deux Etats immédiatement après l'échange des ratifications.

Art. 34. La présente convention sera ratifiée et les ratifications en seront échangées à Bukarest, aussitôt que faire se pourra.

En foi de quoi, les plénipotentiaires respectifs ont apposé leurs signatures et l'empreinte de leurs sceaux.

Fait à Bukarest, en double original, le 17/5 août 1880.

Italien—San Marino

Convenzione di amicizia e di buon vicinato fra il Regno d'Italia e la Repubblica di San Marino. 31 marzo 1939. Raccolta ufficiale delle leggi 1939 VI, S. 4773.

Capo II.

Dell'assistenza giudiziaria in materia civile.

Art. 5. Le decisioni, in materia civile, commerciale e amministrativa, pronunciate da autorità giurisdizionali di uno dei due Stati, hanno l'autorità della cosa giudicata nel territorio dell'altro, quando concorrono le seguenti condizioni:

1° che la decisione sia stata regolarmente notificata ed abbia acquistato forza di giudicato nel Paese nel quale è stata emanata;

2° che la decisione non sia in contraddizione con altra già pronunciata, sulla stessa controversia, da un'autorità giurisdizionale dello Stato nel quale la decisione viene invocata;

3° che, al momento della emanazione della decisione, non fosse pendente, nello Stato ove essa viene invocata, un giudizio per la stessa controversia;

4° che la decisione non contenga disposizioni contrarie all'ordine pubblico dello Stato nel quale viene invocata.

Art. 6. Le decisioni indicate nel precedente articolo e gli altri provvedimenti delle autorità giurisdizionali di uno dei due Stati, in materia civile, commerciale ed amministrativa, possono costituire titolo per l'esecuzione forzata, sia mobiliare che immobiliare, o per l'iscrizione di ipoteca o per la trascrizione, nell'altro Stato, quando siano stati dichiarati esecutori.

L'esecutorietà può essere dichiarata soltanto se concorrono le condizioni prevedute dall'art. 5 e se si tratta di decisione e di provvedimento esecutorio secondo la legge dello Stato dal quale dipende l'autorità che lo ha emanato.

L'esecutorietà è dichiarata, su istanza della parte interessata, con decreto pronunciato senza contradditorio, nel Regno, dal presidente della corte di appello nella cui circoscrizione deve aver luogo l'esecuzione, e, nella Repubblica, dal commissario della legge.

Contro il decreto che pronuncia sulla domanda di dichiarazione di esecutorietà è ammesso ricorso, nel termine di 15 giorni dalla notificazione del decreto stesso, rispettivamente alla corte di appello o al giudice di appello.

Contro la decisione della corte di appello o del giudice di appello non è ammesso alcun ulteriore gravame.

Art. 7. La parte, che invoca l'autorità della decisione, o che chiede la dichiarazione di esecutorietà della decisione o del provvedimento, ne deve presentare un e emplare, spedito in forma autentica.

L'autenticità della spedizione, come pure il concorso della condizione preveduta dal n. 1° dell'art. 5, risultano da una attestazione apposta in calce alla sentenza o al provvedimento:

a) se si tratta di decisione dell'autorità giudiziaria italiana, dal presidente della corte di appello nella cui circoscrizione la decisione o il provvedimento è stato emanato;

b) se si tratta di decisioni o provvedimenti di altre autorità giurisdizionali italiane, dall'autorità stessa, o, qualora questa sia organo collegiale, dal suo presidente;

c) se si tratta di decisioni o provvedimenti di autorità giurisdizionale sammarinese, dal Segretario di Stato per gli affari esteri della Repubblica.

. . .

La presente Convenzione sarà ratificata dalle Parti contraenti, e lo scambio delle ratifiche avrà luogo in Roma al più presto possibile.

Essa entrerà in vigore dal giorno dello scambio delle ratifiche e avrà, a decorrere da tale data, una durata di dieci anni, salvo tacita proroga di anno in anno fino a denuncia, da notificarsi sei mesi prima della scadenza.

Dalla data di entrata in vigore della presente Convenzione, cesseranno di avere vigore fra le parti la Convenzione di amicizia e buon vicinato stipulata in Firenze il 28 giugno 1897 e le relative Convenzione addizionali.

In fede di che i Plenipotenziari hanno firmato la presente Convenzione.
Fatto in Roma il 31 marzo 1939

Italien—Schweiz

Convention entre l'Italie et la Suisse, sur la reconnaissance et l'exécution de décisions judiciaires. Signée à Rome, le 3 janvier 1933.

Texte officiel français. SdN. 142 (1933), S. 18.

Art. 1. Les décisions rendues en matière civile et commerciale par les juridictions de l'un des deux Etats ont l'autorité de la chose jugée sur le territoire de l'autre Etat, si elles réunissent les conditions suivantes:

1° Que la décision émane d'une juridiction compétente selon l'article 2 de la présente convention ou, à défaut de règles conventionnelles, selon les règles de compétence judiciaire internationale admises par le droit de l'Etat où la décision est invoquée;

2° Que la reconnaissance de la décision ne soit pas contraire à l'ordre public ou aux principes du droit public de l'Etat où la décision est invoquée, en particulier que celle-ci ne soit pas en contradiction avec une décision déjà rendue sur la même contestation par une juridiction dudit Etat;

3° Que la décision soit passée en force de chose jugée d'après la loi de l'Etat où elle a été rendue;

4° Qu'en cas de jugement par défaut, la citation qui a introduit l'instance ait été remise en temps utile à la partie défaillante ou à son mandataire autorisé à la recevoir. Si la notification devait avoir lieu sur le territoire de l'Etat où la décision est invoquée, il est nécessaire qu'elle ait été faite par la voie de l'entr'aide judiciaire réciproque.

La procédure à suivre pour la reconnaissance de l'autorité de la chose jugée est régie par la loi de l'Etat requis.

Art. 2. La compétence des juridictions de l'Etat où la décision a été rendue est fondée au sens de l'article premier, N° 1, si elle est prévue par une convention internationale, ou dans les cas mentionnés ci-après:

1° Lorsque le défendeur avait son domicile dans cet Etat;

2° Lorsque, par une convention expresse en vue de contestations déterminées, le défendeur s'était soumis à la compétence du tribunal qui a rendu la décision, sauf si toutes les parties avaient leur domicile dans l'Etat où la décision est invoquée;

Il en est de même si le défendeur est entré en matière, sans réserve, sur le fond du litige;

3° Lorsque le défendeur ayant un établissement commercial ou industriel ou une succursale sur le territoire de l'Etat où la décision a été rendue y a été cité pour des contestations ayant trait à l'exploitation de l'établissement ou de la succursale;

4° S'il s'agit d'une demande reconventionnelle en connexité avec la demande principale ou avec les moyens de défense invoqués contre celle-ci;

5° En matière d'état, de capacité ou de droit de famille des ressortissants du pays où la décision a été rendue;

6° Lorsqu'il s'agit d'une contestation successorale entre les héritiers d'un ressortissant du pays où la décision a été rendue;

7° Lorsqu'il s'agit d une action réelle ayant pour objet un immeuble situé dans l'Etat où la décision a été rendue.

Néanmoins, les dispositions contenues aux Nos 1 à 4 ne s'appliquent pas aux contestations pour lesquelles le droit de l'Etat requis reconnaît comme exclusivement compétentes ses propres juridictions ou celles d'un tiers Etat.

Art. 3. Les décisions rendues par les juridictions de l'un des deux Etats et qui réunissent les conditions énumérées à l'article premier, pourront, après avoir été déclarées exécutoires, donner lieu à l'exécution forcée dans l'autre Etat ou y faire l'objet de formalités telles que l'inscription ou la transcription sur les registres publics.

Ne seront déclarées exécutoires dans l'Etat requis que les décisions qui ont pleine force exécutoire dans l'Etat où elles ont été rendues.

La procédure à suivre est régie par la loi de l'Etat requis.

Art. 4. Les juridictions de l'Etat dans lequel la décision est invoquée ne sont pas liées, lors de l'examen des faits qui déterminent la compétence des juridictions de l'autre Etat, par les constatations rapportées dans la décision.

Elles ne procèdent pas à un nouvel examen du fond de la décision.

Art. 5. La partie qui invoque la décision doit produire:

1° Une expédition de la décision réunissant les conditions nécessaires à son authenticité;

2° Les pièces de nature à établir que la décision est passée en force de chose jugée et, s'il y a lieu, qu'elle est exécutoire;

3° L'original ou une copie certifiée conforme de l'assignation de la partie qui a fait défaut à l'instance;

4° Une traduction des pièces énumérées ci-dessus, certifiée conforme par un représentant diplomatique ou consulaire de l'un des deux Etats, sauf dispense de cette obligation par l'autorité compétente.

Si ces documents sont dressés, délivrés ou légalisés par les tribunaux de l'une des Hautes Parties contractantes, ou par les autorités visées à l'article 11 de la présente convention, ils n'ont besoin d'aucune légalisation pour être utilisés sur le territoire de l'autre partie, pourvu qu'ils soient munis du sceau ou du timbre du tribunal ou de l'autorité susdite.

Art. 6. La partie admise à l'assistance judiciaire gratuite dans l'un des deux Etats en bénéficiera de plein droit dans la procédure tendant à faire reconnaître ou déclarer exécutoire sur le territoire de l'autre Etat la décision qui a été rendue en sa faveur.

Art. 7. Les sentences arbitrales rendues dans l'un des deux Etats et y ayant la même autorité que les décisions judiciaires seront reconnues et déclarées exécutoires dans l'autre Etat, si elles satisfont aux prescriptions des articles précédents, en tant que celles-ci sont applicables.

Il en est de même pour les transactions judiciaires.

Art. 8. Les autorités judiciaires de l'un des deux Etats doivent, si l'une des parties le demande se dessaisir des contestations portées devant elles lorsque ces contestations sont déjà pendantes devant une juridiction de l'autre Etat, pourvu que celle-ci soit compétente selon es règles de la présente convention.

Art. 9. La présente convention ne s'applique pas aux décisions ordonnant un séquestre ou toute autre mesure provisionnelle, ni aux décisions rendues dans un procès pénal sur conclusion de la partie civile, ni aux décisions rendues en matière de faillite.

Art. 10. Les mesures provisoires ou conservatoires organisées par la législation d'un des deux pays peuvent être requises des autorités de ce pays, quelle que soit la juridiction compétente pour connaître du fond.

Art. 11. Les décisions d'autorités non judiciaires chargées en Suisse d'organiser et de surveiller la tutelle sont assimilées aux décisions judiciaires, quant aux effets de la présente convention, uniquement pour ce qui concerne les ressortissants suisses.

Art. 12. Le mot domicile désigne aux effets de la présente convention:

1° Pour le majeur jouissant de sa capacité, le mineur émancipé, le majeur auquel est seulement imposée l'assistance d'un conseil pour l'accomplissement de certains actes, le lieu où il réside, dans l'un des deux Etats, avec l'intention de s'y établir ou, à défaut d'un tel lieu, le lieu où se trouve dans l'un des deux Etats le siège principal de ses intérêts;

2° Pour les personnes sous puissance paternelle ou sous tutelle, le lieu de domicile du représentant légal;

3° Pour la femme mariée, le lieu du domicile de son mari. Toutefois, si le domicile du mari est inconnu ou si la femme est séparée de corps ou autorisée à avoir un domicile séparé, le domicile de la femme est déterminé par le N° 1;

4° Pour les sociétés, le lieu où est établi le siège social.

Art. 13. La présente convention ne déroge pas aux dispositions des accords réglant la compétence judiciaire et l'exécution des jugements au sujet des matières spéciales.

Art. 14. Les décisions relatives aux frais et dépens visées à l'article 18, premier et deuxième alinéas, de la Convention[1] sur la procédure civile conclue à La Haye le 17 juillet 1905, et rendues dans l'un des deux Etats, seront déclarées exécutoires sur le territoire de l'autre Etat à la requête directe de la partie intéressée.

Art. 15. Les dispositions de la présente convention s'appliquent quelle que soit la nationalité des Parties.

Art. 16. Les Hautes Parties contractantes se réservent d'appliquer d'un commun accord, par échange de notes, la présente convention aux colonies italiennes.

Art. 17. Les contestations qui s'élèveraient entre les Hautes Parties contractantes, relativement à l'interprétation ou à l'application de la présente convention, seront réglées conformément aux disposition du Traité[2] de conciliation et de règlement judiciaire, conclu le 20 septembre 1924, à moins que les Hautes Parties contractantes ne soient d'accord pour admettre un autre moyen de règlement.

Art. 18. La présente convention sera ratifiée. Les ratifications en seront échangées à Berne aussitôt que faire se pourra.

Cette convention entrera en vigueur un mois après l'échange des ratifications. Elle ne s'appliquera pas aux décisions judiciaires ou aux sentences arbitrales passées en force de chose jugée avant son entrée en vigueur, ni aux transactions conclues avant ce moment.

---

[1] de Martens, Nouveau Recueil général de Traités, troisième série, tome II, page 243.

[2] Vol. XXXIII, page 91, de ce recueil.

Cette convention pourra être dénoncée par chacun des deux Etats. Toutefois, elle demeurera en vigueur encore un an après la dénonciation.

En foi de quoi les plénipotentiaires ont signé la présente convention. Fait à Rome, en double exemplaire, le 3 janvier 1933.

Italien (Sardinien)—Spanien

Convenio para el cumplimiento de las sentencias de los tribunales entre S. M. C. y el Rey de Cerdeña. Firmado en Madrid á 30 de junio de 1851.

Marqués de Olivart, Colección de los tratados, convenios y documentos internacionales celebrados por nuestros gobiernos con los estados extranjeros. Madrid, II 1893, S. 124.

Art. I. Le sentenze od ordinanze in materia civile ordinaria o commerciale emanate dai tribunali di prima istanza o d'appello di Sua Maestà il Re di Sardegna, o da quelli di Sua Maestà Cattolica, e debitamente legalizzate, saranno reciprocamente eseguite dai tribunali dei due Stati in conformità di quanto è stabilito cogli articoli seguenti.

Art. II. Tale esecuzione sarà chiesta da un tribunale di prima istanza o d'appello all'altro col mezzo di requisitorie.

Quando si tratti di sentenze definitive, la requisitoria sarà accompagnata dal corrispondente decreto di esecuzione.

Qualora invece si tratti di sentenze non definitive, prima di ordinare la spedizione delle requisitorie, il richiedente si accerterà e ne farà quindi menzione motivata nella sua provvidenza, che non vi ha più luogo ad appellarsi da dette sentenze, se pella loro natura le medesime richiedessero questa circostanza per poter essere eseguite.

Art. III. Perchè possano eseguirsi dai tribunali di prima istanza o di appello competenti di ciascun paese le sentenze od ordinanze dei tribunali dell'altro, dovranno le medesime essere previamente dichiarate esecutorie dal tribunale superiore nella cui giurisdizione o territorio dovrà aver luogo l'esecuzione. Non si addiverrà però a questa dichiarazione nei seguenti casi:

Primo. Quando la sentenza od ordinanza fosse peccante di manifesta ingiustizia.

Secondo. Quando fosse nulla per difetto di giurisdizione, di citazione o di mandato.

Tercio. Quando fosse contraria alle leggi proibitive del Regno nel quale se ne chiede l'eseguimento.

Art. IV. Le sentenze pronunciate dai tribunali di Sua Maestà il Re di Sardegna avranno forza di produrre ipoteca sui beni situati negli Stati di Sua Maestà Cattolica, e reciprocamente, allorchè saranno state dichiarate esecutorie nel modo sovra indicato.

Art. V. Gli atti autentici rogati negli Stati di Sua Maesta il Re di Sardegna avranno forza di conferire ipoteca nei beni situati negli Stati di Sua Maestà Cattolica, semprechè questi beni saranno stati specialmente designati nel contratto, e viceversa.

Art. VI. L'ipoteca di cui si tratta nei due precedenti articoli (IV e V) non colpirà se non li beni che ne saranno passibili conformemente alle leggi del paese in cui sono situati.

L'adempimento di tutte le formalità dalle leggi prescritte perchè l'ipoteca sortisca il suo effetto, resterà a carico della persona, a favore di cui sarà stata acquistata od acconsentita.

Art. VII. Gli atti di giurisdizione volontaria passati negli Stati di Sua Maestà Sarda sortiranno il loro effetto negli Stati di Sua Maestà Cattolica, e viceversa, allorchè si sarà dichiarato nulla ostare all'esecuzione dei medesimi dal tribunale superiore nella cui giurisdizione debbono gli atti eseguirsi.

Art. VIII. La presente Convenzione è conchiusa per anni cinque, i quali decorsi, senza che una delle Alte Parti contraenti abbia dichiarato all'altra, sei mesi prima della scadenza di detto termine, di volerne far cessare gli effetti, continuerà ad essere in vigore per un anno, e così di seguito a meno di disdetta come sopra.

La medesima sarà ratificata, e le rispettive ratifiche saranno scambiate nello spazio di tre mesi, od anche prima ove sia possibile.

In fede di che i Plenipotenziarii suddetti l'hanno munita della loro firma, apponendovi il sigillo delle loro armi.

Fatto nel Real Palazzo in Madrid, addì 30 Giugno 1851.

Italien—Tschechoslowakei

Accordo. 6 aprile 1922. Raccolta ufficiale delle leggi 1924 VI, S. 4397.

La Cecoslovacchia e l'Italia, desiderose di regolare le questioni che riguardano l'esecutorietà delle sentenze, ecc., in materia civile e commerciale, volendo concludere un accordo a questo riguardo, le Alte Parti Contraenti hanno nominato come loro plenipotenziari: . . .

Art. 1. Le decisioni pronunciate in materia civile o commerciale dalle autorità giudiziarie di una delle Alte Parti Contraenti hanno nel territorio dell'altra l'autorità della cosa giudicata, quando concorrano le condizioni seguenti:

1° Che, secondo le norme vigenti nello Stato in cui la decisione è prodotta, le autorità giudiziarie dello Stato in cui fu pronunciata potessero conoscere della controversia;

2° Che la decisione abbia acquistato forza di cosa giudicata secondo le leggi del paese in cui è stata pronunziata;

3° Che, secondo le stesse leggi, le parti siano state legalmente citate, rappresentate o dichiarate contumaci;

4° Che la decisione non sia contraria ad altra decisione pronunciata sullo stesso oggetto dalle autorità giudiziarie dello Stato in cui è prodotta;

5° Che non contenga disposizioni contrarie all'ordine pubblico o al diritto pubblico interno del paese.

Art. 2. Le sentenze delle autorità giudiziarie di una delle Alte Parti Contraenti saranno rese esecutive nel territorio dell'altra, sui beni mobili o immobili, e per gli effetti della trascrizione in pubblici registri, premesso un giudizio di delibazione nel quale deve essere verificato il concorso delle condizioni indicate all' art. 1 del presente Accordo, senza esame in merito.

Art. 3. Se il convenuto, già contumace davanti l'autorità giudiziaria straniera, non sia comparso nel giudizio di delibazione e se la citazione non gli sia stata notificata in persona propria o nelle forme equipollenti secondo la legge del luogo, sarà ammessa l'opposizione alla decisione che avesse dato forza esecutiva alla sentenza straniera.

Art. 4. Nel giudizio di delibazione saranno conservate le forme stabilite dalla legge del paese nel quale l'esecuzione è richiesta.

Art. 5. Le norme stabilite agli articoli precedenti si osservano, in quanto siano applicabili, per ciò che concerne:

a) provvedimenti aventi forza di titolo esecutivo, emessi dalle autorità giudiziarie civili;

b) le decisioni dei collegi arbitrali permanenti o degli arbitri nominati per compromesso dalle parti;

c) le transazioni dinanzi le autorità giudiziarie e gli atti notarili muniti di clausola di esecuzione.

Art. 6. Le decisioni e gli atti a cui si riferiscono gli articoli precedenti saranno presentati o trasmessi in copia autentica, accompagnati, quando occorra, dai documenti che attestino il concorso dei requisiti di cui ai nn. 2 e 3 dell' art. 1 del presente Accordo, e da una traduzione, certificata conforme, nella lingua del paese in cui la decisione o l'atto prodotto, o l'esecuzione è richiesta.

La trasmissione in via ufficiale contemplata nella convenzione per 'assistenza giudiziaria esime dall'obligo di qualsiasi legalizzazione.

Art. 7. Le decisioni pronunciate dall'autorità giudiziaria di una delle Alte Parti Contraenti in favore di una Parte che abbia ottenuto il gratuito patrocinio saranno rese esecutive gratuitamente nel territorio dell'altra senza che la Parte che chiede l'esecuzione debba ottenere di nuovo, a questo fine, il beneficio della gratuita assistenza.

Art. 8. Il presente Accordo sarà ratificato e gli atti di ratifica saranno scambiati al più presto possibile.

Esso non entrerà in vigore che dopo lo scambio delle ratifiche e resterà in vigore fino a sei mesi dopo il giorno della denunzia da parte di una delle Alte Parti Contraenti.

In fede di che i plenipotenziari suddetti hanno firmato il presente Accordo.

Fatto a Roma, il 6 aprile 1922, in italiano e in cecoslovacco, i due testi facendo egualmente fede in due esemplari, uno dei quali sarà consegnato a ciascuno degli Stati firmatari.

Italien—Türkei

Convention entre le Royaume d'Italie et la République Turque concernant la protection judiciaire et l'assistance réciproque des autorités judiciaires en matière civile et pénale et l'exécution des décisions judiciaires. 10 août 1926. Raccolta ufficiale delle leggi 1930 III, S. 2412.

Partie II.

Exécution des décisions judiciaires.

Art. 19. — Les décisions rendues en matière civile ou commerciale par les autorités judiciaires d'une des Hautes Parties Contractantes seront déclarées exécutoires dans le territoire de l'autre Partie Contractante par une décision y relative du tribunal compétent de cette dernière Partie, tant sur les meubles que sur les immeubles, et reconnues valable aux effets de la transcription dans les registres publics, si elles réunissent les conditions suivantes:

1) que la décision ait été rendue par une autorité judiciaire compétente à la rendre selon les principes généraux du droit international et selon les lois du pays où la décision même a été rendue;

2) que la citation ait été signifiée conformément à la loi du pays où le jugement a eu lieu et avec un terme pour comparaître réellement suffisant en rapport à la distance et aux autres circonstances spéciales;

3) que les parties aient été légalement représentées selon la loi du pays ou déclarées défaillantes en conformité de la même loi;

4) que la décision soit revêtue de l'autorité de la chose jugée et que elle possède toujours sa pleine force exécutoire d'après la loi du pays où elle a été rendue;

5) que la décision ne soit pas en contradiction avec une autre décision rendue sur le même objet et entre les mêmes parties par les autorités judiciaires du pays où l'exécution est requise, ou bien qu'une autre contestation sur le même objet et entre les mêmes parties ne soit déjà pendante devant ces autorités au moment où la demande d'exequatur a été signifiée;

6) que la décision ne contienne rien de contraire à l'ordre public ou aux principes du droit public du pays où elle est invoquée;

7) que la cause ne rentre pas dans la compétence exclusive des tribunaux du pays requis.

Dans le jugement de délibation seront observées les formes établies par la loi du pays où l'exécution est demandée.

Art. 20. — Si le défendeur, déjà en contumace devant l'autorité judiciaire qui a rendu la décision, n'a pas comparu pendant le jugement de délibation, et si la signification y relative ne lui a pas été notifiée personnellement, l'opposition à la décision qui a ordonné l'exécution sera admise, même si la signification a été renouvelée.

Art. 21. — L'autorité judiciaire compétente à donner force exécutive à la décision étrangère examinera de nouveau intégralement la controverse lorsque un des cas suivants sera présenté par le défendeur:

1) que la décision ait été l'effet du dol de l'autre partie;

2) que la décision soit fondée sur des documents reconnus faux par l'autorité judiciaire;

3) qu'après la décision on ait recouvré un document décisif qui ne fut pas produit auparavant par faute imputable à l'autre partie;

4) que la décision soit l'effet direct d'une erreur de fait résultant des actes et des documents du procès.

Art. 22. — Les règles établies dans les articles précédents sont applicables aux sentences prononcées par les arbitres entre les sujets de chacune des deux Parties ou entre les sujets de l'une et les sujets de l'autre, à condition que ces décisions aient la valeur et l'efficacité des décisions de l'autorité judiciaire selon la loi du pays où elles furent rendues.

Art. 23. — Les décisions seront transmises par voie diplomatique en copie authentique, ou présentées à l'autorité compétente, pour le jugement de délibation, en copie authentique et légalisée, avec les documents qui attestent le concours des conditions susindiquées et avec une traduction, certifiée conforme, dans la langue du pays où l'exequatur a été demandé.

Partie III.

Dispositions générales.

Art. 24. — La présente convention sera ratifiée et les ratifications seront échangées à Angora aussitôt que faire se pourra.

Art. 25. — La présente convention entrera en vigueur trois mois après l'échange des ratifications et restera en vigueur six mois après le jour de la dénonciation de la part d'une des Hautes Parties Contractantes.

En foi de quoi, les plénipotentiaires susnommés ont signé la présente convention et l'ont munie de leurs sceaux.

Fait à Rome, le 10 août 1926, en deux exemplaires, dont un sera remis à chacun des Etats signataires.

Italien—Vatikanstadt

Trattato fra la Santa Sede e l'Italia (sog. Lateranvertrag). 11 febbraio 1929. Raccolta ufficiale delle leggi 1929 IV, S. 3981.

Art. 23. Per l'esecuzione nel Regno delle sentenze emanate dai tribunali della Città del Vaticano si applicheranno le norme del diritto internazionale.

Avranno invece senz'altro piena efficacia giuridica, anche a tutti gli effetti civili, in Italia le sentenze ed i provvedimenti emanati da autorità ecclesiastiche ed ufficialmente communicati alle autorità civili, circa persone ecclesiastiche o religiose e concernenti materie spirituali o disciplinari.

Art. 27. Il presente Trattato, non oltre quattro mesi dalla firma sarà sottoposto alla ratifica del Sommo Pontefice e del Re d'Italia ed entrerà in vigore all'atto stesso dello scambio delle ratifiche.

Roma, addì 11 febbraio 1929.

Jugoslawien—Österreich

Staatsvertrag zwischen der Republik Österreich und dem Königreiche der Serben, Kroaten und Slowenen über den wechselseitigen rechtlichen Verkehr. Vom 1. Mai 1928. Bundesgesetzblatt für die Republik Österreich 1929, S. 539.

6. Abschnitt.

Zwangsvollstreckung.

Art. 37. (1) Eine Zwangsvollstreckung findet auf Grund der Bestimmungen des vorliegenden Vertrages nur wegen vermögensrechtlicher Ansprüche und nur dann statt, wenn es sich nicht um streitige Eigentums- oder andere dingliche Rechte an unbeweglichen Gütern handelt, die in dem um Vollstreckung ersuchten Staate gelegen sind.

(2) Die Bestimmung des Absatzes 1 schließt aber nicht aus, daß die unbeweglichen Güter, die in dem um Vollstreckung ersuchten Staate gelegen sind, der Zwangsvollstreckung unterworfen werden, wenn nur der Exekutionstitel nicht Eigentums- oder andere dingliche Rechte an unbeweglichen Gütern zum Gegenstande hat, die in dem Staate gelegen sind, wo die Vollstreckung durchgeführt werden soll.

Art. 38. Die Zwangsvollstreckung wird beiderseits zugelassen:

1. auf Grund von Urteilen, Zahlungsbefehlen oder anderen Beschlüssen der Zivil- oder Handelsgerichte;

2. auf Grund von Erkenntnissen eines Schiedsgerichtes, sofern dieses zufolge eines schriftlichen Schiedsvertrages oder einer gesetzlichen Bestimmung zur Entscheidung der Streitsache berufen war;

3. auf Grund von Vergleichen, die vor den in Zahl 1 und 2 genannten Gerichten und Schiedsgerichten abgeschlossen worden sind;

4. auf Grund von Notariatsakten, die mit der Vollstreckbarkeitsklausel versehen sind.

Art. 39. Die Zwangsvollstreckung wird jedoch versagt, wenn dadurch ein Rechtsverhältnis zur Anerkennung oder ein Anspruch zur Verwirklichung gelangen soll, dem durch das Gesetz des Ortes der Zwangsvollstreckung aus Rücksichten der öffentlichen Ordnung oder der Sittlichkeit die Gültigkeit oder Klagbarkeit versagt ist.

Art. 40. Auf Grund einer gerichtlichen Entscheidung findet die Zwangsvollstreckung nur unter der Bedingung statt,

1. daß die Zuständigkeit des Gerichtes, das in der Sache erkannt hat, gemäß Artikel 41 dieses Vertrages als begründet anzusehen ist,

2. daß die Entscheidung rechtskräftig und vollstreckbar geworden ist.

Art. 41. Die Zuständigkeit des Gerichtes, das in der Sache erkannt hat, gilt im Sinne des Artikels 40 für begründet, wenn die Rechtssache nach den Gesetzen des ersuchten Staates bei einem Gerichte des anderen vertragschließenden Staates anhängig gemacht werden konnte.

Art. 42. Auf Grund eines schiedsgerichtlichen Erkenntnisses findet die Zwangsvollstreckung nur statt, wenn es rechtskräftig und vollstreckbar geworden ist.

Art. 43. Auf Grund eines gerichtlichen oder schiedsgerichtlichen Vergleiches findet die Zwangsvollstreckung nur statt, wenn der Vergleich nach den Gesetzen des Ortes des Vergleichsabschlusses vollstreckbar ist.

Art. 44. Auf Grund eines Notariatsaktes findet die Zwangsvollstreckung nur statt, wenn er nach den Gesetzen des Ortes seiner Errichtung vollstreckbar ist.

Art. 45. (1) Dem Ersuchen um Zwangsvollstreckung sind folgende Beilagen anzuschließen:

1. eine Ausfertigung der Entscheidung samt Gründen oder des Vergleiches oder des Notariatsaktes;

2. eine amtliche Bestätigung, daß die Entscheidung rechtskräftig geworden ist und einen Exekutionstitel darstellt oder daß der Vergleich oder der Notariatsakt vollstreckbar ist. Diese Bestätigung hat das Gericht des ersuchenden Staates auszustellen, das nach seinen Gesetzen zur Bewilligung der Zwangsvollstreckung zuständig wäre.

(2) Das Ersuchen um Zwangsvollstreckung kann von dem in Absatz 1, Zahl 2, bezeichneten Gerichte an die zuständige Behörde des ersuchten Staates nach den Bestimmungen der Artikel 8 und 9 übersendet werden.

Art. 46. Über die Zulässigkeit der Zwangsvollstreckung entscheidet die zuständige Behörde des ersuchten Staates ohne Einvernehmung des Verpflichteten. Die Vollstreckung ist zu bewilligen, wenn die einschlägigen durch die Artikel 37 bis 45 dieses Übereinkommens festgesetzten Bedingungen erfüllt sind. In eine Prüfung der Rechtssache selbst darf sich das ersuchte Gericht nicht einlassen.

Art. 47. Wenn in dem Ersuchschreiben um Zwangsvollstreckung ein Bevollmächtigter der betreibenden Partei nicht namhaft gemacht ist, hat die die Vollstreckung vollziehende Behörde ihr nötigenfalls einen Vertreter zu bestellen.

Art. 48. Wurde die Zwangsvollstreckung bewilligt, so sind die nötigen Maßnahmen zu ihrem Vollzuge bis zur Sicherstellung der betreibenden Partei unverzüglich von Amts wegen zu treffen.

Art. 49. (1) Die verpflichtete Partei kann unbeschadet des durch die Gesetze des Landes eingeräumten Rekurses gegen die gemäß Artikel 48 vollzogene Vollstreckung folgende Einwendungen geltend machen:

1. daß eine der in den Artikeln 37 bis 45 dieses Vertrages festgesetzten Bedingungen nicht gegeben ist;

2. daß die den Prozeß einleitende Verfügung dem Beklagten, der sich in dem die Grundlage der Entscheidung bildenden Verfahren auf den Streit nicht eingelassen hatte, nicht ordnungsmäßig zugestellt worden ist;

3. daß infolge einer anderen Unregelmäßigkeit des Verfahrens der Person, wider welche die Zwangsvollstreckung geführt werden soll, die Möglichkeit, sich an dem Verfahren zu beteiligen, entzogen war;

4. daß nach der Gesetzgebung des Ortes, wo die Entscheidung erlassen, der Vergleich geschlossen oder der Notariatsakt errichtet wurde, deren Vollstreckbarkeit erloschen ist;

5. daß nach der Gesetzgebung des Ortes der Zwangsvollstreckung dem Anspruche, wegen dessen die Zwangsvollstreckung stattfinden soll, die Einrede der entschiedenen Sache im Wege steht.

(2) Die Zustellung hat als ordnungsmäßig im Sinne der Zahl 2 nur dann zu gelten, wenn die den Prozeß einleitende Verfügung dem Beklagten oder seinem zur Empfangnahme berechtigten Vertreter zu eigenen Händen zugestellt wurde. Hatte die Zustellung in den Gebieten jenes vertragschließenden Staates, dessen Behörden mit der Zwangsvollstreckung befaßt werden, zu geschehen, so muß sie im Rechtshilfewege bewirkt worden sein.

(3) Die Gründe, die gegen die Zwangsvollstreckung geltend gemacht werden, müssen, außer in den in Artikel 39 und in Zahl 4 und 5 dieses Artikels vorgesehenen Fällen, binnen 14 Tagen nach Zustellung des Vollstreckungsbeschlusses vorgebracht werden.

(4) Wenn die verpflichtete Partei gemäß den vorstehenden Bestimmungen gegen die Zwangsvollstreckung Einsprache erhebt, hat das zuständige Gericht nach mündlicher Verhandlung über die Frage zu erkennen, ob die Vollstreckung aus einem der oben angeführten Gründe abzulehnen ist.

(5) Die Tagfahrt muß auf möglichst kurze Frist und keinesfalls später als 14 Tage nach dem Tag anberaumt werden, an dem die verpflichtete Partei einen Ablehnungsgrund geltend gemacht hat.

(6) Wenn die vorgebrachten Ablehnungsgründe unbegründet befunden oder wenn derartige Gründe innerhalb der 14tägigen Anmeldefrist überhaupt nicht vorgebracht wurden, ist die bis zur Sicherstellung durchgeführte Vollstreckung von Amts wegen bis zur Befriedigung der Forderung fortzusetzen.

Art. 50. Beim Vollzuge der Zwangsvollstreckung sind, sofern dieser Vertrag nicht besondere Bestimmungen enthält, die Gesetze des ersuchten Staates anzuwenden.

Art. 51. (1) Wenn eine Zwangsvollstreckung wegen Mangels der geforderten Voraussetzungen abgelehnt wurde, hat der betreibende Gläubiger das Recht, Rekurs zu ergreifen.

(2) Das Ersuchen um Vollstreckung kann übrigens von dem ersuchenden Gericht oder von der beteiligten Partei erneuert werden, wenn die in diesem Vertrage festgesetzten Bedingungen nachträglich erfüllt wurden.

Art. 52. (1) Die Gerichtskosten, die durch die Vollstreckung von Entscheidungen, Vergleichen, Notariatsakten verursacht werden, fallen den beteiligten Parteien zur Last und müssen entsprechend den im Vollstreckungsgebiet in Kraft stehenden Gesetzen bezahlt werden; sie werden nötigenfalls von dem ersuchten Staate vorgestreckt.

(2) Kann der Ersatz dieser Kosten von den Parteien nicht erlangt werden, so sind sie vom ersuchenden Staate zu tragen.

(3) Sind anläßlich der Zwangsvollstreckung Gebühren zu bezahlen, so werden sie nach den Gesetzen des Landes, wo die Vollstreckung stattfinden soll, bemessen. Aus dem Grunde, daß die erwähnten Gebühren nicht bezahlt worden sind, darf aber die Vollstreckung nicht verzögert werden.

Art. 53. Die in den Gebieten eines der vertragschließenden Staaten erflossenen Entscheidungen, die dort abgeschlossenen Vergleiche und die dort errichteten vollstreckbaren Notariatsakte haben in den Gebieten des anderen Staates die nämliche Kraft und die nämliche Wirkung, wie die inländischen Entscheidungen, Vergleiche und Notariatsakte, vorausgesetzt, daß sie daselbst auf Grund des gegenwärtigen Übereinkommens vollstreckbar wären.

Art. 62. (1) Der gegenwärtige Vertrag soll ratifiziert werden. Die Ratifikationsurkunden sind so bald wie möglich in Beograd auszutauschen.

(2) Der Vertrag tritt einen Monat nach dem Austausche der Ratifikationsurkunden in Kraft. Der Vertrag kann zur Gänze oder hinsichtlich einzelner Abschnitte von jedem der vertragschließenden Staaten gekündigt werden. Die gekündigten Bestimmungen bleiben jedoch nach erfolgter Kündigung noch durch sechs Monate in Kraft.

Urkund dessen haben die Bevollmächtigten den gegenwärtigen Vertrag unterzeichnet und mit ihren Siegeln versehen.

Geschehen zu Beograd, am 1. Mai eintausendneunhundertachtundzwanzig in deutscher und in serbischer Sprache in je zwei Ausfertigungen. Da die Verhandlungen in deutscher Sprache geführt wurden, gilt im Zweifelsfalle der deutsche Text als authentisch.

Schlußprotokoll.

Bei Fertigung des Vertrages über den wechselseitigen rechtlichen Verkehr haben die Unterzeichneten Bevollmächtigten die Erklärung abgegeben, daß über folgende Punkte Einverständnis besteht: ...

Zu den Art. 37—53. Die Bestimmungen dieser Artikel über die Zwangsvollstreckung beziehen sich auf jene Exekutionstitel, die nach dem 5. April 1924 in einem der beiden vertragschließenden Staaten entstanden sind, sofern es sich nicht um Exekutionstitel handelt, die schon nach den gegenwärtigen Vorschriften gegenseitig vollstreckbar sind.

Zu Art. 41. Unter dem Ausdruck „nach den Gesetzen des ersuchten Staates" sind die Gesetze zu verstehen, die an dem Orte gelten, wo sich die unbewegliche oder bewegliche Sache befindet, auf die Exekution geführt werden soll, bei Forderungspfändungen, wo der Schuldner den Wohnsitz hat oder wo die sonstige Vollstreckungshandlung vorgenommen werden soll.

In Beograd, am 1. Mai 1928.

Jugoslawien—Tschechoslowakei

Convention relative au règlement des rapports judiciaires conclue entre le Royaume des Serbes, Croates et Slovènes et la République Tchécoslovaque. Signée à Belgrade le 17 mars 1923. Traduction. SdN. 30 (1924), S. 218.

Chapitre XIII.

Exécution des actes exécutoires.

Art. 38. Chacune des Parties contractantes s'engage à admettre et à assurer, sur son territoire, conformément aux dispositions de la présente Convention, l'exécution des actes, énumérés plus loin, qui ont été dressés sur le territoire de l'autre Partie contractante et qui y sont des actes exécutoires en vertu de la loi.

Art. 39. Actes exécutoires.

Au sens de l'article précédent, sont actes exécutoires:

1. Les jugements, ordres de paiement, décisions et autres arrêts rendus par les tribunaux civils, y compris les tribunaux municipaux, portant sur une somme d'argent ou sur d'autres biens, si suivant les lois appliquées par le tribunal qui les a rendus, aucun recours suspensif n'est plus admis à leur égard. Le tribunal devra en outre certifier qu'aucun recours suspensif n'est plus admis à leur égard et confirmer l'authenticité de l'acte.

2. Les transactions concernant les mêmes demandes et effectuées devant les tribunaux civils, y compris les tribunaux municipaux, si elles sont accompagnées d'une déclaration du tribunal certifiant qu'elles sont exécutoires et authentiques.

3. Les jugements et décisions rendus par des arbitres ou par des tri bunaux arbitraux, ou les transactions passées par devant des arbitres ou des tribunaux arbitraux, en tant que ces derniers sont appelés à statuer sur la cause soit en vertu d'une disposition légale, soit à la suite d'un compromis dressé par écrit et dans des formes prescrites par la loi. Ces pièces devront être munies d'une déclaration émanant du tribunal compétent de première instance, sur le territoire duquel résidait l'arbitre ou le tribunal arbitral au moment soit du prononcé du jugement ou de la décision, soit de la passation de la transaction, déclaration certifiant qu'aucun recours suspensif n'est admis à l'égard desdits actes et établissant leur authenticité.

Art. 40. Sauf dispositions contraires établies par la présente Convention, les lois de l'Etat où l'exécution devrait être admise ou assurée régiront l'admissibilité et la mise à effet de la demande d'exécution.

Art. 41. Procédure relative à la présentation des demandes d'exécution et procédure suivie par le tribunal requis d'exécuter la demande.

La demande d'exécution devra être présentée par la Partie intéressée au tribunal de l'endroit où l'acte exécutoire a été établi. En ce qui concerne les actes exécutoires résultant d'une procédure, soit par devant des tribunaux municipaux soit par devant des arbitres ou des tribunaux arbitraux, la demande sera présentée au tribunal compétent de première instance de l'endroit où l'acte exécutoire a été établi. Le tribunal qui aura reçu la demande d'exécution, la transmettra sans retard au tribunal compétent de l'autre Partie contractante, en y ajoutant les déclarations dont il est question à l'article 39 et les pièces à l'appui nécessaires conformément aux prescriptions réglant l'échange de communications entre les tribunaux des deux pays.

La partie intéressée pourra saisir directement d'une demande d'exécution le tribunal compétent de l'autre Etat contractant.

Le tribunal compétent pour accorder l'exécution examinera, d'après les pièces qui lui ont été remises si les conditions requises pour l'admissibilité et la mise à effet de la demande d'exécution ont été remplies. Cet examen, qui devra être terminé dans un délai maximum de 30 jours à partir de la date où le tribunal aura reçu les pièces, ne pourra avoir pour objet que les points suivants:

1. L'autorité qui a statué en la cause, doit-elle être considérée comme compétente? Cette compétence sera considérée comme établie, si, d'après les lois de l'Etat requis, un tribunal de l'Etat requérant peut être saisi de l'affaire.

2. S'agit-il d'un acte exécutoire, conformément à l'article 39?

3. Le défendeur a-t-il été, dans le cas où la loi le prescrit, régulièrement invité à prendre part à la procédure qui a donné lieu à la décision? En particulier, la demande qui a provoqué la procédure sur le territoire de l'autre Partie contractante, a-t-elle été signifiée au défendeur en personne, ou le jugement ou la décision sur lequel se fonde l'acte exécutoire, lui a-t-il été régulièrement signifié? En cas de jugement par contumace, il y aura lieu d'examiner sur demande du défendeur, si une irrégularité quelconque a empêché le défendeur de prendre part à la procédure ou d'y être régulièrement représenté.

Au cours de l'examen des points mentionnés à l'alinéa précédent, le défendeur ou son représentant pourra être entendu avant qu'une décision soit prise.

4. L'exequatur accordé à l'exécution exige-t-il des mesures qui, en vertu des lois en vigueur dans L'Etat requis sont interdits ou inapplicables, ou oblige-t-il à la reconnaissance d'une situation de droit ou au recouvrement d'une créance qui porterait atteinte au droit de souveraineté de l'Etat requis, serait contraire aux bonnes moeurs ou, selon les lois de l'Etat requis, ne pourrait faire l'objet d'une action en justice ou être exécutoire?

Il est interdit au tribunal requis d'entrer dans l'examen du fond de l'affaire.

Art. 42. Dès que le Tribunal recevra les pièces (article 41), le Tribunal compétent pour statuer sur la demande d'exécution prenda, sans tarder et suivant les prescriptions en vigueur sur son propre territoire, des mesures provisoires à l'égard du défendeur en vue d'assurer le recouvrement de la créance faisant l'objet de l'acte exécutoire. Ces mesures provisoires ne pourront être rapportées que dans les cas où le défendeur fournirait un cautionnement pour le recouvrement complet de la créance faisant l'objet de l'acte exécutoire.

Chapitre XVIII.

Ratification et Dénonciation de la Convention.

Art. 67. La présente Convention sera établie dans la langue officielle de chacune des deux Parties contractantes, les deux textes faisant foi.

Elle sera ratifiée et les instruments de ratification seront échangés à Prague dans le plus bref délai possible.

Elle entrera en vigueur un mois après l'échange des instruments de ratification et conservera sa validité jusqu'à expiration d'un délai de six mois à dater du jour où elle aura été dénoncée par l'une des deux Parties contractantes.

En foi de quoi, les Plénipotentiaires ont signé la présente Convention et y ont apposé leurs sceaux.

Fait en double original, à Belgrade, le 17 mars 1923.

Mongolei—Sowjetrußland

Abkommen zwischen Sowjetrußland und der Mongolei über die Urteilsvollstreckung in gewissen zivilrechtlichen Angelegenheiten. In Kraft am 16. April 1931.

Mitgeteilt von J. A. Taraconzio in: Am. Journ. of Intern. Law 31 (1937), S. 63ff.

Circular of the People's Commissariat of Justice No. 48 of 1931, containing instructions to the courts in regard to the application of the provisions contained therein:

In applying the convention between the U.S.S.R. and the Mongolian People's Republic in regard to the execution of judgments in certain civil cases, which came into force on April 16, 1931, the judicial organs of the R.S.F.S.R. must be guided by the following rules:

A. In instances of decisions of courts of the R.S.F.S.R. to be executed in the Mongolian People's Republic:

1. In cases where the judgment of a court of the R.S.F.S.R. is to be executed in the territory of the Mongolian People's Republic, the plaintiff must file a petition with the court which rendered the judgment, asking to transmit the executory papers to the Mongolian People's Republic for execution.

2. The petition must state the nature of the execution, and in particular instances when money is to be collected, the amount of the same, to whom it belongs, and where it is located.

3. The filing of such petitions is allowed exclusively in the cases stipulated in Article 2 of the convention, namely:

(a) in cases involving maintenance of parents, children, and parties to marriage (alimony);

(b) in cases flowing out of damages done to government institutions, undertakings and civic organization (embezzlement, theft, [illegal] appropriation, etc.);

(c) in cases involving labor relations;

(d) in cases involving collection of debts to the state banks of the U.S.S.R. and Mongolian People's Republic, as well as to the governmental cooperative and civic organizations of the U.S.S.R. and the Mongolian People's Republic.

4. Upon receipt of such petition, the court transmits it, together with executory papers, to the People's Commissariat for Foreign Affaires, which in its turn forwards them, provided no objections to so doing are found, to the Ministry of Justice of the Mongolian People's Republic.

5. After the execution of the judgment in the Mongolian People's Republic, the plaintiff will receive all information through the Soviet representative in the Mongolian People's Republic.

B. In instances of judgments of the courts of the Mongolian People's Republic to be executed in the R.S.F.S.R.:

6. Petitions for execution in the R.S.F.S.R. of the judgments of the courts of the Mongolian People's Republic are filed with the People's Commissariat of Justice of the R.S.F.S.R., or of the A.S.S.R.[1] These, upon verification that the judgment is subject to execution in the R.S.F.S.R. in conformity with the convention between the U.S.S.R. and the Mongolian People's Republic, transmit the correspondence to the court where the execution is to take place. Otherwise, they return the correspondence to the People's Commissariat for Foreign Affairs, giving motives for refusal [of execution] as prescribed in Article 3 of the convention.

7. Upon receipt of the said correspondence, the court orders the execution of the judgment by the appropriate organ [duly] charged with the execution of ordinary judgments (village Soviets, etc.).

8. In cases when the executory organ must have some additional information and data from the plaintiff, it communicates with the latter through the People's Commissariat for Foreign Affairs exclusively.

9. After the execution of the judgment, the executory organ notifies the People's Commissariat of Justice to that effect.

10. The transmittal to the plaintiff of property or money collected in virtue of the execution of the judgment takes place exclusively in conformity with the instructions of the People's Commissariat of Justice.

Österreich—Schweiz

Vertrag zwischen der Schweiz und Österreich über die Anerkennung und Vollstreckung gerichtlicher Entscheidungen. Abgeschlossen in Bern am 15. März 1927. Eidgenössische Gesetzsammlung 45 (1929), S. 29.

Art. 1. Die in einem der beiden Staaten gefällten gerichtlichen Entscheidungen in Zivil- und Handelssachen werden im andern Staat anerkannt, wenn sie folgende Voraussetzungen erfüllen:

---

[1] Presumably . . . Autonomous Socialist Soviet Republics.

1. daß die Grundsätze, die in dem Staate, wo die Entscheidung geltend gemacht wird, über die zwischenstaatliche Zuständigkeit der Gerichte bestehen, die Gerichtsbarkeit des andern Staates nicht ausschließen;

2. daß die Anerkennung der Entscheidung nicht gegen die öffentliche Ordnung des Staates verstößt, wo die Entscheidung geltend gemacht wird, insbesondere daß ihr nicht nach dem Rechte dieses Staates die Einrede der entschiedenen Rechtssache entgegensteht;

3. daß die Entscheidung nach dem Rechte des Staates, wo sie gefällt wurde, die Rechtskraft erlangt hat;

4. daß im Fall eines Versäumnisurteils die den Prozeß einleitende Verfügung oder Ladung der säumigen Partei oder ihrem zur Empfangnahme berechtigten Vertreter zu eigenen Handen rechtzeitig zugestellt wurde. Hatte die Zustellung im Gebiete des Staates zu geschehen, wo die Entscheidung geltend gemacht wird, so muß sie im Rechtshilfewege bewirkt worden sein.

Die Behörden des Staates, wo die Entscheidung geltend gemacht wird, dürfen nur prüfen, ob die in Z. 1 bis 4 angeführten Voraussetzungen erfüllt sind. Diese Prüfung erfolgt von Amts wegen.

Art. 2. Die Gerichtsbarkeit des Staates, wo die Entscheidung gefällt wurde, gilt für persönliche Ansprüche gegen einen zahlungsfähigen Schuldner insbesondere dann im Sinne des Art. 1, Z. 1, als ausgeschlossen, wenn der Schuldner zur Zeit der Erhebung der Klage seinen Wohnsitz in dem Staat hatte, wo die Entscheidung geltend gemacht wird.

Diese Bestimmung ist jedoch nicht anzuwenden:

1. wenn sich der Beklagte durch eine ausdrückliche Vereinbarung der Zuständigkeit des Gerichtes unterworfen hat, das in der Sache erkannt hat;

2. wenn sich der Beklagte vorbehaltlos auf den Rechtsstreit eingelassen hat;

3. wenn es sich um eine Widerklage handelt;

4. wenn der Schuldner am Orte seiner geschäftlichen Niederlassung oder Zweigniederlassung für Ansprüche aus dem Betriebe dieser Niederlassung belangt worden ist.

Als persönliche Ansprüche im Sinne dieses Artikels gelten nicht: familienrechtliche und erbrechtliche Ansprüche, dingliche Rechte und pfandrechtlich versicherte Forderungen.

Art 3. Die in einem der beiden Staaten gefällten gerichtlichen Entscheidungen in Zivil- und Handelssachen werden im andern Staate vollstreckt, wenn sie die in Art. 1, Z. 1 bis 4, angeführten Voraussetzungen erfüllen und in dem Staate, wo sie gefällt wurden, vollstreckbar sind.

Die Behörden des Staates, wo die Vollstreckung beantragt wird, dürfen nur prüfen, ob die im Abs. 1 angeführten Voraussetzungen erfüllt sind. Diese Prüfung erfolgt von Amts wegen.

Art. 4. Die Partei, die die Entscheidung geltend macht oder die Vollstreckung beantragt, hat beizubringen:

1. eine Ausfertigung oder Abschrift der Entscheidung;

2. eine Bescheinigung über die Rechtskraft und gegebenenfalls über die Vollstreckbarkeit der Entscheidung; die Bescheinigung ist von der Behörde, die die Entscheidung gefällt hat, oder vom Gerichtsschreiber auszustellen;

3. im Fall eines Versäumnisurteils eine Abschrift der den Prozeß einleitenden Verfügung oder Ladung und eine Bescheinigung über die Art und Zeit ihrer Zustellung an die nicht erschienene Partei;

4. wenn die Entscheidung den ihr zugrunde liegenden Sachverhalt nicht soweit erkennen läßt, daß die Prüfung im Sinne des Art. 1 möglich ist, eine Abschrift der Klage oder andere geeignete Urkunden;

5. gegebenenfalls eine Übersetzung der in Z. 1 bis 4 bezeichneten Urkunden in die Amtssprache der Behörde, bei der die Entscheidung geltend gemacht oder die Vollstreckung beantragt wird. Die Übersetzung muß nach dem Recht eines der beiden Staaten als richtig bescheinigt sein.

Auf die Beglaubigung der in diesem Artikel erwähnten Urkunden sind die Bestimmungen des Staatsvertrages vom 21. August 1916 anzuwenden.

Art. 5. Die in einem der beiden Staaten gefällten Schiedssprüche werden im andern Staat anerkannt und vollstreckt, wenn sie den Vorschriften der vorstehenden Artikel, soweit diese Anwendung finden können, genügen.

Dies gilt auch für gerichtliche oder vor Schiedsgerichten abgeschlossene Vergleiche.

Die Bescheinigung über die Rechtskraft und über die Vollstreckbarkeit des Schiedsspruchs oder des vor einem Schiedsgericht abgeschlossenen Vergleichs wird in Österreich durch die Behörde, die zur Bewilligung der Zwangsvollstreckung in diesem Staate zuständig wäre, in der Schweiz durch die zuständige Behörde des Kantons, wo der Schiedsspruch gefällt oder der Vergleich geschlossen wurde, ausgestellt.

Art. 6. In einem Strafverfahren ergangene Entscheidungen über privatrechtliche Ansprüche, in einem Zivilprozesse verhängte Ordnungsstrafen, Entscheidungen über die Eröffnung des Konkurses und andere Entscheidungen im Konkurs- und Ausgleichsverfahren, sowie Entscheidungen über die Bestätigung eines Nachlaßvertrages gelten nicht als gerichtliche Entscheidungen im Sinne dieses Vertrages.

Art. 7. Entscheidungen anderer als gerichtlicher Behörden, die zur Führung von Vormundschaften oder Pflegschaften berufen sind, sowie die vor solchen Behörden abgeschlossenen Vergleiche sind den gerichtlichen Entscheidungen und Vergleichen im Sinne dieses Vertrages gleichgestellt. Die beiden Regierungen werden einander diese Behörden mitteilen.

Die Vollstreckung von Ansprüchen auf Herausgabe Minderjähriger oder Pflegebefohlener kann aufgeschoben werden, wenn der Durchführung vorläufige Verfügungen der zuständigen Behörden des Staates, wo die Vollstreckung beantragt wird, entgegenstehen, die auf Grund der diesen Behörden obliegenden Fürsorgepflicht wegen veränderter persönlicher Verhältnisse der beteiligten Personen getroffen werden. Die Behörde, von der die zu vollstreckende Entscheidung ausgegangen ist, sowie die Partei, die die Vollstreckung beantragt hat, sind von der Aufschiebung ungesäumt in Kenntnis zu setzen.

Art. 8. Die Zuständigkeit und das Verfahren für die Zwangsvollstreckung bestimmen sich nach dem Rechte des Staates, wo die Vollstreckung beantragt wird, und zwar in der Schweiz, wenn sie auf Geldzahlung oder Sicherheitsleistung gerichtet ist, nach den bundesrechtlichen Vorschriften über Schuldbetreibung und Konkurs (Bundesgesetz vom 11. April 1889 samt Nachträgen), in den übrigen Fällen nach dem Prozeßrechte des Kantons, wo die Vollstreckung erfolgen soll, in Österreich nach den Bestimmungen der österreichischen Exekutionsordnung (Gesetz vom 27. Mai 1896, Reichsgesetzblatt Nr. 79, samt Nachträgen).

Art. 9. Die Bestimmungen zwischenstaatlicher Abkommen, an denen beide Staaten beteiligt sind, werden durch diesen Vertrag nicht berührt.

Die in Art. 18, Abs. 1 und 2, der Übereinkunft über Zivilprozeßrecht vom 17. Juli 1905 genannten Kostenentscheidungen, die in einem der beiden Staaten ergangen sind, werden im andern Staat auf ein von der beteiligten Partei unmittelbar zu stellendes Begehren vollstreckt.

Art. 10. Die Bestimmungen dieses Vertrages sind ohne Rücksicht auf die Staatsangehörigkeit der Parteien anzuwenden.

Art. 11. Das österreichische Bundeskanzleramt (Justiz) und das eidgenössische Justiz- und Polizeidepartement werden einander unmittelbar über Fragen, zu denen die Anwendung dieses Vertrages Anlaß geben sollte, auf Ersuchen Rechtsauskunft erteilen. Die Entscheidungsfreiheit der Gerichte bleibt unberührt.

Art. 12. Dieser Vertrag ist auch auf gerichtliche Entscheidungen, Schiedssprüche und Vergleiche anzuwenden, die vor seinem Inkrafttreten erlassen oder geschlossen worden sind.

Art. 13. Dieser Vertrag soll ratifiziert und die Ratifikationsurkunden sollen in Wien ausgetauscht werden.

Der Vertrag tritt zwei Monate nach dem Austausche der Ratifikationsurkunden in Kraft und bleibt nach Kündigung, die jederzeit zulässig ist, noch ein Jahr in Kraft.

Zu Urkund dessen haben die Bevollmächtigten diesen Vertrag in doppelter Ausfertigung unterzeichnet.

So geschehen in Bern am 15. März 1927.

Österreich—Türkei

Übereinkommen zwischen Österreich und der Türkei über die wechselseitigen rechtlichen Beziehungen in Zivil- und Handelssachen und über die Vollstreckungsrechtshilfe. Vom 22. Juni 1930. Bundesgesetzblatt für die Republik Österreich 1932, S. 251.

III. Abschnitt.

Vollstreckungsrechtshilfe.

Art. 18. Die in Zivil- und Handelssachen von den Gerichtsbehörden des einen Vertragsstaates gefällten Entscheidungen sind auf dem Gebiete des andern Vertragsstaates durch eine Entscheidung des zuständigen Gerichtes des letzteren sowohl in das bewegliche als auch in das unbewegliche Vermögen für vollstreckbar zu erklären, wenn sie folgenden Bedingungen entsprechen:

1. Die Entscheidung muß von einer zuständigen Gerichtsbehörde gefällt worden sein. Die Behörde ist als zuständig anzusehen, wenn die Rechtssache nach dem Rechte des Landes, wo die Vollstreckbarerklärung begehrt wird, bei einem Gerichte des andern vertragschließenden Teiles anhängig gemacht werden konnte;

soferne die rechtlichen Erwägungen, aus denen sich das Gericht für zuständig erachtet hat, nicht aus dem Wortlaute der Entscheidung selbst hervorgehen, können sie durch eine diesbezügliche Bestätigung des Gerichtes dargetan werden;

2. die Ladung muß gemäß dem Rechte des Staates, wo die Entscheidung gefällt worden ist, zugestellt worden sein und es muß hiebei für das Erscheinen eine Frist gesetzt worden sein, die mit Rücksicht auf die Entfernung und die besonderen Umstände des Falles tatsächlich ausreichend war;

3. die Parteien müssen nach dem Rechte des Landes, wo die Entscheidung gefällt worden ist, gesetzmäßig vertreten oder gemäß diesem Rechte für säumig erklärt worden sein, es sei denn, daß der Gegner das Fehlen dieser Bedingung nicht geltend macht;

4. die Entscheidung muß nach dem Rechte des Landes, wo sie gefällt worden ist, in Rechtskraft erwachsen und jederzeit ungehindert vollstreckbar sein;

zum Nachweis dafür, daß die angeführten Bedingungen zutreffen, genügt die Vorlage einer Erklärung der Behörde, von der die Entscheidung ausgeht, über die Rechtskraft und Vollstreckbarkeit der Entscheidung;

5. die Entscheidung darf nicht mit einer anderen Entscheidung, die über denselben Gegenstand zwischen denselben Parteien von den Gerichtsbehörden des Landes, in dem die Vollstreckbarerklärung begehrt wird, gefällt worden ist, in Widerspruch stehen und es darf auch nicht vor diesen Behörden in dem Zeitpunkt, in dem der Antrag auf Volstreckbarerklärung zugestellt worden ist, bereits ein anderer Rechtsstreit über denselben Gegenstand zwischen denselben Parteien anhängig sein;

6. die Entscheidung darf nichts enthalten, was der öffentlichen Ordnung oder den Grundsätzen des öffentlichen Rechtes des Landes, wo die Vollstreckbarerklärung begehrt wird, widersprechen würde;

7. die Entscheidung darf nicht den Personen- oder Familienstand betreffen;

8. die Angelegenheit darf nicht in die ausschließliche Zuständigkeit der Gerichte des ersuchten Landes fallen.

Art. 19. Die für die Vollstreckbarerklärung der ausländischen Entscheidung zuständige Gerichtsbehörde hat den Streit neuerlich zur Gänze zu überprüfen, wenn vom Beklagten einer der folgenden Umstände vorgebracht wird:

1. daß die Entscheidung auf eine bösliche Handlungsweise der anderen Partei zurückzuführen ist;

2. daß die Entscheidung sich auf Urkunden stützt, die von der Gerichtsbehörde für gefälscht erklärt worden sind;

3. daß nach der Fällung der Entscheidung eine entscheidende Urkunde zum Vorschein gekommen ist, die durch Verschulden der anderen Partei nicht früher vorgelegt worden ist;

4. daß die Entscheidung unmittelbar auf einem Tatsachenirrtum beruht, der sich aus den Akten und Urkunden des Rechtsstreites ergibt.

Art. 20. Die von Schiedsrichtern in dem Gebiet eines der Vertragsstaaten gefällten Schiedssprüche sind in dem Gebiete des andern Teiles für vollstreckbar zu erklären, wenn ihnen nach dem Rechte des Landes, wo sie gefällt wurden, die Rechtswirksamkeit gerichtlicher Entscheidungen zukommt und wenn nach dem Rechte des Landes, wo sie geltend gemacht werden, der Gegenstand der Entscheidung im Schiedswege geregelt werden kann.

Die Partei, welche die Vollstreckbarerklärung beantragt, hat vorzulegen:

1. den Schiedsvertrag oder das die Schiedsklausel enthaltende Übereinkommen;
2. eine Ausfertigung des Schiedsspruches;
3. eine Bestätigung darüber, daß der Schiedsspruch rechtskräftig und vollstreckbar ist. Diese Bestätigung ist zu erteilen:
   a) wenn der Schiedsspruch in dem Gebiete der Republik Österreich gefällt wurde, von dem Gerichte, das zur Bewilligung der Zwangsvollstreckung auf Grund dieses Schiedsspruches in Österreich zuständig wäre;
   b) wenn der Schiedsspruch in dem Gebiete der Türkischen Republik gefällt wurde, von dem Gerichte, das zur Bestätigung (Homologisierung) des Schiedsspruches in der Türkei zuständig ist.

Die Bestimmungen der Artikel 18 und 19 sind auf die Vollstreckung von Schiedssprüchen anzuwenden.

Art. 21. Die gerichtlichen Entscheidungen (Artikel 18), die Schiedssprüche (Artikel 20) sowie die zum Nachweise der Voraussetzungen der Vollstreckbarerklärung erforderlichen Urkunden sind in Urschrift oder in Abschrift entweder im diplomatischen Wege oder von der beteiligten Partei unmittelbar an die zur Vollstreckbarerklärung zuständige Behörde zu übersenden. Wenn die angeführten Schriftstücke nicht in der Sprache des Staates, wo die Vollstreckbarerklärung begehrt wird, abgefaßt sind, so ist eine Übersetzung in dieser Sprache anzuschließen.

Die Echtheit der Urschrift sowie die Richtigkeit der Abschriften und Übersetzungen sind von einem diplomatischen oder konsularischen Vertreter eines der beiden vertragschließenden Teile zu bestätigen.

Art. 22. (1) Das vorliegende Übereinkommen soll ratifiziert werden. Die Ratifikationsurkunden sollen möglichst bald in Ankara ausgetauscht werden.

(2) Das Übereinkommen tritt drei Monate nach Austausch der Ratifikationsurkunden in Kraft. Es kann von jedem der beiden Staaten gekündigt werden; es bleibt jedoch während sechs Monaten von dem Tage, an dem es gekündigt worden ist, in Kraft.

Geschehen in Ankara, am 22. Juni 1930.

Österreich—Ungarn

Verordnung des Justizministers vom 26. Oktober 1914 über die Regelung der Vollstreckungsrechtshilfe zwischen den im Reichsrate vertretenen Königreichen und Ländern und den Ländern der ungarischen heiligen Krone. Reichsgesetzblatt für die im Reichsrate vertretenen Königreiche und Länder 1914, S. 1160.

Auf Grund des § 84 des Gesetzes vom 27. Mai 1896, RGBl. Nr. 79, wird verordnet:

Für die Vollstreckungsrechtshilfe im Verhältnisse der im Reichsrate vertretenen Königreiche und Länder zu den Ländern der ungarischen heiligen Krone haben auf Grund eines mit der ungarischen Regierung getroffenen Übereinkommens sowie eines Nachtragsübereinkommens zu Artikel 21, das durch die im Zusammenhange mit den kriegerischen Ereignissen eingeführte Stundung von privatrechtlichen Verpflichtungen veranlaßt wurde, vom 1. Jänner 1915 an die folgenden Bestimmungen zu gelten. Insoweit hienach anderes zu gelten hat als bisher, finden die Vorschriften des § 86 EO. mangels der verbürgten Gegenseitigkeit keine Anwendung.

Im Verhältnisse zwischen den im Reichsrate vertretenen Königreichen und Ländern und Kroatien-Slavonien bleiben bis auf weiteres die für die wechselseitige Vollstreckung von Exekutionstiteln bestehenden Vorschriften in Geltung.

Art. 1. Folgende einen vermögensrechtlichen Anspruch betreffende Akte und Urkunden werden wechselseitig als vollstreckbar anerkannt:

1. Die im bürgerlichen Streitverfahren erflossenen rechtskräftigen Entscheidungen, nämlich Urteile, Beschlüsse, Zahlungsaufträge im Mandats-, Wechsel- und Scheckverfahren (Aufträge auf Grund von Wechseln, kaufmännischen Anweisungen, Verpflichtungsscheinen und Schecks).

2. Die im bürgerlichen nichtstreitigen Verfahren ergangenen rechtskräftigen Beschlüsse über Unterhaltsansprüche.

3. Vergleiche, die im bürgerlichen streitigen oder nichtstreitigen Verfahren abgeschlossen wurden.

4. Die im Konkursverfahren abgeschlossenen rechtskräftig bestätigten Vergleiche und Zwangsausgleiche, die während eines solchen Verfahrens ergangenen rechtskräftigen gerichtlichen Beschlüsse, die amtlichen Auszüge aus dem während des Konkursverfahrens aufgenommenen Liquidierungsprotokolle und die rechtskräftig bestätigten Beitragsberechnungen im Konkurse einer Erwerbs- und Wirtschaftsgenossenschaft.

5. Die rechtskräftigen Entscheidungen der Börsenschiedsgerichte und der Börsengerichte sowie die vor ihnen geschlossenen Vergleiche, und zwar auch dann, wenn sich die Parteien ihnen durch schriftliche Vereinbarung oder vorbehaltlose Annahme eines Schlußbriefes, in dem die Bestimmung enthalten ist, daß Rechtsstreitigkeiten aus dem Geschäfte vor dem Börsenschiedsgerichte oder Börsengerichte zu entscheiden sind, unterworfen haben.

6. Notariatsakte (Artikel 5).

Als bürgerliches streitiges oder nichtstreitiges Verfahren im Sinne dieses Vertrages gilt das Verfahren in bürgerlichen Rechtsangelegenheiten vor den ordentlichen und den Sondergerichten (Obersthofmarschallamt, Obersthofmarschallgericht, Gewerbegericht und andere). Als Sondergerichte im Sinne dieses Vertrages gelten auch die Gemeindevermittlungsämter, die ungarischen Gemeindegerichte und die Friedensrichter sowie die Schiedsgerichte, die ohne Rücksicht auf einen Schiedsvertrag vermöge einer besonderen staatlichen Anordnung zuständig sind.

Art. 2. Als vollstreckbar werden nicht anerkannt:

1. die im Mahnverfahren ergangenen Zahlungsbefehle;

2. die im bürgerlichen streitigen oder nichtstreitigen Verfahren ergangenen Entscheidungen, welche eine Geldbuße oder Geldstrafe verhängen.

Art. 3. Die Vollstreckung von gerichtlichen Entscheidungen im Sinne des Artikels 1, Z. 1, kann gegen den Verpflichteten nur bewilligt werden, wenn einer der in den folgenden Ziffern 1 bis 15 bezeichneten Zuständigkeitsgründe bei dem erkennenden Gerichte vorhanden war und nicht ein Gericht des Vollstreckungsstaates ausschließlich zur Entscheidung zuständig ist:

1. Der allgemeine Gerichtsstand des Beklagten nach dem Rechte des erkennenden Gerichtes.

2. Der Gerichtsstand des Aufenthaltsortes für Ansprüche gegen prozeßfähige Personen, die sich an einem Orte unter Umständen aufhalten, die ihrer Natur nach auf einen Aufenthalt von längerer Dauer hinweisen (zum Beispiel als Dienstboten, Hand- oder Fabriksarbeiter, Gewerbegehilfen oder Lehrlinge, als Studierende oder Schüler). Dieser Gerichtsstand gilt für die Mitglieder der bewaffneten Macht, die im aktiven Dienste stehen und nur ihre Wehrpflicht erfüllen, derart, daß an die Stelle des Gerichtes des Aufenthaltsortes das Gericht der ständigen Garnison tritt.

3. Der Gerichtsstand der geführten Verwaltung.

Vermögensrechtliche Ansprüche gegen ausländische öffentliche Anstalten, Körperschaften, Handelsgesellschaften, Genossenschaften, Vereine, Stiftungen und andere Vermögensmassen können bei dem Gerichte geltend gemacht werden, in dessen Sprengel sie ihre ständige Vertretung, in Ermanglung einer solchen aber ihre mit der Besorgung der Geschäfte betrauten Organe haben.

4. Der Gerichtsstand der Niederlassung.

Personen, die außerhalb des Gerichtssprengels ihres Wohnsitzes eine Fabriks-, Handels- oder gewerbliche Niederlassung oder eine Betriebsstätte ihres Geschäftes oder Berufes haben, von der aus sie sich unmittelbar mit dem Abschlusse von Geschäften befassen, können in streitigen Rechtssachen, die sich auf diese Niederlassung oder auf ihre geschäftliche oder berufliche Tätigkeit beziehen, bei dem Gerichte des Ortes geklagt werden, an dem sich ihre Niederlassung oder Betriebsstätte befindet. Personen, die auf einem mit Wohn- und Wirtschaftsgebäuden versehenen Landgute eine Wirtschaft betreiben, können aus allen auf die Bewirtschaftung dieses Landgutes sich beziehenden Rechtsverhältnissen beim Gerichte geklagt werden, in dessen Sprengel das Landgut oder der Ort gelegen ist, von dem aus die Wirtschaft betrieben wird.

5. Der Gerichtsstand des Erfüllungsortes.

Klagen auf Feststellung des Bestehens oder Nichtbestehens, auf Erfüllung oder Aufhebung eines Vertrages sowie auf Entschädigung wegen Unterlassung vertragsmäßiger Leistungen können auch bei dem Gerichte des Ortes erhoben werden, an dem der Vertrag nach der Vereinbarung zu erfüllen ist, wenn der Erfüllungsort sich aus einer Urkunde ergibt oder wenn die Ladung dem Beklagten im Sprengel oder am Sitze des

Gerichtes zugestellt werden kann. Von mehreren Erfüllungsorten begründet jeder die Zuständigkeit. Eine besondere Form ist für diese Urkunde nicht erforderlich. Der Gerichtsstand gilt auch dann als gegeben, wenn in die Urkunde die Erklärung aufgenommen ist, daß durch die Vereinbarung des Erfüllungsortes auch die Berechtigung zur Klage an diesem Orte begründet ist.

Für Forderungen aus Ratengeschäften kann die Zuständigkeit auf Grund der Bestimmungen über den Gerichtsstand des Erfüllungsortes nicht festgestellt werden.

6. Der Gerichtsstand des Zahlungsortes des Wechsels oder Schecks für Klagen des Inhabers gegen die aus dem Wechsel oder Scheck verpflichteten Personen.

7. Der Gerichtsstand des früheren Wohnsitzes.

Kaufleute und Gewerbetreibende können wegen ihrer Forderungen aus einem im Kreise ihres Geschäftes abgeschlossenen Rechtsgeschäfte auch bei dem nach dem früheren Wohnsitze des Vertragsgegners zuständigen Gerichte klagen, wenn sie urkundlich nachweisen, daß seit der Änderung des Wohnsitzes bis zur Anbringung der Klage nicht mehr als 90 Tage verstrichen sind. Eine besondere Form ist für diese Urkunde nicht erforderlich.

8. Der Gerichtsstand für Warenforderungen der Kaufleute.

Gegen Kaufleute können protokollierte Kaufleute wegen ihrer Forderungen aus einem im Kreise ihres Geschäftes erfolgten Verkaufe innerhalb zweier Jahre von der letzten Bestellung an gerechnet auch vor dem Gerichte des Ortes ihrer Niederlassung klagen, wenn sie die als Grundlage der Forderung dienende Bestellung und die tatsächliche Übernahme der Ware urkundlich nachweisen. Bei Geschäften, die auf Grund einer Bevollmächtigung abgeschlossen wurden, muß die Vollmacht des Bestellers urkundlich nachgewiesen werden. Eine besondere Form ist für diese Urkunde nicht erforderlich.

Für Forderungen aus Ratengeschäften kann die Zuständigkeit auf Grund der Bestimmungen über den Gerichtsstand für Warenforderungen der Kaufleute nicht festgestellt werden.

9. Der Gerichtsstand des Schadensortes.

Klagen auf Ersatzleistung wegen einer Ereignung im Verkehre einer Eisenbahn oder auf Ersatz von Schäden, die durch den Betrieb eines Kraftfahrzeuges verursacht sind, können auch bei dem Gerichte erhoben werden, in dessen Sprengel das schädigende Ereignis stattfand.

10. Der Gerichtsstand der belasteten Sache.

Vor dem nach der Lage der unbeweglichen Sache zuständigen Gerichte kann auch mit der Klage zur Geltendmachung des Pfandrechtes die Klage auf Zahlung der pfandrechtlich versicherten Forderung, mit der Klage auf Aufhebung (Löschung) des Pfandrechtes die Klage auf Feststellung des Nichtbestehens der pfandrechtlich versicherten Forderung verbunden werden, wenn beide Klagen wider denselben Beklagten gerichtet sind.

Klagen auf die aus einer Reallast rückständigen Leistungen können gegen den Besitzer des belasteten Grundstückes bei dem Gerichte erhoben werden, in dessen Sprengel das belastete Grundstück gelegen ist.

11. Der Gerichtsstand der Widerklage, insoweit eine solche nach dem Gesetze des Erkenntnisstaates zulässig ist.

12. Der Gerichtsstand für Forderungen der Nachlaßgläubiger.

Nachlaßgläubiger können, solange der Nachlaß nicht eingeantwortet ist, wegen ihrer Forderungen an den Erblasser oder Erben als solchen vor dem sachlich zuständigen Gerichte klagen, das durch den Sitz des Nachlaßgerichtes örtlich bestimmt ist.

13. Der Gerichtsstand der Unterwerfung.

Die Parteien können sich durch ausdrückliche Vereinbarung der Zuständigkeit eines bestimmten Gerichtes unterwerfen. Die Unterwerfung gilt nur dann, wenn sie sich auf einen bestimmten Rechtsstreit oder die aus einem bestimmten Rechtsverhältnisse entspringenden Rechtsstreitigkeiten bezieht und wenn der Beklagte seinen allgemeinen Gerichtsstand im Erkenntnisstaat hatte. Sie muß durch eine öffentliche oder eine vollen Glauben verdienende Privaturkunde nachgewiesen sein.

Für Forderungen aus Ratengeschäften kann die Zuständigkeit auf Grund der Bestimmungen über den Gerichtsstand der Unterwerfung nicht festgestellt werden.

14. Der Gerichtsstand der Streitgenossenschaft nach Maßgabe des Rechtes des Erkenntnisstaates unter der Voraussetzung, daß, abgesehen von der Streitgenossenschaft ein Gericht des Erkenntnisstaates im Sinne der Bestimmungen dieses Vertrages zuständig wäre.

15. Die Zuständigkeit des durch ein höheres Gericht bestimmten Gerichtes, wenn die Gerichtsbarkeit des Erkenntnisstaates begründet ist, aber Tatsachen fehlen, welche die örtliche Zuständigkeit begründen, ferner im Falle von Zuständigkeitsstreitigkeiten unter mehreren Gerichten und im Falle der Delegation. Die Zuständigkeit gilt jedoch im Sinne dieser Bestimmung nur dann als gegeben, wenn abgesehen von dieser Verfügung ein Gericht des Erkenntnisstaates im Sinne der Bestimmungen dieses Vertrages zuständig wäre.

Art. 4. Entscheidungen über den Ersatz von Prozeßkosten sind in den im Artikel 18 des Haager Prozeßübereinkommens vom 17. Juli 1905 bezeichneten Fällen ohne Rücksicht auf die Zuständigkeit der Behörde, die erkannt hat, wechselseitig vollstreckbar.

Art. 5. Die Vollstreckung auf Grund eines vollstreckbaren Notariatsaktes (Artikel 1, Z. 6) findet nur statt, wenn darin eine Schuld an Geld oder anderen vertretbaren Sachen festgestellt ist und die Person des Berechtigten und des Verpflichteten, der Rechtsgrund, der Gegenstand und die Zeit der Leistung genau bestimmt sind und wenn zugleich der Verpflichtete in der Urkunde zugestimmt hat, daß sie in Ansehung der Schuld sofort vollstreckbar sein soll. Es ist jedoch die Vollstreckung auch auf Grund von Notariatsakten ohne Vollstreckbarkeitsklausel zu gewähren, wenn sie vor Beginn der Wirksamkeit dieses Vertrages errichtet wurden und nach dem Gesetze des Errichtungsortes vollstreckbar sind.

Vollmachten, auf Grund deren ein Notariatsakt errichtet werden soll, müssen, um dem Akte die Vollstreckbarkeit zu sichern, gerichtlich oder notariell beglaubigt sein, sofern sie nicht schon öffentliche Urkunden sind.

Insoweit die Ausstellung von Urkunden, die den notariellen gleichgeachtet werden, zur Zuständigkeit der Gerichte gehört, können unter den oben genannten Voraussetzungen auch solche Gerichtsurkunden vollstreckt werden.

Art. 6. Das Ersuchen um Vollstreckung gegen den Verpflichteten kann nur vom Gerichte gestellt werden.

In dem Ersuchen hat das Gericht die Vollstreckbarkeit und, wenn der Exekutionstitel gemäß Artikel 1 und 19 rechtskräftig sein muß, auch die Rechtskraft zu bestätigen.

Der Ausfertigung eines besonderen Ersuchschreibens bedarf es nicht.

Art. 7. Dem Ersuchen ist eine Ausfertigung der Urkunde anzuschließen, auf Grund deren die Vollstreckung erfolgen soll.

Die Voraussetzungen für die Zuständigkeit des erkennenden Gerichtes im Sinne des Artikels 3 sind nur anzugeben.

Das Vorhandensein der übrigen Voraussetzungen der Vollstreckung ist, soweit nicht schon die Urkunde, auf Grund deren die Vollstreckung bewilligt werden soll, oder das amtliche Ersuchen um die Vollstreckung sie entnehmen läßt, durch öffentliche Urkunden darzutun.

Art. 8. Die Gerichte der vertragschließenden Staaten verkehren unmittelbar miteinander.

Geht das Ersuchen um Vollstreckung von einem Gerichte der Länder der ungarischen heiligen Krone aus, so wird es in der amtlichen Sprache des ersuchenden Gerichtes ausgefertigt, geht es von einem österreichischen Gerichte aus, so wird es in deutscher Sprache ausgefertigt oder mit einer deutschen Übersetzung versehen sein.

Das Gleiche gilt für die Beilagen des Ersuchens.

Art. 9. Wird den Anordnungen des Artikels 6, Absatz 2, oder der Artikel 7 und 8 nicht entsprochen, so hat das ersuchte Gericht die Beseitigung der Mängel und, wenn sich gegründete Anhaltspunkte für das Vorliegen eines Versagungsgrundes ergeben, die zu dessen Ausschließung erforderlichen Nachweise zu verlangen.

Art. 10. Das zur Entscheidung über das Ersuchen zuständige Gericht hat darüber ohne Einvernehmung des Verpflichteten Beschluß zu fassen. Es kann jedoch vorher das Organ, von dem der Exekutionstitel herrührt, oder das Gericht, das um die Vollstreckung ersucht hat, um Aufklärung ersuchen.

Das ersuchte Gericht prüft die Zulässigkeit der Exekution auch dann, wenn das ersuchende Gericht die Exekution schon bewilligt hat. Es hat jedoch nicht zu prüfen, ob das ersuchende Gericht zur Entgegennahme des Gesuches und zur Bewilligung nach seinem Rechte zuständig war.

Die Gesetzmäßigkeit der zu vollstreckenden Entscheidung darf das Gericht nicht überprüfen.

Art. 11. Wenn die in den vorhergehenden Artikeln bezeichneten Voraussetzungen für die Bewilligung der Vollstreckung fehlen, ist das Ersuchen von Amts wegen abzulehnen.

Ungeachtet des Vorhandenseins dieser Voraussetzungen ist die Vollstreckung zu versagen, wenn durch sie ein Rechtsverhältnis zur Anerkennung oder ein Anspruch zur Verwirklichung gelangen soll, dem durch das Gesetz des Vollstreckungsstaates aus Rücksichten der öffentlichen Ordnung oder der Sittlichkeit die Gültigkeit oder Klagbarkeit versagt ist, oder wenn über den Anspruch im Vollstreckungsstaate rechtskräftig entschieden wurde.

Art. 12. Die Vollstreckung auf Grund gerichtlicher Entscheidungen ist außerdem zu versagen:

1. wenn über Ansprüche gegen den Vollstreckungsstaat erkannt wurde, es sei denn, daß er sich durch Staatsvertrag der Zuständigkeit des Erkenntnisrichters ausdrücklich unterworfen hat, daß es sich um Ansprüche handelt, die gegen den Staat als Erben oder Vermächtnisnehmer erhoben wurden oder daß es sich um Forderungen handelt, die aus einem geschäftlichen Unternehmen herrühren, das vom Vollstrekkungsstaate im Gebiete des Erkenntnisstaates betrieben wird und dort seinen Sitz hat;

2. wenn über Ansprüche aus der Eigenschaft eines Mitgliedes einer Korporation, Gesellschaft, Genossenschaft oder eines Vereines gegen den Verband oder dessen Organe oder wenn über Ansprüche aus Teilschuldverschreibungen, staatlichen oder sonstigen öffentlichen Anlehen, aus Pfandbriefen oder fundierten Bankschuldverschreibungen von einem anderen Gerichte als dem des allgemeinen Gerichtsstandes des Beklagten erkannt wurde.

Art. 13. Wird die Vollstreckung bewilligt, so ist der Vollzug unverzüglich von Amts wegen einzuleiten, es sei denn, daß der betreibende Gläubiger sich vorbehalten hat, wegen der Vornahme des Vollzuges noch besonders einzuschreiten.

Art. 14. Gegen die Bewilligung der Vollstreckung kann der Verpflichtete, unbeschadet der nach den Gesetzen des Vollstreckungsstaates zulässigen Einbringung eines Rechtsmittels, Widerspruch erheben:

1. wenn die in den Artikeln 1 bis 8 für die Bewilligung der Vollstreckung bezeichneten Voraussetzungen nicht gegeben sind oder wenn ein Versagungsgrund im Sinne der Artikel 11, Absatz 2, und 12 vorliegt;

2. wenn in der Entscheidung bei Beurteilung der Handlungs- oder Prozeßfähigkeit des Verpflichteten oder seiner gesetzlichen Vertretung oder aber bei der Beurteilung eines für den Anspruch maßgebenden Familien- oder erbrechtlichen Verhältnisses oder der dafür maßgebenden Feststellung des Todes einer Person zum Nachteile des Verpflichteten andere als die nach dem Rechte des Vollstreckungsstaates anzuwendenden Gesetze zugrunde gelegt wurden;

3. wenn die Vollstreckung auf Grund der gerichtlichen Entscheidung gegen den Beklagten, der an dem Streite nicht teilgenommen hat, geführt werden soll und ihm die Ladung oder Verfügung, durch die das Verfahren eingeleitet worden ist, nicht ordnungsmäßig zugestellt wurde;

4. wenn infolge einer anderen Unregelmäßigkeit des Verfahrens der Person, gegen welche die Vollstreckung geführt werden soll, die Möglichkeit, sich an dem Verfahren zu beteiligen, vollständig entzogen war;

5. wenn nach den Gesetzen des Ortes, wo die zu vollstreckende Urkunde entstanden ist, deren Vollstreckbarkeit erloschen ist.

Als ordnungsmäßig im Sinne der Z. 3 hat die Zustellung nur dann zu gelten, wenn die Ladung oder Verfügung, durch die das Verfahren eingeleitet worden ist, dem Beklagten oder seinem zur Empfangnahme berechtigten Vertreter (Kurator) zu eigenen Händen oder im Gebiete des Vollstreckungsstaates nach den für die Zustellung von Klagen oder von Ladungen zur ersten Tagsatzung geltenden Vorschriften zugestellt worden ist.

Art. 15. Der Widerspruch ist, soweit er sich nicht auf die Bestimmung der Artikel 11, Absatz 2, oder 14, Z. 5, stützt, in den im Reichsrate vertretenen Königreichen und Ländern binnen 14 Tagen, in den Ländern der ungarischen heiligen Krone binnen 15 Tagen nach Zustellung des die Vollstreckung bewilligenden Beschlusses zu erheben.

Art. 16. Über den Widerspruch ist nach dem Verfahren des Vollstreckungsgerichtes, jedoch nach vorangehender Anhörung der Gegenpartei zu entscheiden.

Nach Erhebung des Widerspruches können die über die Sicherstellung des Anspruches hinausgehenden Vollstreckungshandlungen bis zur Entscheidung über den Widerspruch aufgeschoben werden.

Art. 17. Insoweit dieser Vertrag nicht besondere Bestimmungen enthält, sind die im Vollstreckungsstaate geltenden Vorschriften über das Verfahren, insbesondere die Bestimmungen über die Aufschiebung und Einstellung der Exekution, ferner über Klagen behufs Einstellung der Exekution wegen Erlöschens oder Hemmung des Anspruches und über Exszindierungsklagen auch auf Vollstreckungen anzuwenden, die auf Grund des Ersuchens der Gerichte des anderen Staates bewilligt werden.

Art. 18. Wenn gegen einen Zahlungsauftrag im Mandats-, Wechsel- oder Scheckverfahren (Auftrag auf Grund eines Wechsels, einer kaufmännischen Anweisung, eines Verpflichtungsscheines oder Schecks) Einwendungen erhoben werden, findet die Exekution zur Sicherstellung statt.

Auf die Exekution zur Sicherstellung sind die Artikel 3 und 6 bis 17 dieses Vertrages entsprechend anzuwenden.

Art. 19. Außer den im Artikel 1 bezeichneten Akten und Urkunden werden wechselseitig als vollstreckbar erklärt die nach den Gesetzen des Errichtungsortes gegen den Verpflichteten vollstreckbaren Entscheidungen und Verfügungen der Gerichte und Pflegschaftsbehörden auf Herausgabe von Minderjährigen und Pflegebefohlenen sowie die rechtskräftigen Beschlüsse der administrativen Pflegschaftsbehörden über Unterhaltsansprüche.

Insoweit die Entscheidung einer administrativen Pflegschaftsbehörde zusteht, wird das Ersuchen um Vollstreckung von dieser Pflegschaftsbehörde unmittelbar gestellt. Das Ersuchen um Vollstreckung einer Entscheidung oder Verfügung auf Herausgabe eines Minderjährigen oder Pflegebefohlenen ist an die zur Vornahme pflegschaftsbehördlicher Maßnahmen berufene Behörde unmittelbar zu richten.

Ist der Minderjährige oder Pflegebefohlene Angehöriger des Vollstreckungsstaates, so ist die Mitwirkung zur Herausgabe zu versagen. Die Vollstreckung ist in erster Linie durch zwangsweise Abnahme durchzuführen.

Im übrigen sind die Bestimmungen der Artikel 6 bis 11 und 13 bis 17 auch auf solche Vollstreckungen sinngemäß anzuwenden.

Art. 20. Die Wirksamkeit der Bestimmungen dieses Vertrages erstreckt sich nicht auf Kroatien-Slavonien.

Art. 21. Der gegenwärtige Vertrag tritt am 1. Jänner 1915 in Wirksamkeit und bleibt bis zum Ablaufe des Jahres 1917 in Kraft. Falls keiner der vertragschließenden Teile zwölf Monate vor dem Ende dieses Zeitraumes seine Absicht, den Vertrag außer Kraft zu setzen, anzeigt, bleibt er bis zum Ablaufe eines Jahres von dem Tage an in Geltung, an dem ihn der eine oder der andere der vertragschließenden Teile kündigt.

Bis zum 1. Juli 1915 ist jedoch auf Grund von Exekutionstiteln, die vor dem 1. Jänner 1915 entstanden sind, die Vollstreckung auch dann zu bewilligen, wenn sie nach den bei Beginn der Wirksamkeit dieses Vertrages geltenden Vorschriften bewilligt werden konnte.

Zusatz zu Art. 21. Für Forderungen oder Forderungsteilbeträge, die im Erkenntnisstaate aus Anlaß der kriegerischen Ereignisse durch besondere Vorschriften gestundet wurden und für die bis zum 30. April 1915 ein Exekutionstitel entstanden ist, ist im anderen Staate bis zum 1. Oktober 1915 die Vollstreckung auch dann zu bewilligen, wenn sie nach den bei Beginn der Wirksamkeit des Vollstreckungsrechtshilfevertrages geltenden Vorschriften bewilligt werden konnte.

Falls das Moratorium sich auf eine längere Zeitdauer als bis Ende November 1914 erstrecken würde, wird die Bestimmung des vorstehenden Absatzes mit der Abänderung anzuwenden sein, daß dem Gläubiger eine Fristverlängerung von ebensolcher Dauer zustehe, als er durch die Stundung verliert.

Polen—Tschechoslowakei

Convention entre la République de Pologne et la République Tchécoslovaque relative aux rapports judiciaires mutuels en matière civile et pénale. Signée à Varsovie, le 21 janvier 1949. Traduction. UN. 31 (1949), S. 263.

Chapitre IV

Reconnaissance des sentences judiciares et des sentences des tribunaux arbitraux

Conditions générales de la reconnaissance

Art. 32. 1) Les décisions judiciaires de l'une des Parties qui, conformément à ses lois, ont acquis force de chose jugée, seront reconnues sur le territoire de l'autre Partie.

2) Par décisions judiciaires, au sens du paragraphe premier, on entend les jugements et les autres décisions équivalentes (quelle qu'en soit la désignation) rendus par les tribunaux civils, tant sur le fond de l'affaire que sur les frais de procédure.

3) Sont assimilées aux décisions judiciaires, au sens des paragraphes précédents, les décisions ayant force de chose jugée, rendues par des tribunaux spéciaux, ainsi que les décisions des tribunaux arbitraux. Toutefois, les décisions des tribunaux arbitraux ne leur sont assimilées que lorsque le compromis d'arbitrage a été établi par écrit et que l'arbitre ou les arbitres ont été désignés soit par les Parties soit par une tierce personne à laquelle les Parties avaient confié la désignation soit, enfin, par le tribunal. Le choix de l'arbitre ou la désignation d'une tierce dersonne chargée de choisir l'arbitre devra être confirmé par écrit.

4) Les décisions des tribunaux de l'une des Parties seront reconnues sur le territoire de l'autre Partie, si la validité en est certifiée par le tri-

bunal qui a jugé l'affaire en premier ressort. La validité des décisions rendues par les tribunaux arbitraux sera certifiée par le tribunal qui est compétent en vertu de la loi de la Partie sur le territoire de laquelle le jugement a été prononcé.

Refus de reconnaître une décision

Art. 33. 1) La décision ne sera pas reconnue:

1. Si, en vertu des dispositions de la présente convention ou de la loi de la Partie sur le territoire de laquelle la décision doit être reconnue, les tribunaux de cette Partie sont exclusivement compétents;

2. Si l'acte introductif d'instance n'avait pas été signifié à la Partie qui a succombé dans le procès, dans les formes légales et en temps utile, et si cette Partie ne s'est pas présentée au procès;

3. Si, en ce qui concerne la capacité de faire des actes juridiques et la capacité d'ester en justice ainsi que la représentation légale, et en outre dans les affaires relatives à la validité du mariage et du divorce (ainsi que de la séparation de corps), dans les affaires d'adoption, d'interdiction ainsi que dans les affaires de succession, il n'a pas été fait application de la loi qu'il y avait lieu d'appliquer en vertu de la législation de la Partie sur le territoire de laquelle la reconnaissance de la décision est sollicitée, à moins que la présente convention n'en dispose autrement ou que la loi qui a été appliquée ne soit analogue quant au fond à la loi de la Partie dont il y avait lieu d'appliquer la législation nationale;

4. Si elle est contraire à l'ordre public ou aux bonnes moeurs;

5. En matière de dépens si la décision rendue au principal ne peut être reconnue.

2) Les décisions mettant les dépens à la charge d'un requérant ou intervenant qui a été exempté de la caution conformément à l'art. 2 de la présente convention, seront reconnues, indépendamment de l'existence des conditions posées au paragraphe premier.

Examen des décisions dont la reconnaissance est demandée

Art. 34. Lorsqu'ils examinent les motifs de refus, le tribunal ou les autres autorités de la Partie sur le territoire de laquelle la décision doit être reconnue ne sont pas liés par les constatations de fait contenues dans la décision. L'examen du bien-fondé de la décision à d'autres égards n'est pas admis.

Exécution

Dispositions générales

Art. 35. 1) Les décisions judiciaires et les sentences des tribunaux arbitraux rendues sur le territoire de l'une des Parties seront exécutées sur le territoire de l'autre Partie si les conditions de reconnaissance énoncées aux articles 32 à 34 sont remplies et si l'exequatur a été prononcé sur le territoire de l'autre Partie de la manière prévue par la présente convention.

2) Sauf dispositions contraires de la présente convention, la procédure ayant pour objet l'octroi de l'exequatur et la procédure d'exécution

auront lieu conformément aux prescriptions de la législation en vigueur sur le territoire de la Partie où doit avoir lieu l'exécution avec cette réserve qu'il pourra être fait appel de la décision d'exequatur. Si, d'après ces prescriptions, le tribunal qui a statué sur l'affaire est compétent pour veiller à l'exécution ou pour connaître des réclamations relatives à l'exécution, c'est le tribunal dans le ressort duquel doit avoir lieu l'exécution qui se substituera à lui.

Demande d'exequatur

Art. 36. 1) La demande d'exequatur pourra être introduite auprès du tribunal de la Partie sur le territoire de laquelle a été rendue la décision judiciaire ou la sentence du tribunal arbitral. Ce tribunal transmettra la demande du (au ?) tribunal de l'autre Partie qui est compétent aux termes de l'art. 37.

2) La demande pourra également être introduite directement auprès du tribunal compétent aux termes de l'art. 37 par le créancier qui poursuit l'exécution.

Art. 37. La décision concernant l'octroi de l'exequatur est rendue à la requête du créancier demandeur et sans convocation des Parties, par le tribunal de la Partie sur le territoire de laquelle la décision doit être exécutée; le défendeur pourra être entendu. Le tribunal compétent est le tribunal ayant compétence générale à l'égard du débiteur ou, à défaut, le tribunal dans le ressort duquel il doit être procédé à l'exécution.

Pièces à joindre à la demande

Art. 38. Le créancier qui poursuit l'exécution devra présenter:

a) une expédition de la décision judiciaire ou de la sentence du tribunal arbitral munie d'une formule constatant que celle-ci a force de chose jugée et qu'elle est exécutoire; la force de chose jugée et la force exécutoire devront être attestées par des documents officiels, à moins qu'elles ne ressortent de l'expédition même; lorsqu'il s'agit d'une sentence de tribunal arbitral, il y aura lieu de tenir compte des dispositions du paragraphe 4 de l'article 32;

b) une traduction des documents indiqués à l'alinéa a) faite par un traducteur assermenté de l'une des Parties.

Suspension de l'exécution

Art. 39. 1) Si, à la suite d'une action en renouvellement (en annulation) du titre exécutoire, l'exécution a été suspendue ou annulée sur le territoire de la Partie dont le tribunal a rendu la décision, il y aura lieu de surseoir à l'octroi de l'exequatur et, si celui-ci a déjà été accordé, se suspendre l'exécution sur le territoire de la Partie où la décision doit être exécutée.

2) Dans les autres cas, la suspension ou l'annulation de l'exécution ordonnée sur le territoire de la Partie dont le tribunal a rendu la décision n'a d'effet ni sur la procédure introduite sur le territoire de l'autre Partie sur la base de cette décision en vue d'obtenir l'exequatur, ni sur l'exécution elle-même.

Procédure d'exécution des transactions et des actes notariés

Art. 40. Seront également susceptibles d'exécution les transactions judiciaires et les actes notariés aux termes desquels le débiteur s'est soumis à l'exécution. Les dispositions des articles 35 à 39 seront applicables mutatis mutandis à cet égard.

Exécution des décisions relatives aux frais et dépens

Art. 41. L'exequatur sera accordé sans frais en ce qui concerne les décisions condamnant aux dépens un demandeur, requérant ou intervenant qui a été exempté de la caution en vertu de l'article 2.

. . .

Chapitre XII

Dispositions finales

Art. 89. La présente convention, établie en langue polonaise et en langue tchèque, les deux textes faisant également foi, sera soumise à ratification. Les instruments de ratification seront échangés à Prague dans le plus bref délai.

La convention entrera en vigueur un mois après l'échange des instruments de ratification et demeurera en vigueur six mois après que l'une ou l'autre des Parties l'aura dénoncée.

Seront abrogées, du jour de l'entrée en vigueur de la présente convention:

a) . . .; b) . . .;

c) La convention entre la République de Pologne et la République tchécoslovaque concernant l'exécution réciproque des titres exécutoires et la réciprocité en matière de faillites, signée à Prague, le 10 février 1934.

En foi de quoi, les plénipotentiaires des deux Parties ont signé la présente convention et y ont apposé leurs sceaux.

Fait à Varsovie, en double original, le 21 janvier 1949.

Portugal—Tschechoslowakei

Convention entre la République Portugaise et la République Tchécoslovaque, relative à la reconnaissance et à l'exécution de décisions judiciaires. Signée à Lisbonne, le 23 novembre 1927. Texte officiel français. SdN. 123 (1931), S. 418.

Art. 1. Seront considérées comme des décisions judiciaires, au sens de la convention, les décisions rendues en matière civile ou commerciale, dans la procédure soit contentieuse soit non contentieuse, par les tribunaux ordinaires, les tribunaux spéciaux, les tribunaux arbitraux et, en Tchécoslovaquie, par les autorités de tutelle (curatelle).

Les décisions rendues dans un procès pénal, sur conclusion de la partie civile, et les décisions prononçant la faillite ou homologuant un concordat ne seront pas considérées comme des décisions judiciaires en matière civile ou commerciale au sens de la convention.

Art. 2. L'autorité des décisions judiciaires au sens de l'article premier rendues dans l'un des Etats contractants sera reconnue dans l'autre si elles remplissent les conditions suivantes:

1° Que, pour l'affaire en question, les règles de compétence judiciaire internationale admises par le droit de l'Etat dans lequel la décision est invoquée n'excluent pas la juridiction de l'autre Etat;

2° Que la reconnaissance de la décision ne soit pas contraire à l'ordre public ou aux principes du droit public de l'Etat, où la décision est invoquée;

3° Que, d'après la loi de l'Etat où la décision a été rendue, celle-ci soit passée en force de chose jugée;

4° Qu'en cas de jugement par défaut, la partie défaillante contre laquelle la décision est invoquée ait été régulièrement citée, conformément à la loi de l'Etat où la décision a été rendue, et que la citation l'ait atteinte en temps utile.

L'examen par les autorités de l'Etat où la décision est invoquée ne portera que sur les conditions énumérées sous chiffres 1 à 4. Ces autorités devront examiner d'office si lesdites conditions sont remplies. Cet examen devra être terminé au plus tard dans les deux mois à compter du jour où l'autorité compétente a reçu les actes.

Art. 3. Les décisions judiciaires rendues dans l'un des Etats contractants seront mises à exécution dans l'autre Etat si elles remplissent les conditions énumérées dans l'article 2, chiffres 1 à 4, et si elles sont exécutoires dans l'Etat où elles ont été rendues.

L'examen par les autorités de l'Etat où l'exécution est demandée ne portera que sur les exigences indiquées au précédent alinéa. Ces autorités devront examiner d'office s'il est satisfait auxdites exigences. Cet examen devra être terminé au plus tard dans les deux mois à compter du jour où 'autorité compétente a reçu les actes.

Art. 4. La partie qui invoque la décision ou qui en demande l'exécution devra produire:

1° Une expédition de la décision remplissant les conditions nécessaires à son authenticité;

2° Une attestation que la décision est passée en force de chose jugée et, s'il y a lieu, qu'elle est devenue exécutoire; cette attestation sera délivrée par l'autorité qui a rendu la décision;

3° En cas de jugement par défaut, une copie authentique de l'acte ou de l'assignation qui introduisait l'instance, ainsi qu'une attestation indiquant le mode et la date de la notification à la partie défaillante;

4° Une traduction des pièces énumérées ci-dessus certifiée conforme d'après les prescriptions de l'un ou l'autre Etat; la traduction sera produite en Tchécoslovaquie en langue tchécoslovaque, en Portugal, dans la langue portugaise.

Art. 5. Les sentences arbitrales rendues dans l'un des Etats contractants et y ayant acquis la même autorité que les décisions judiciaires seront reconnues et mises à exécution dans l'autre Etat si elles satisfont aux prescriptions des articles précédents, en tant que celles-ci sont applicables.

Il en sera de même pour les transactions judiciaires et pour les transactions conclues devant des arbitres ou des tribunaux arbitraux.

Les attestations que les sentences, décisions ou transactions mentionnées dans cet article sont passées en force de chose jugée et qu'elles sont devenues exécutoires seront délivrées dans chacun des deux Etats contractants par l'autorité qui y serait compétente pour autoriser l'exécution sur la base desdits titres exécutoires.

Art. 6. L'exécution sera requise par la partie intéressée directement auprès du tribunal dans la juridiction duquel elle doit avoir lieu.

La procédure en matière d'exécution sera réglée par la loi de l'Etat requis. Il en sera de même quant aux mesures prévues aux articles 9 à 11.

Art. 7. L'exécution des décisions relatives aux frais et dépenses visées à l'article 18, alinéas 1 et 2, de la Convention de La Haye[1] du 17 juillet 1905 sur la procédure civile, et prononcées dans l'un des deux Etats, est réglée à l'article 6 de l'Accord conclu entre les deux Etats contractants sur l'assistance judiciaire réciproque en matière civile et commerciale.

Art. 8. Les dispositions de la présente convention s'appliqueront quelle que soit la nationalité des parties.

Art. 9. Le tribunal compétent à autoriser l'exécution accordera à la demande de la partie, conformément à ses lois, la prise de mesures de sûreté pour assurer les droits résultants du titre exécutoire à l'égard du débiteur. Ce tribunal révoquera éventuellement ces mesures, conformément à ses lois.

Art. 10. Avant même que les décisions indiquées aux articles premier et 5 soient passées en force de chose jugée, ou que le délai prévu dans les décisions pour l'accomplissement se soit écoulé, le tribunal compétent à autoriser l'exécution pourra, sur demande, accorder la prise de mesures conservatoires d'après les dispositions en vigueur dans l'Etat requis.

Art. 11. Des mesures provisoires seront accordées déjà avant le procès ou au cours du procès sur la demande de la partie dont les intérêts se trouvent menacés, et cela conformément aux lois de l'Etat requis, même si un tribunal de l'autre Etat est compétent pour statuer dans l'affaire en question.

Art. 12. Si des doutes surgissent au sujet des questions que l'application de la présente Convention pourrait soulever, le Ministère de la Justice et des Cultes, à Lisbonne, et le Ministère de la Justice, à Prague, se communiqueront directement, sur demande des renseignements juridiques nécessaires.

Art. 13. La présente convention sera ratifiée et les ratifications en seront échangées à Prague.

Cette convention entrera en vigueur un mois après l'échange des ratifications et produira ses effets encore un an après la dénonciation qui pourra avoir lieu en tout temps.

En foi de quoi les plénipotentiaires ont signé la présente convention en deux exemplaires.

Fait à Lisbonne, le 23 novembre 1927.

---

[1] de Martens, Nouveau Recueil général de Traités, troisième série, tome II, page 243.

Rumänien—Tschechoslowakei

Convention entre la Tchécoslovaquie et la Roumanie relative à la protection et à l'assistance judiciaire réciproques, en matière de droit civil et commercial, ainsi que dans les affaires non contentieuses. Signée à Bucarest, le 7 mai 1925. Texte officiel français. SdN. 54 (1926), S. 18.

Chapitre XIII.

Article 43.

Exécution réciproque des titres exécutoires.

Chacune des Parties contractantes s'engage à autoriser l'exécution et sa mise à effet sur son territoire des titres énumérés cidessous, émanant des autorités de l'autre Partie contractante, et qui, d'après les lois en vigueur, y constituent des titres exécutoires.

Art. 44. Seront considérés comme titres exécutoires:

a) Les sentences, les ordres (mandats) de payer, les arrêts et autres décisions des tribunaux civils de toute sorte, y compris ceux de commerce, pour autant qu'ils sont certifiés conformes et que, d'après la législation de l'Etat requérant, ils ne sont plus sujets à aucune voie de recours avec effet dilatoire.

Il en sera de même quant aux sentences rendues en matière pénale et concernant le dédommagement des parties lésées et les frais de procédure.

b) Les transactions conclues devant les tribunaux mentionnés ci-dessus, si elles sont certifiées conformes et munies de l'attestation du tribunal d'être exécutoires.

c) Les sentences et les décisions d'arbitres ou des tribunaux d'arbitrage, en tant que d'après la loi ou d'après une convention écrite des parties, conclue dans la forme légale, l'arbitre ou le tribunal d'arbitrage est autorisé à juger.

Ces sentences, décisions ou transactions devront être munies de l'attestation du tribunal de première instance dans le ressort duquel l'arbitre ou le tribunal d'arbitrage ont prononcé la sentence ou la décision, ou dans le ressort duquel la transaction a été conclue, les certifiant conformes et affirmant qu'aucune voie de recours avec effet dilatoire n'est plus recevable.

Art. 45. L'autorisation d'exécution et l'exécution elle-même, seront régies par les prescriptions en vigueur dans l'Etat où elles doivent avoir lieu, à moins que la présente convention n'y apporte des dérogations.

Art. 46. 1. La demande d'autorisation d'exécution et de l'exécution elle-même, sera déposée par le demandeur au tribunal duquel le titre émane. Lorsqu'il s'agira de l'exécution de titre émanant d'un tribunal d'arbitrage ou d'un arbitre, la demande sera déposée au tribunal de première instance indiqué à l'article 44, alinéa c).

Ces tribunaux transmettront sans retard, par la voie du Ministère de la Justice, la demande d'autorisation et d'exécution au tribunal compétent, après l'avoir munie des attestations prévues à l'article 44 et avec les autres documents à l'appui.

2. La partie intéressée sera pourtant libre de saisir directement de sa demande d'autorisation et d'exécution le tribunal compétent de l'autre Etat contractant.

3. Le tribunal compétent à autoriser l'exécution examinera, sur la base des pièces reçues, si toutes les conditions sont remplies pour l'autoriser. Cet examen qui devra être terminé au plus tard dans les quinze jours à compter de celui où le tribunal a reçu les actes, se bornera aux questions suivantes:

a) Si la compétence du tribunal qui a décidé l'affaire peut être considérée comme fondée d'après les lois de l'Etat où le titre exécutoire a été établi. Dans ce cas, il suffira que, d'après les prescriptions sur la compétence judiciaire en vigueur dans l'Etat saisi de la demande d'autorisation et d'exécution, aucun tribunal de cet Etat n'ait été exclusivement compétent pour juger l'affaire en question;

b) S'il s'agit d'un titre exécutoire d'après l'article 44;

c) Si le défendeur a été, toutes les fois que la loi l'exige, dûment assigné pour prendre part à la procédure, notamment si soit la demande ou la requête, soit la sentence ou la décision formant le titre exécutoire lui a été dûment signifiée. Si le jugement a été rendu par défaut, le tribunal devra, lorsque le défendeur le demande, constater, si ce dernier n'a pas été mis dans l'impossibilité, par une irrégularité de procédure, de participer au procès ou de s'y faire représenter valablement.

Avant de rendre sa décision, le tribunal pourra entendre sur ces questions la partie, ou le représentant de la partie, contre laquelle l'exécution est demandée;

d) Si l'exécution n'a pas pour but, soit d'obtenir un acte qui, d'après les lois en vigueur dans l'Etat où elle doit avoir lieu, est interdit, soit de faire reconnaître un état de droit, soit de faire droit à une réclamation, contraire à la souveraineté de l'Etat requis ou aux bonnes moeurs, ou bien qui, d'après les lois de l'Etat requis, ne peut faire l'objet d'une action en justice, ou est inexécutable.

4. Ni le tribunal qui autorise l'exécution, ni celui qui l'effectue, n'est en droit d'examiner le fond de l'affaire.

Art. 47. Le tribunal compétent à autoriser l'exécution accordera, conformément à ses lois, la prise de mesures provisoires (mesures de sûreté) pour assurer les droits résultant du titre exécutoire à l'égard de la personne contre laquelle l'exécution est demandée, et cela tant dans sa propre circonscription que dans celles d'autres tribunaux du même pays où se trouvent ses biens.

Ces mesures ne pourront être révoquées que si cette personne fournit une garantie suffisante pour satisfaire tous les droits découlant du titre exécutoire.

Article 48.

Exécution conservatoire.

Avant même que les titres prévus à l'article 44 soient devenus définitifs, ou que le délai prévu pour l'accomplissement soit écoulé, le tribunal compétent à autoriser l'exécution pourra, sur la demande faite dans la forme prescrite, accorder la prise de mesures conservatoires d'après les dispositions en vigueur dans l'Etat requis.

Article 49.

Mesures provisoires (conservatoires).

Des mesures provisoires (conservatoires) seront accordées même avant le procès ou au cours du procès sur la demande de la partie dont les intérêts se trouvent menacés, même si un tribunal de l'autre Etat est compétent pour statuer dans l'affaire en question.

Chapitre XIV.

Article 50.

Dispositions finales.

La présente convention sera ratifiée et les ratifications seront échangées le plus tôt possible à Praha.

Elle entrera en vigueur un mois après l'échange des ratifications et restera en vigueur six mois à compter du jour où elle aura été dénoncée par l'une des Parties contractantes.

En foi de quoi les plénipotentiaires ont signé la présente convention et l'ont revêtue de leurs sceaux.

Fait en double exemplaire à Bucarest, le 7 mai 1925.

Schweden—Schweiz

Abkommen zwischen der Schweiz und Schweden über die Anerkennung und Vollstreckung von gerichtlichen Entscheidungen und Schiedssprüchen. Abgeschlossen in Stockholm am 15. Januar 1936. Eidgenössische Gesetzsammlung 52 (1936), S. 225.

Art. 1. Die im einen Vertragsstaate in Zivilsachen gefällten Entscheidungen der streitigen Gerichtsbarkeit, mit Einschluß der in einem Strafverfahren gefällten Entscheidungen über zivilrechtliche Ansprüche, werden im andern Staat anerkannt, wenn sie die in den nachstehenden Artikeln bezeichneten Voraussetzungen erfüllen.

Art. 2. Als gerichtliche Entscheidungen im Sinne des gegenwärtigen Abkommens gelten die von den ordentlichen Gerichten gefällten Entscheidungen, die über die Streitsache selbst befinden. Das gleiche gilt für die Verurteilungen in Prozeßkosten, die infolge der Entscheidung über die Streitsache selbst ergehen. Als ordentliche Gerichte werden auch die oberen schwedischen Vollstreckungsbehörden („Oeverexekutor"), soweit sie über schriftlich anerkannte Schuldverpflichtungen („lagsökning") urteilen, sowie die schweizerischen Handelsgerichte und gewerblichen Schiedsgerichte betrachtet.

Die gerichtlichen Vergleiche werden in Ansehung ihrer Wirkungen den gerichtlichen Entscheidungen gleichgestellt.

Art. 3. Die Entscheidungen, die über Gütertrennung, Trennung und Scheidung der Ehe ergehen, werden als Entscheidungen der streitigen Gerichtsbarkeit angesehen, auch wenn sie auf Begehren der Beteiligten ergangen sind. Dagegen werden die in Vormundschafts- und Entmündigungssachen ergangenen Entscheidungen in keinem Falle als Entscheidungen der streitigen Gerichtsbarkeit betrachtet.

Art. 4. Die Anerkennung der Entscheidung ist an folgende Voraussetzungen geknüpft:

1. daß die Entscheidung von einem nach den Bestimmungen des Art. 5 zuständigen Gerichte gefällt wurde;
2. daß die Anerkennung der Entscheidung nicht mit der öffentlichen Ordnung des Staates, in dem die Entscheidung geltend gemacht wird, offensichtlich unvereinbar sei;
3. falls es sich um eine in Personenstands-, Familienrechts- oder Erbrechtssachen ergangene Entscheidung handelt, daß sie nicht auf einem Gesetze beruhe, dessen materielle Bestimmungen im Widerspruch stehen zu jenen des Gesetzes, das nach dem internationalen Privatrecht des Staates, in dem die Entscheidung geltend gemacht wird, anwendbar ist;
4. daß die Entscheidung nach dem Rechte des Staates, in dem sie gefällt wurde, die Rechtskraft erlangt hat;
5. daß im Falle eines Versäumnisurteils die den Prozeß einleitende Verfügung oder Ladung rechtzeitig der säumigen Partei, sei es persönlich oder an ihren ermächtigten Vertreter, zugestellt wurde.

Art. 5. Die Zuständigkeit der Gerichte des Staates, in dem die Entscheidung gefällt wurde, ist im Sinne des gegenwärtigen Abkommens in den folgenden Fällen begründet:

1. wenn der Beklagte im Zeitpunkt der Klageerhebung seinen tatsächlichen Wohnsitz oder, falls es sich nicht um eine natürliche Person handelt, seinen Sitz in diesem Staate hatte; als tatsächlicher Wohnsitz ist der Ort verstanden, wo der Beklagte sich mit der Absicht dauernden Verbleibens aufhält;
2. wenn der Beklagte sich durch ausdrückliche Vereinbarung der Zuständigkeit des Gerichts unterworfen hatte, das die Entscheidung gefällt hat;
3. wenn der Beklagte sich vorbehaltlos auf den Rechtsstreit eingelassen hat;
4. im Falle einer Widerklage, die mit der Hauptklage in rechtlichem Zusammenhange steht;
5. wenn der Beklagte, der im Gebiete des Staates, wo die Entscheidung gefällt wurde, eine geschäftliche Niederlassung oder Zweigniederlassung hat, dort für Streitigkeiten aus ihrem Betriebe belangt worden ist;
6. wenn der Beklagte, der im Gebiete des Staates, wo die Entscheidung gefällt wurde, einen Vertreter hat, zu dessen Bestellung er durch das Gesetz dieses Staates verpflichtet war, dort für Streitigkeiten aus dessen Tätigkeit in diesem Staate belangt worden ist;
7. wenn die Entscheidung Ansprüche aus einer unerlaubten Handlung betrifft, die vom Beklagten im Staate begangen worden ist, wo die Entscheidung gefällt wurde, und die Ladung ihm persönlich während seiner Anwesenheit in diesem Staate zugestellt worden ist; dabei besteht die Meinung, daß diesen Ansprüchen gleichgestellt sind solche aus Unfällen, die durch den Gebrauch irgend eines Transportmittels verursacht worden sind;

8. wenn die Entscheidung von einem Gerichte gefällt wurde, dessen Zuständigkeit durch einen Staatsvertrag vorgesehen ist, der selbst keine Bestimmungen über die Anerkennung und Vollstreckung enthält.

Die Bestimmungen des vorstehenden Absatzes finden keine Anwendung auf Personenstands-, Familienrechts- und Erbrechtssachen. In diesen Sachen ist die Zuständigkeit des Gerichts des Staates, wo die Entscheidung gefällt wurde, dann anzuerkennen, wenn unter analogen Voraussetzungen ein Gericht des Staates, wo die Entscheidung geltend gemacht wird, zuständig wäre.

Art. 6. Die Behörden des Staates, in dem die Entscheidung geltend gemacht wird, haben sich auf die Prüfung zu beschränken, ob die in den vorstehenden Artikeln vorgesehenen Voraussetzungen erfüllt sind. Bei dieser Prüfung sind sie nicht an die tatsächlichen Feststellungen der Entscheidung gebunden.

Art. 7. Die Gerichte des einen der beiden Staaten haben das Eintreten auf ihnen vorgelegte Streitigkeiten abzulehnen, wenn sie davon Kenntnis haben, daß diese Streitigkeiten schon vor einem Gerichte des andern Staates anhängig sind, vorausgesetzt, daß dieses Gericht nach Maßgabe der Bestimmungen des gegenwärtigen Abkommens zuständig ist.

Art. 8. Die im einen Vertragsstaate gefällten Entscheidungen, die gemäß den Bestimmungen der vorstehenden Artikel im Gebiete des andern Staates anzuerkennen sind, sollen auf Begehren einer Partei im andern Staate vollstreckt werden.

Art. 9. In der Schweiz bestimmen sich die Zuständigkeit und das Verfahren für die Zwangsvollstreckung, wenn diese auf eine Geldzahlung oder Sicherheitsleistung gerichtet ist, nach den bundesrechtlichen Vorschriften über Schuldbetreibung und Konkurs (Bundesgesetz vom 11. April 1889 und Nachträge) und in den übrigen Fällen nach dem Prozeßrechte des Kantons, wo die Vollstreckung stattfinden soll.

In Schweden ist das Begehren um Vollstreckbarerklärung an den Appellationshof in Stockholm (Svea hovrätt) zu richten.

Art. 10. Die Partei, die die Vollstreckung nachsucht, hat beizubringen:

1. Die Entscheidung in der Urschrift oder in einer beweiskräftigen Ausfertigung;
2. eine Bescheinigung darüber, daß die Entscheidung in Rechtskraft erwachsen ist;
3. die Gerichtsprotokolle oder andere Urkunden, die dartun, daß die im Art. 5, Abs. 1, vorgesehenen Voraussetzungen erfüllt sind;
4. im Falle eines Versäumnisurteils die Urschrift oder eine als richtig bescheinigte Abschrift der Urkunden, aus denen hervorgeht, daß die säumige Partei gemäß den Bestimmungen von Art. 4, Ziff. 5, oder gegebenenfalls von Art. 5, Abs. 1, Ziff. 7, geladen worden ist.

Betrifft das Begehren um Vollstreckung einen Vergleich, so muß es von einer durch die zuständige Behörde als richtig bescheinigten Abschrift des Protokolls und von einer Bescheinigung begleitet sein, daß der Vergleich vor einem Gericht abgeschlossen oder von diesem bestätigt worden ist und daß er im Staate, in dem er geschlossen wurde, vollstreckbar ist.

Die vorstehend erwähnten Urkunden werden

in Schweden durch die Kanzlei des Groß-Gouverneurs von Stockholm oder von einer Provinzialverwaltung ausgestellt oder beglaubigt und

in der Schweiz durch die zuständigen Behörden ausgestellt und durch die Bundeskanzlei beglaubigt.

Alle vorzulegenden Urkunden müssen von einer Übersetzung in die Amtssprache der ersuchten Behörde begleitet sein; die Übersetzung muß durch einen diplomatischen oder konsularischen Vertreter des einen oder des andern Vertragsstaates oder durch einen öffentlichen Dolmetscher des Landes, wo die Entscheidung geltend gemacht wird, als richtig bescheinigt sein.

Art. 11. Das gegenwärtige Abkommen findet keine Anwendung auf Entscheidungen und Vergleiche:

1. in Konkurs- oder Nachlaßvertragssachen, mit Einschluß der Anfechtung von Verträgen des Schuldners;
2. betreffend jedes dingliche Recht an Grundstücken, die außerhalb des Staates, wo die Entscheidung gefällt wurde, gelegen sind, sowie betreffend die Verpflichtung, in bezug auf solche Rechte Verfügungen zu treffen oder die Rechtsfolgen aus der Nichterfüllung einer solchen Verpflichtung; jedoch bleibt das Abkommen auf die Entscheidungen und Vergleiche in Familien- und Erbrechtssachen anwendbar.

Art. 12. Das Abkommen findet keine Anwendung auf die vor seinem Inkrafttreten gefällten Entscheidungen oder abgeschlossenen Vergleiche.

Art. 13. Die Anerkennung und Vollstreckung der in einem der beiden Staaten gefällten Schiedssprüche bestimmt sich im andern Staate nach dem in Genf am 26. September 1927 abgeschlossenen Abkommen zur Vollstreckung ausländischer Schiedssprüche. Jedoch wird die Anerkennung und die Vollstreckung nicht an die Voraussetzungen geknüpft, die in Art. 1, Abs. 1 des genannten Abkommens vorgesehen sind.

Art. 9 und Art. 10, letzter Absatz, des gegenwärtigen Abkommens finden Anwendung auf das Verfahren zur Erwirkung der Vollstreckbarkeit von Schiedssprüchen.

Art. 14. Die Bestimmungen der Vereinbarungen, die hinsichtlich besonderer Rechtsgebiete die Gerichtszuständigkeit und die Urteilsvollstreckung regeln, werden durch das gegenwärtige Abkommen nicht berührt.

Art. 15. Das gegenwärtige Abkommen soll durch den schweizerischen Bundesrat und durch seine Majestät den König von Schweden, mit Zustimmung des Riksdag, ratifiziert werden, und die Ratifikationsurkunden sollen sobald als möglich in Bern ausgetauscht werden.

Es tritt in Kraft am 1. Januar oder 1. Juli, der auf den Ablauf einer Frist von zwei Monaten nach dem Zeitpunkt des Austausches der Ratifikationsurkunden folgt; es bleibt in Kraft bis zum 1. Januar oder 1. Juli, der auf den Ablauf einer Frist von einem Jahre nach dem Zeitpunkt der Kündigung durch einen Vertragsstaat folgt.

Zu Urkund dessen haben die Bevollmächtigten dieses Abkommen unterzeichnet.

So geschehen, in doppelter Ausfertigung, in Stockholm am 15. Januar 1936.

Schweiz-Spanien

Traité entre la Suisse et l'Espagne sur l'exécution réciproque des jugements ou arrêts en matière civile ou commerciale. Du 19 novembre 1896. Bundesblatt der schweizerischen Eidgenossenschaft 1897 III, S. 499.

Art. 1. Les jugements ou arrêts définitifs en matière civile ou commerciale, rendus dans l'un des deux Etats contractants, soit par les tribunaux ordinaires, soit par des arbitres ou des tribunaux de prud'hommes, légalement constitués, seront exécutoires dans l'autre Etat aux conditions suivantes.

Art. 2. L'exécution sera requise directement par la partie intéressée, auprès du tribunal ou de l'autorité du lieu où l'exécution doit avoir lieu et à qui appartient la compétence pour accorder l'exequatur.

La demande d'exécution sera accompagnée:

1° D'une copie littérale du jugement ou de l'arrêt, dûment légalisée par le représentant diplomatique ou consulaire du pays dans lequel l'exécution est requise;

2° d'un document établissant que la partie adverse a été dûment citée et que le jugement ou l'arrêt lui a été notifié;

3° d'un certificat délivré par le greffier du tribunal qui a rendu le jugement, certificat légalisé dans les formes prévues au chiffre 1, constatant que le jugement ou l'arrêt dont l'exécution est requise est définitif et exécutoire, attendu qu'il n'existe ni appel ni opposition.

Art. 3. L'autorité compétente statuera sur la demande d'exécution dans la forme prévue par la loi, après avoir entendu le Ministère public, si la loi le prescrit.

Elle accordera à la partie contre laquelle l'exécution est requise le délai légal ou d'usage pour défendre ses droits.

Elle indiquera aux deux parties le jour où il sera prononcé sur la demande.

Art. 4. La décision qui accorde l'exécution est transcrite par l'autorité de qui elle émane dans le jugement ou dans l'arrêt. Elle sortira ses effets dans la procédure d'exécution ultérieure.

Art. 5. L'autorité saisie de la demande d'exécution n'entrera point dans la discussion du fond de l'affaire.

La décision qui accorde ou qui refuse l'exécution ne sera point susceptible d'opposition à raison de la non-comparution d'une partie, mais elle pourra être l'objet d'un recours devant l'autorité compétente dans les délais légaux et suivant les formes déterminées par la loi du pays où elle a été rendue, si toutefois cette loi prévoit un tel recours.

Art. 6. L'exécution pourra être refusée dans les cas suivants:

1° Si la décision émane d'une juridiction incompétente.

2° Si elle a été rendue sans que les parties aient été dûment citées ou légalement représentées.

3° Si les règles du droit public du pays où l'exécution est demandée s'opposent à ce que la décision de la juridiction étrangère y reçoive son exécution.

Art. 7. Quand l'exécution emportera contrainte par corps, cette partie du jugement ou de l'arrêt ne sera pas exécutoire si la législation du pays où l'exécution doit avoir lieu n'admet pas la contrainte par corps dans le cas dont il s'agit.

Art. 8. Les actes judiciaires, tels que citations, notifications, sommations, commissions rogatoires et autres actes de procédure seront transmis à qui de droit par les agents diplomatiques ou consulaires des gouvernements respectifs; le gouvernement du pays requis veillera à leur signification, soit exécution, à moins que les règles du droit public du pays requis ne s'y opposent.

Les frais resteront à la charge du pays requis.

Ces actes, citations, notifications, sommations, etc., devront être accompagnés de traductions françaises dûment certifiées, s'ils étaient rédigés dans une autre langue.

Art. 9. Le présent Traité sera ratifié et les ratifications seront échangées à Madrid dans le plus bref délai possible.

En foi de quoi les Plénipotentiaires respectifs l'ont signé, en double expédition, et y ont apposé leurs cachets à Madrid le dix-neuf Novembre mil huit cent quatre-vingt seize.

Schweiz—Tschechoslowakei

Convention entre la Suisse et la République Tchécoslovaque, relative à la reconnaissance et à l'exécution de décisions judiciaires. Signée à Berne, le 21 décembre 1926. Texte officiel français. SdN. 86 (1929), S. 444.

Art. 1. L'autorité des décisions judiciaires rendues en matière civile ou en matière commerciale dans l'un des Etats contractants sera reconnue dans l'autre Etat si elles remplissent les conditions suivantes:

1° Que, pour l'affaire en question, les règles de compétence judiciaire internationale admises par le droit de l'Etat dans lequel la décision est invoquée n'excluent pas la juridiction de l'autre Etat;

2° Que la reconnaissance de la décision ne soit pas contraire à l'ordre public ou aux principes du droit public de l'Etat où la décision est invoquée;

3° Que, d'après la loi de l'Etat où la décision a été rendue, celle-ci soit passée en force de chose jugée;

4° Qu'en cas de jugement par défaut, la partie défaillante contre laquelle la décision est invoquée ait été régulièrement citée, conformément à la loi de l'Etat où la décision a été rendue, et que la citation l'ait atteinte en temps utile.

L'examen par les autorités de l'Etat où la décision est invoquée ne portera que sur les conditions énumérées sous chiffres 1° à 4°. Ces autorités devront examiner d'office si lesdites conditions sont remplies.

Art. 2. En considération des cas où la Suisse, sur la base de l'article 59 de la constitution fédérale, ne reconnaît pas, dans le sens de l'article premier, chiffre 1° de la présente convention, la juridiction d'un autre Etat, il est disposé par analogie ce qui suit:

La juridiction suisse ne sera pas reconnue en Tchécoslovaquie à l'égard des réclamations personnelles contre le débiteur solvable qui avait son domicile en Tchécoslovaquie au moment de l'ouverture d'action, si ce débiteur n'a pas convenu d'un for en Suisse ou n'est pas entré en matière, sans réserve, sur le fond de l'action introduite devant le juge suisse.

Cette disposition ne mettra pas obstacle à ce que la juridiction suisse soit reconnue lorsque le débiteur sera recherché au for de son établissement commercial ou industriel ou de sa succursale pour des réclamations dont la cause remonte à l'exploitation de cet établissement, ou encore lorsqu'une demande reconventionnelle en connexité avec la demande principale aura été introduite au for de cette dernière.

Ne seront pas considérées comme réclamations personnelles au sens du présent article les actions fondées sur le droit de la famille et le droit des successions, ainsi que les actions réelles et les actions mixtes.

Art. 3. Les décisions judiciaires rendues dans l'un des Etats contractants pourront être mises à exécution dans l'autre Etat si elles sont exécutoires dans l'Etat où elles ont été rendues et si elles remplissent les conditions énumérées dans l'article premier, chiffres 1⁰ à 4⁰.

L'examen par les autorités de l'Etat où l'exécution est demandée ne portera que sur les exigences indiquées au précédent alinéa. Ces autorités devront examiner d'office s'il est satisfait auxdites exigences.

Art. 4. La partie qui invoque la décision ou qui en demande l'exé. cution devra produire:

1⁰ Une expédition de la décision remplissant les conditions nécessaires à son authenticité;

2⁰ Les pièces de nature à établir que la décision est passée en force de chose jugée et, s'il y a lieu, qu'elle est devenue exécutoire;

3⁰ Une copie authentique de l'assignation (article premier, chiffre 4⁰) de la partie qui a fait défaut à l'instance;

4⁰ Une traduction des pièces énumérées ci-dessus certifiée conforme d'après les prescriptions de l'un ou l'autre Etat, sauf dispense de cette obligation par l'autorité compétente; la traduction sera produite en Tchécoslovaquie en langue tchécoslovaque, en Suisse dans la langue de l'autorité requise.

Art. 5. Les sentences arbitrales rendues dans l'un des Etats contractants et y ayant la même autorité que les décisions judiciaires seront reconnues et mises à exécution dans l'autre Etat si elles satisfont aux prescriptions des articles précédents, en tant que celles-ci sont applicables.

Il en sera de même pour les transactions judiciaires et pour les transactions conclues devant des arbitres ou des tribunaux arbitraux.

Art. 6. La loi de l'Etat requis régira la compétence et la procédure en matière d'exécution.

Art. 7. Les dispositions de la présente convention s'appliqueront, quelle que soit la nationalité des parties.

Art. 8. La présente convention sera ratifiée et les ratifications en seront échangées à Prague.

Cette convention entrera en vigueur un mois après l'échange des ratifications et produira ses effets encore un an après la dénonciation qui pourra avoir lieu en tout temps.

En foi de quoi les plénipotentiaires ont signé la présente convention, en deux exemplaires.

Fait à Berne, le vingt et un décembre mil neuf cent vingt-six.

Protocole additionnel

Les plénipotentiaires des Parties contractantes, en passant à la signature de la Convention entre la République tchécoslovaque et la Suisse relative à la reconnaissance et à l'exécution de décisions judiciaires, se sont mis d'accord pour constater ce qui suit:

I.

Seront considérées comme des décisions judiciaires au sens de la convention les décisions rendues en matière civile ou commerciale, dans la procédure soit contentieuse soit non contentieuse, par les tribunaux ordinaires, les tribunaux spéciaux, les tribunaux arbitraux ou les autorités de tutelle (curatelle).

Les décisions rendues, dans un procès pénal, sur conclusion de la partie civile, et les décisions prononçant la faillite ou homologuant un concordat ne seront pas considérées comme des décisions judiciaires en matière civile ou commerciale au sens de la convention.

II.

Si des doutes surgissent quant à la portée de l'article 2, le Département fédéral de Justice et Police et le Ministère de la Justice tchécoslovaque se communiqueront les renseignements utiles, sous réserve toutefois de la liberté de décision des tribunaux.

III.

Il est constaté, à la demande du plénipotentiaire suisse, que la convention s'appliquera aussi aux décisions judiciaires, sentences arbitrales et transactions judiciaires passées en force de chose jugée avant son entrée en vigueur.

IV.

Le présent protocole fait partie intégrante de la convention.

En foi de quoi les plénipotentiaires ont signé ce protocole.

Fait à Berne, en deux exemplaires, le 21 décembre 1926.

Spanien—Tschechoslowakei

Convention entre le Royaume d'Espagne et la République Tchécoslovaque relative à la reconnaissance et à l'exécution de décisions judiciaires. Signée à Madrid, le 26 novembre 1927. Texte officiel français. SdN. 121 (1931), S. 312.

Art. 1. Seront considérées comme des décisions judiciaires au sens de la convention les décisions rendues en matière civile ou commerciale, dans la procédure soit contentieuse soit non contentieuse, par les tribunaux ordinaires, les tribunaux spéciaux, les tribunaux arbitraux ou les autorités de tutelle (curatelle).

Les décisions rendues dans un procès-pénal, sur conclusion de la partie civile, et les décisions prononçant la faillite ou homologuant un concordat ne seront pas considérées comme des décisions judiciaires en matière civile ou commerciale au sens de la convention.

Art. 2. L'autorité des décisions judiciaires au sens de l'article pemier rendues dans l'un des Etats contractants sera reconnue dans l'autre Etat si elles remplissent les conditions suivantes:

1° Que, pour l'affaire en question, les règles de compétence judiciaire internationale admises par le droit de l'Etat dans lequel la décision est invoquée, n'excluent pas la juridiction de l'autre Etat;

2° Que la reconnaissance de la décision ne soit pas contraire à l'ordre public ou aux principes du droit public de l'Etat où la décision est invoquée;

3° Que, d'après la loi de l'Etat où la décision a été rendue, celle-ci soit passée en force de chose jugée;

4° Qu'en cas de jugement par défaut, la partie défaillante contre laquelle la décision est invoquée ait été régulièrement citée, conformément à la loi de l'Etat où la décision a été rendue et que la citation l'ait atteinte en temps utile.

L'examen par les autorités de l'Etat où la décision est invoquée ne portera que sur les conditions énumérées sous chiffres 1 à 4. Ces autorités devront examiner d'office si lesdites conditions sont remplies. Cet examen devra être terminé au plus tard dans les deux mois à compter du jour où l'autorité compétente a reçu les actes.

Art. 3. Les décisions judiciaires rendues dans l'un des Etats contractants seront mises à exécution dans l'autre Etat si elles remplissent les conditions énumérées dans l'article 2, chiffres 1 à 4 et si elles sont exécutoires dans l'Etat où elles ont été rendues.

L'examen par les autorités de l'Etat où l'exécution est demandée ne portera que sur les exigences indiquées au précédent alinéa. Ces autorités devront examiner d'office s'il est satisfait auxdites exigences. Cet examen devra être terminé au plus tard dans les deux mois à compter du jour où l'autorité compétente a reçu les actes.

Art. 4. La partie qui invoque la décision ou qui en demande l'exécution devra produire:

1° Une expédition de la décision remplissant les conditions nécessaires à son authenticité;

2° Une attestation que la décision est passée en force de chose jugée et, s'il y a lieu, qu'elle est devenue exécutoire; cette attestation sera délivrée par l'autorité qui a rendu la décision;

3° En cas de jugement par défaut une copie authentique de l'acte ou de l'assignation qui introduisait l'instance, ainsi qu'une attestation indiquant le mode et la date de la notification à la partie défaillante;

4° Une traduction des pièces énumérées ci-dessus certifiée conforme d'après les prescriptions de l'un ou l'autre Etat; la traduction sera produite en Tchécoslovaquie en langue tchécoslovaque, en Espagne dans la langue espagnole.

Art. 5. Les sentences arbitrales rendues dans l'un des Etats contractants et y ayant acquis la même autorité que les décisions judiciaires seront reconnues et mises à exécution dans l'autre Etat si elles satisfont aux prescriptions des articles précédents, en tant que celles-ci sont applicables.

Il en sera de même pour les transactions judiciaires et pour les transactions conclues devant des arbitres ou des tribunaux arbitraux.

Les attestations que les sentences, décisions ou transactions mentionnées dans cet article sont passées en force de chose jugée et qu'elles sont devenues exécutoires seront délivrées dans chacun des deux Etats contractants par l'autorité qui y serait compétente pour autoriser l'exécution sur la base desdits titres exécutoires.

Art. 6. L'exécution sera requise par la partie intéressée directement auprès du tribunal dans la juridiction duquel elle doit avoir lieu.

La procédure en matière d'exécution sera réglée par la loi de l'Etat requis. Il en sera de même quant aux mesures prévues aux articles 9 à 11.

Art. 7. L'exécution des décisions relatives aux frais et dépenses visées à l'article 18, alinéas 1 et 2 de la Convention[1] de la Haye de 17 juillet 1905 sur la procédure civile et prononcée dans l'un des deux Etats est réglée à l'article 6 de l'accord[2] conclu entre les deux Etats contractants sur l'assistance judiciaire réciproque en matière civile et commerciale.

Art. 8. Les dispositions de la présente convention s'appliqueront quelle que soit la nationalité des parties.

Art. 9. Le tribunal compétent à autoriser l'exécution accordera à la demande de la partie, conformément à ses lois, la prise de mesures de sûreté pour assurer les droits résultants du titre exécutoire à l'égard du débiteur. Ce tribunal révoquera éventuellement ces mesures, conformément à ses lois.

Art. 10. Avant même que les décisions indiquées aux articles premier et 5 soient passées en force de chose jugée, ou que le délai prévu dans la décision pour l'accomplissement se soit écoulé, le tribunal compétent à autoriser l'exécution pourra, sur demande, accorder la prise de mesures conservatoires d'après les dispositions en vigueur dans l'Etat requis.

Art. 11. Des mesures provisoires seront accordées déjà avant le procès ou au cours du procès sur la demande de la partie dont les intérêts se trouvent menacés, même si un tribunal de l'autre Etat est compétent pour statuer dans l'affaire en question.

Art. 12. Si des doutes surgissent au sujet des questions que l'application de la présente convention pourrait soulever, le Ministère de la Justice à Prague et le Ministère de Grâce et Justice à Madrid se communiqueront directement, sur demande, des renseignements juridiques nécessaires.

Art. 13. La présente convention sera ratifiée et les ratifications en seront échangées à Prague.

Cette convention entrera en vigueur un mois après l'échange des ratifications et produira ses effets encore un an après la dénonciation qui pourra avoir lieu en tout temps.

En foi de quoi les plénipotentiaires ont signé la présente convention en deux exemplaires.

Fait à Madrid, le 26 novembre 1927.

---

[1] de Martens, Nouveau Recueil général de Traités, troisième série, tome II, page 243.

[2] Voir page 287, de ce volume.

Anhang

Haager Entwurf 1925

Conférence de la Haye de droit international privé
Actes de la cinquième session, tenue du 12 octobre au 7 novembre 1925
Protocole final.

Les soussignés, Délégués des Gouvernements de l'Allemagne, de l'Autriche, de la Belgique, du Danemark, de l'Espagne, de la Finlande, de la France, de la Grande-Bretagne, de la Hongrie, de l'Italie, du Japon, de la Lettonie, du Luxembourg, de la Norvège, des Pays-Bas, de la Pologne, du Portugal, de la Roumanie, de l'Etat serbe-croate-slovène, de la Suède, de la Suisse et de la Tchécoslovaquie se sont réunis à La Haye, le 12 octobre 1925, sur l'invitation du Gouvernement des Pays-Bas, dans le but d'arriver à une entente sur divers points de droit international privé.

A la suite des délibérations consignées dans les procès-verbaux des séances plénières et des commissions, ils sont convenus de soumettre à l'appréciation de leurs Gouvernements

A. les projets de Convention suivants:

I. Projet d'une Convention sur la faillite. Art. 1—17.

II. Projet d'une Convention sur la reconnaissance et l'exécution de décisions judiciaires.

Art. 1. L'autorité des décisions judiciaires, rendues en matière civile ou en matière commerciale dans l'un des Etats contractants, sera reconnue dans l'autre Etat si elles réunissent les conditions suivantes:

1° que, pour le litige en question, les règles de compétence judiciaire internationale, admises par le droit de l'Etat dans lequel la décision est invoquée, n'excluent pas la juridiction de l'autre Etat;

2° que la reconnaissance de la décision ne soit pas contraire à l'ordre public ou aux principes du droit public de l'Etat où la décision est invoquée;

3° que d'après la loi de l'Etat où la décision a été rendue, elle soit passée en force de chose jugée;

4° qu'en cas de jugement par défaut, la partie ait été déclarée défaillante conformément à la loi du pays où le jugement a été rendu et aux dispositions des traités en vigueur entre les Etats contractants.

L'examen à faire par les autorités de l'Etat où la décision est invoquée, se borne aux conditions énumérées dans l'alinéa 1er, n°. 1—4. Ces autorités doivent examiner d'office, si ces conditions sont remplies.

Art. 2. Les décisions judiciaires rendues dans un des Etats contractants peuvent être mises à exécution dans l'autre Etat après y avoir été déclarées exécutoires.

L'exequatur est accordé, si la décision est exécutoire dans l'Etat où elle a été rendue et si elle remplit les conditions énumérées dans l'article 1er, alinéa 1er, n°. 1—4. L'alinéa 2 de cet article s'applique à l'examen à faire par les autorités de l'Etat où l'exécution est demandée.

Art. 3. La partie qui invoque la décision ou qui demande l'exequatur doit produire:

1° une expédition de la décision réunissant les conditions nécessaires à son authenticité;

2° les pièces de nature à établir que la décision est passée en force de chose jugée, et, s'il y a lieu, qu'elle est devenue exécutoire;

3° une copie authentique dûment légalisée de l'assignation de la partie qui a fait défaut à l'instance;

4° une traduction des pièces énumérées ci-dessus, certifiée conforme d'après les règles admises par l'Etat dans lequel l'exequatur est demandé, sauf dispense de cette obligation par l'autorité compétente.

Art. 4. Les sentences arbitrales rendues dans l'un des Etats contractants et y ayant la même autorité que les décisions judiciaires seront reconnues et déclarées exécutoires dans l'autre Etat, si elles satisfont aux prescriptions des articles précédents, en tant qu'elles sont applicables.

Il en est de même pour les transactions judiciaires.

Art. 5. Les dispositions de la présente Convention s'appliquent, quelle que soit la nationalité des parties.

La Conférence juge utile de demander aux Gouvernements de faire connaître, aussi promptement que possible, au Gouvernement des Pays-Bas s'ils sont disposés à signer les projets ci-dessus ou l'un d'eux.

B. les modifications suivantes à apporter aux traités de La Haye de 1902 et 1905:

1° à ajouter à l'article 19 de la Convention du 17 juillet 1905 relative à la procédure civile l'alinéa suivant:

»L'autorité compétente pour statuer sur la demande d'exequatur évaluera, pourvu que la partie le demande en même temps, le montant des frais de traduction et de légalisation visés à l'alinéa 2, numéro 3. Ces frais seront considérés comme des frais et dépens du procès.«

Haager Questionnaire 1925

Conférence de la Haye de droit international privé
Documents relatifs à la cinquième session, tenue du 12 octobre au 7 novembre 1925.

Exécution et reconnaissance de jugements étrangers

Première Question.

Faut-il conclure un traité collectif ou bien est-il préférable de concevoir un modèle de convention à conclure d'Etat à Etat?

Question 2.

Le traité doit-il viser seulement les jugements en matière personnelle et mobilière ou doit-il avoir un champ d'application plus étendu?

Question 3.

La partie gagnante qui veut procéder à l'exécution dans un des autres pays contractants, doit-elle y intenter de nouveau son action — comme en Angleterre — afin d'obtenir une nouvelle condamnation, la revision du fond étant pourtant exclue et les débats étant limités à quelques questions à désigner spécialement (p. ex. la compétence, etc.) ?

Ou bien le juge de l'autre pays autorisera-t-il l'exécution de la décision étrangère après une procédure spéciale destinée seulement à vérifier les conditions dont dépend l'exequatur ?

Question 4.

L'exequatur sera-t-il accordé quelle que soit la nationalité des parties au procès tranché par la décision étrangère ?

Question 5.

Quelles conditions doit réunir la décision dont l'exequatur est demandé :

a) la compétence du juge qui a rendu la décision.

Doit-on se contenter de la condition que la décision émane d'un juge compétent d'après la loi du pays où elle a été rendue ?

Ou faut-il exiger que le juge soit compétent d'après la loi du pays où l'exequatur est demandé ? Ou bien d'après les lois tant de l'un que de l'autre pays ?

Serait-il bon d'exclure en tout cas de fors exceptionnels comme par exemple celui de l'art. 14 C. c., de l'art. 53 de la loi belge de 1876 sur la compétence et de l'art. 127 Code de pr. civ. néerl. (forum evocationis) ?

Ou bien le traité doit-il établir lui-même, en cette matière, des règles de compétence ?

Fors à considérer :

1. le for du domicile du défendeur avec ou sans définition du domicile soit de fait soit légal (femme mariée, mineur, etc.) ?

2. le for du domicle élu :

le commerçant qui a une succursale sera-t-il considéré comme ayant élu domicile pour toutes les contestations concernant cet établissement ?

3. le for du siège social des personnes morales et des associations civiles ou commerciales sans personnalité civile ?

4. les fors spéciaux, soit principaux soit subsidiaires, pour actions entre associés etc., celles relatives aux titres au porteur, celles fondées sur des contrats ou des actes illicites etc. ?

5. — à titre subsidiaire — le for de la résidence du défendeur sans domicile ?

Faut-il, en outre, tenir compte des actions reconventionnelles, des actions en garantie ou en intervention et des autres actions incidentes comme p. ex. celles qui se rapportent à la connexité, etc. ?

Faut-il attribuer au juge de l'autre pays la faculté de contrôler le bien-fondé, tant en droit qu'en fait, de la décision à exécuter en ce qui concerne la compétence du juge qui l'a rendue ?

b) Faut-il permettre de refuser l'exequatur, parce que l'exécution de la décision porte atteinte à l'ordre public de l'autre pays ?

En cas d'affirmative, le traité doit-il disposer que les règles relatives à la compétence, à la preuve et à la procédure ne concernent pas l'ordre public ?

Si, par rapport à l'assignation du défendeur, on ne veut reconnaître que sous réserve de l'ordre public, l'autorité de la loi du pays où la décision a été rendue, faut-il que le traité détermine lui-même les conditions auxquelles l'assignation doit satisfaire? Ou peut-il passer la question sous silence, le juge qui accorde l'exequatur ayant en principe la faculté de vérifier les conditions que l'assignation devant le tribunal étranger doit remplir?

Le traité doit-il contenir une disposition expresse refusant l'exequatur si la décision étrangère est contraire à une décision rendue par un juge national?

Faut-il qu'une réserve analogue soit faite par rapport aux décisions obtenues par dol, sous l'influence d'erreur manifeste, etc.?

L'examen du fond, en tant qu'il ne concerne pas les points énumérés ci-dessus, doit-il être défendu au juge qui connaît de la demande en exequatur?

c) L'exequatur ne sera-t-il accordé qu'à des jugements passés en force de chose jugée, c'est-a-dire n'étant plus susceptibles d'aucun pourvoi ordinaire (opposition, appel, pourvoi en cassation)?

Ou faut-il permettre l'exécution à la condition que le jugement étranger soit exécutoire dans le pays d'origine?

d) Quelles pièces doivent être produites par la partie qui demande 'exequatur? Quelles conditions doivent-elles remplir?

Question 6.

Sera-ce le traité ou la loi nationale de l'autre pays contractant qui décide:

a) à qui revient le droit de demander l'exequatur;

b) quel juge est compétent pour l'accorder;

c) quelles sont les formalités de procédure y compris les pourvois contre le jugement d'exequatur, les délais d'appel etc.;

d) si le jugement d'exequatur est susceptible d'exécution par provision?

Le défendeur à la demande en exequatur est-il en droit d'y répondre par une demande reconventionnelle?

Question 7.

Faut-il appliquer des règles analogues à la simple reconnaissance de l'autorité d'un jugement étranger, prononcée par le juge de l'autre pays soit expressément, soit implicitement?

Question 8.

Le juge de l'autre pays doit-il procéder, d'office, à la vérification des conditions dont dépendent l'exequatur à accorder à la décision étrangère et la reconnaissance de son autorité?

Question 9.

La reconnaissance une fois prononcée peut-elle être invoquée envers tous dans le pays du juge? En cas d'affirmative, ce principe s'applique-t-il aussi à la reconnaissance impliquée dans la décision qui accorde l'exequatur?

Question 10.

Serait-il bon pour des raisons d'ordre pratique, d'attribuer au juge d'un des Etats contractants la faculté de surseoir à l'instance, introduite devant lui, pour un délai à déterminer par lui, si la même affaire est déjà pendante devant le juge d'un autre pays compétent en vertu du traité?

Question 11.

Faut-il assimiler aux jugements, et à quelles conditions, les ordonnances des autorités judiciaires permettant des mesures conservatoires?

Question 12.

Faut-il régler de la même manière, sauf en ce qui concerne la compétence, l'exécution des sentences arbitrales et la reconnaissance de leur autorité?

Question 13.

Serait-il bon de régler l'exécution des actes authentiques portant reconnaissance de dette? En cas d'affirmative, de quelles conditions doit dépendre l'octroi de l'exequatur?

Question 14.

Faut-il régler dans le traité la compétence du juge qui accorde l'exequatur, prévu aux questions 11 et 12 précédentes, et la procédure y compris les délais etc.? Ou sera-ce la loi nationale de l'autre Etat contractant à qui incombe de pourvoir à ces matières?

Question 15.

Afin d'éviter des sentences contradictoires, le traité doit-il contenir la clause que les Etats contractants s'obligent de porter devant la Cour Permanente de Justice Internationale tout différend entre Eux concernant l'interprétation du texte?

Haager Zusätze 1928

Conférence de la Haye de droit international privé

Actes de la sixième session tenue du 5 au 28 janvier 1928

Protocole final.

Les soussignés, Délégués des Gouvernements de l'Allemagne, de l'Autriche, de la Belgique, du Danemark, de l'Espagne, de la Finlande, de la France, de la Grande-Bretagne, de la Hongrie, de l'Italie, du Japon, de la Lettonie, du Luxembourg, de la Norvège, des Pays-Bas, de la Pologne, du Portugal, de la Roumanie, de l'Etat Serbe-Croate-Slovène, de la Suède, de la Suisse et de la Tschécoslovaquie se sont réunis à La Haye, le 5 janvier 1928, sur l'invitation du Gouvernement des Pays-Bas, dans le but d'arriver à une entente sur divers points de droit international privé.

A la suite des délibérations consignées dans les procès-verbaux des séances plénières et des commissions, ils sont convenus de soumettre à l'appréciation de leurs Gouvernements: . . .

G. la rédaction suivante de l'article 4 du projet de Convention sur la reconnaissance et l'exécution des décisions judiciaires étrangères, élaboré en 1925:

«Les transactions judiciaires intervenues entre parties à un procès dans l'un des Etats contractants seront reconnues et déclarées exécutoires dans un autre Etat contractant, si elles satisfont aux prescriptions des articles précédents, en tant qu'elles sont applicables.»

Alphabetische Register

(Die Zahlen bezeichnen die Seiten)

I. Namensverzeichnis

II. Staatsverträge

(T) bedeutet Vertragstext

III. Sachverzeichnis

FSC
www.fsc.org
MIX
Papier | Fördert gute Waldnutzung
FSC® C083411

Kolibri 360 GmbH
Ferdinand-Jühlke-Straße 7
99095 Erfurt, Deutschland
produktsicherheit@kolibri360.de